PRIVACY

WHAT EVERYONE NEEDS TO KNOW®

PRIVACY

WHAT EVERYONE NEEDS TO KNOW®

LESLIE P. FRANCIS
JOHN G. FRANCIS

OXFORD
UNIVERSITY PRESS

OXFORD
UNIVERSITY PRESS

Oxford University Press is a department of the University of Oxford.
It furthers the University's objective of excellence in research, scholarship,
and education by publishing worldwide.

Oxford is a registered trade mark of Oxford University
Press in the UK and certain other countries.

"What Everyone Needs to Know" is a registered trademark of
Oxford University Press.

Published in the United States of America by Oxford University Press
198 Madison Avenue, New York, NY 10016, United States of America.

© Oxford University Press 2017

Library of Congress Cataloging-in-Publication Data
Names: Francis, John G., 1943– author. | Francis, Leslie, 1946– author.
Title: Privacy : what everyone needs to know / John G. and Leslie P. Francis.
Description: New York : Oxford University Press, 2017. |
Includes bibliographical references and index.
Identifiers: LCCN 2016046402 (print) | LCCN 2016047121 (ebook) |
ISBN 9780190612252 (pbk. : alk. paper) | ISBN 9780190612269 (cloth :
alk. paper) | ISBN 9780190612276 (updf) | ISBN 9780190612283 (ebook)
Subjects: LCSH: Privacy, Right of—United States. | Civil rights—United
States. | Data protection—Law and legislation—United States. |
Digital communications—United States.
Classification: LCC KF1262 .F73 2017 (print) | LCC KF1262 (ebook) |
DDC 342.7308/58—dc23
LC record available at https://lccn.loc.gov/2016046402

1 3 5 7 9 8 6 4 2
Paperback printed by LSC Communications,
United States of America
Hardback printed by Bridgeport National Bindery, Inc.,
United States of America

To our children: Sarah, Laura, and John

CONTENTS

9 Privacy and Security   239

PREFACE

Imagine you have a ring, round, smooth, and golden. When you slide it on your finger, you become invisible to everyone else. Thus J. R. R. Tolkien wrote about the ring of Sauron, Plato about the ring of Gyges, and Wagner about the ring of Alberich. If you put on the ring, would you have privacy? Or something else? Would using the ring make your life better or worse? Would wearing the ring be good for you? Would you ever want to have such a ring? Would it be a bad thing for everyone else if you had such a ring—perhaps so bad that they should want it buried at the bottom of a river for all time?

Or, imagine that you live in Bentham's panopticon, where everyone may always be under observation, all the time, without ever knowing when (UCL 2016). Or George Orwell's *1984*, with the ever-present suggestion that Big Brother is watching (Singleton 1997; Orwell 1949). Or imagine everyone just believes that they are being observed continuously. Would you have any privacy in such a world, or none? Would you feel safe or threatened? Would it matter who or what was doing the observing, why they were doing it, and whether they kept exact records of what they were seeing? Would it be good for people or for societies to experiment with building panopticons to see how they could work?

These images, and the many questions they bring to mind, lie at the heart of the debates about privacy that we will explore in this volume.

A word about our choice of person. We'll use the second person (you, yours) when we want to address a question or an idea directly to you as an individual reading this volume: What do you think privacy means? How can you protect your privacy? We'll use the third person (they, theirs, people) when we want to refer to people generally: What do people think about privacy? What rights do people in a given society have? We'll use the first person (we) when we want to give you our take on an issue or arguments in moral or political theory that we have developed in our earlier work or for this book.

Finally, several observations about scope. First, much privacy policy is enshrined in or affected by law. It's difficult to write a book about privacy without legal references. We've done our best to keep these to a minimum and to explain them clearly. But we can't avoid them altogether. There's an Appendix available [global.oup.com/us/companion.websites/9780190612252/] for more complete legal explanations. Second, in part because of the role of law in shaping privacy policies, there are significant variations by jurisdiction. We are scholars based in the United States, although with considerable interest in European politics. So, many of our references are to US practices. We have also tried, however, to present important European contrasts. Readers should be aware of two from the beginning: Europe has much more overarching privacy law than the United States does, and Europe has been exploring the contours of a "right to be forgotten" that is unlikely to be recognized in the United States, at least for the near future.

Privacy has long mattered to us as individuals and as members of various communities. But how it matters and the importance we assign to various expressions of privacy change as a result of technological innovations, socio-economic transformations, and political shifts. This volume went to press in the early days of the Trump administration in the United States.

Already, we have seen efforts in Congress to allow employers to request genetic testing of employees in wellness programs through the "Preserving Employee Wellness Programs Act"— a practice that would undermine the protections of the Genetic Information Non-discrimination Act (Gina, discussed in Chapter 3). We have also seen a potential roll-back of the regulation preventing Internet service providers from collecting information about the websites you visit (see Chapter 9). Among the many other changes that may be anticipated with the new administration are an increased reliance on social media and heightened concerns about security. Moreover, the upcoming British exit from the European Union may have implications for how privacy protections are understood in the United Kingdom. Across Europe, concerns about migrants and terrorist threats may fuel increased calls for security protections. We will do our best to post important policy updates in the online legal appendix to this volume, available [global.oup.com/us/companion.websites/9780190612252/].

Privacy, we suggest in this book, is valued, varied, and complex. We hope this volume will stimulate informed and careful thinking among our readers about what privacy means and how it might matter to them.

PRIVACY

WHAT EVERYONE NEEDS TO KNOW®

1

CONCEPTUALIZING PRIVACY

Introduction

What is privacy? What does it mean, and how does it relate to other important values? Is it a human right? When and how did it emerge as an idea? In this introductory chapter, we address these and related questions to set the stage for the discussions about privacy in the remainder of the volume.

Privacy notoriously has many different meanings. The problem is not only that different kinds of privacy matter to different people and in different circumstances and cultures. What you mean by privacy, and why and whether you value it, may have been very different if you lived in contemporary China or Victorian England, or in a small town or a large urban area. Scholars have defended many views about the concept of privacy, with some claiming that it really means just one clear idea, and others contending that it is impossibly confused. In this book, we don't want to leave out important privacy-related ideas—after all, this is supposed to be a book about what *everyone* needs to know about privacy. So this chapter leads off by exploring the many ideas that have come under the rubric of privacy and how they are related to common themes of respect for persons and their freedom.

What is privacy? Is privacy one concept or many?

Privacy, the theme of this volume, is a concept rich in meanings, and it often is highly valued, particularly in its absence. But it is famously difficult to define. It has taken many guises in law, public policy, ethics, and social science—and in film, photography and other arts, novels and poetry, the press, and online. Before reading on, we suggest that you stop for a moment to think about what privacy means to you. Is it a separate bedroom—a "private" room? Control over your sexual life or whom (or whether) to marry? Or is it about information? Does it matter to you whether the world knows what you had for breakfast, what grades you received in high school or college, how much you weigh, or whether you've been treated for HIV or cancer? Is your privacy violated if search engines track you over the Internet to give you ads about shoes, deals on hotel rooms, or restaurants you might like? Do you spend time figuring out who should have access to your Facebook page or Twitter feeds? Are you worried that cyber-criminals might steal your identifying information and open a bank account in your name? Or, is your biggest privacy fear that the government might have access to the GPS coordinates of your cell phone and the numbers that have been dialed from it?

All these ideas, and more, have been included in the idea of privacy. These protean facets of privacy do have an apparent common center, however. Put most succinctly, privacy is the "right to be let alone" (Warren and Brandeis 1890). At its core, privacy protects the self: choosing whether to decline access to your person, to avoid observation by others, or to hold back information about yourself, at least in some situations (Moore 1984). Social psychologist Irwin Altman (1981) characterized this basic idea of privacy as the process by which individuals or groups negotiate boundaries, letting others in or keeping them out.

Although in some respects privacy is a very modern concept, privacy-related ideas have a long history. The effort to distinguish between the private and public spheres of our lives dates back at least to ancient Greece (Moore 1984) and ancient China (Farrell 2008). This distinction was traditionally understood to fall between the state or public authority and the private setting of family or home life (e.g., Whitman 1985). In the nineteenth century, liberal political philosophers who emphasized individual freedom distinguished between actions that could harm others and thus be the subject of social coercion, and so-called self-regarding actions that were solely up to individuals to decide for themselves, whether or not they were acting in the privacy of their homes. For example, for these liberals, individuals could decide what they wanted to do with their property, so long as they did not use it to cause injuries to others. Twentieth-century totalitarianism brought new meaning to the need to insulate the individual from the authority of the state. The power exercised by fascist and communist states gave rise in the aftermath of World War II to the protection of privacy as a right in fundamental international instruments, such as the Universal Declaration of Human Rights adopted in 1948 and the European Convention for the Protection of Human Rights and Fundamental Freedoms adopted in 1950, as well as in many national constitutions and laws.

Especially over the past two centuries, technological innovation has presented some of the most recurring challenges to privacy and its meaning. From mirrors and periscopes to portable cameras and surveillance by closed circuit television (CCTV), from the ever-changing Internet and its creative uses to brain scans and other biosensors, technology has enabled novel forms of observation and intrusion. Through technology, people continue to access and to learn much more about themselves and others, not just in their community but often in other parts of the nation and the world. Assessing the implications of these and other technological developments for privacy remains complex.

Tensions also are ever present between people's expectations for privacy and their interests in knowing about other people and the institutions that govern their lives. The debate is long-standing, not just in the literature on national security, over whether privacy has been overly valued in the face of the need to seek a better political order. Close observation of individuals often has been justified by the state to protect the population from domestic and foreign threats. Beyond such national security, one school of political philosophy, at least since Rousseau, has argued for the value of community and the importance of knowing about others who live among us. From *The Scarlet Letter*'s portrayal of the community's desire to know who among them has been sexually transgressive (Hawthorne 1850) to contemporary published lists of sex offenders, and from concerns about who might be reading materials thought to be subversive to efforts by anti-terrorist investigations to get records of library patrons' activities, communities want to know about their neighbors in order to assess the extent to which they should be trusted, feared, or condemned.

Privacy is often thought of as a value associated with liberalism, but liberal theorists also struggle with the interplay between privacy and other values. Privacy may be in tension with other liberal values, most notably with freedom of expression, transparency in organizational and governmental decision-making, and easy entry into commerce. Journalists seek to publish what others might consider details of their private lives, and artists from photographers to poets capture images of the lives of others. Citizens want to know what their governments and those who work for them are doing. The commercial world of the Internet, with all its convenience, comes with trade-offs in the collection and flow of information.

And then there is the image of privacy as foisting isolation or even the loss of identity. Privacy has kept women in harems and homes, subject to domestication or abuse. Ralph Ellison's *Invisible Man* (1952) experienced the ultimate in destructive privacy: passing through a world in which he went entirely unnoticed because of his race. Anita Allen, in a related twist, explores in her work *Unpopular Privacy* (2011) whether there are some privacies that we must perforce respect, even when they are disliked by both their beneficiaries and those who are required to honor them.

Security of the physical person, space protected from intrusion, liberty of choice, and confidentiality of information are among the more particular ideas that have come under the rubric of privacy in political theory and law. These represent different but related areas that reflect the underlying importance of the ability to control how and when you are left alone. This prolix description of the nature of privacy has been the source of a great deal of confusion, as these concepts are not the same. Nonetheless, they are interrelated, both intrinsically and instrumentally, in complex and rich ways that protect fundamental aspects of respect for persons. So it is not surprising that no single definition of privacy has come to prevail, given the broad scope of privacy in many different areas of individuals' lives and communities.

What is physical security and how is it related to privacy?

Physical security is protection of the body against unwanted physical access. It protects privacy in the sense of control over direct access to the body. Privacy-violating intrusions may include unwanted touching, unwanted medical care, or unwanted sex, among many other similar impositions. At the extreme, forms of unwanted bodily intervention may amount to torture. Critics of waterboarding and other extreme interrogation techniques have invoked privacy as one of the values at stake.

Rape is another very devastating imposition that violates victims' physical privacy, among the many other serious ways in which it harms. Physical searches—strip searches, body cavity searches, or extraction of bodily fluids such as blood for testing—also violate privacy in this sense.

Both criminal and civil law have long recognized the importance of protecting individuals' bodily security. Assault, battery, and rape are among the physical invasions that are punished under criminal law. The tort of battery—unwanted touching—allows individuals to recover damages from those who intentionally intruded upon them. Battery victims can recover damages for the dignitary harm of unwanted intrusion, even when it was beneficial to them—as when a physician operates on you without your consent. Fundamental international and constitutional protections apply to serious violations of physical security. Torture is a violation of Article 5 of the Universal Declaration of Human Rights; Article 3 of the Declaration enshrines the right to security of the person along with the rights to life and liberty. The Fourth Amendment to the US Constitution protects against unreasonable searches and seizures.

Importantly, privacy as physical security is instrumentally related to other aspects of privacy. Without physical security, you may not be able to protect your home or your information. The reverse is also true. Protection of homes or other spaces shields the individuals within them. Protection of privacy in information may ensure that others do not come to have the kind of knowledge that would lead to violations of physical security. For example, if fathers do not know that their daughters have had sexual relations, they will not have the information that goads honor killing; if HIV status is not revealed, communities will not have the information that leads them to stone HIV victims.

What is spatial privacy? Is privacy to be equated with the home or family?

Spatial privacy is protection of a location against unwanted entry. Protected locations may be as varied as a home, a bedroom, a workspace, a purse, or a locked suitcase or car trunk. Unwanted entry may be physical, as when an unauthorized person climbs through your window; or, it may be visual, as when a "peeping Tom" peers into your bedroom when the curtains have been left slightly askew; or, it may be virtual, as when someone gains unauthorized access to view your computer screen or your emails. Technological developments from radar that can peer through walls to infrared heat sensors to drones buzzing overhead raise increasingly complex challenges to spatial privacy (e.g., Heath 2015). Crowded housing conditions may severely restrict spatial privacy. Concentration camps—in the literal origin of the term, camps that concentrate people together so that they can be monitored—deny spatial privacy. Spatial privacy is limited or nonexistent in the crowded refugee camps located all over the world today. Living conditions in cities overwhelmed by migrants from rural areas seeking work may lack spatial privacy. Multiple generations of families sharing housing, or large groups of unrelated strangers cramming into limited space, may find themselves fighting for access to bathrooms or kitchens, unable to secure individual belongings, or unable to choose even when or where to sleep. The British publication *Shelter* (2005) reported that 92% of people living in very crowded housing indicated that what bothered them most was the lack of privacy.

Spatial privacy may be a way to protect privacy in the family, at least when families share a common dwelling area that is protected from intrusion. Privacy in the family may be a double-edged sword, however. On the one hand, the family has been thought of as part of the private sphere and protecting the family as an important reason for protecting the home where the family lives. Nevertheless, even though the family can be a source of strength for its members to pursue their own lives, it can also be the locus of child or spousal abuse, exploitation, or oppression. It can be the site of privacy invasion, too, as when husbands search drawers to find out whether their wives are using birth control, siblings snoop on one another's email, or parents take samples of their children's hair to test for drugs.

Fundamental laws such as constitutions may protect persons or their spaces against unwarranted intrusions by the state or its agents. Article 12 of the Universal Declaration of

Human Rights and Article 8 of the European Convention on Human Rights provide that no one shall be subjected to arbitrary interference with his privacy, family, home, or correspondence. The Third Amendment of the US Constitution protects the quartering of soldiers in homes during peacetime without the consent of their owners. The Fourth Amendment protects against unreasonable search or seizures of persons, houses, papers, and effects.

How is privacy related to liberty?

Several important liberties also have been protected under the banner of privacy. Typically, these liberties involve intimate matters: founding a family, reproducing, or deciding how to raise children. Liberties of thought and spirit, including the free exercise of religion, also have been classified as privacy rights in some views, as have liberties of association. Certain liberties may be thought of as intrinsic to privacy—as part of what it means to be left alone. Or, liberty may be instrumental to other aspects of privacy, or the reverse. For example, some argue that unless people are physically secure, have personal space protected, and are able to maintain control over their information, genuine liberty of choice will not be possible. Husbands' efforts to search their wives' drawers many likely chill freedom of reproductive choice, to take just one example.

Protections for fundamental liberties are typically found at the most basic constitutional level. In the United States, the First Amendment to the Constitution protects liberty of expression and the free exercise of religion; rights to choose with respect to intimate matters such as family formation have been understood as protected liberties under the due process clauses of the Fifth and Fourteenth Amendments. In the European Union Charter, Article 7 guarantees the right to respect for private and family life, home, and communications; Article 9 the right to marry and found a family; Article 10 the right to freedom of thought, conscience, and religion; and Article 11 the freedom of expression and information.

At times in US law, privacy has been identified as a form of liberty. Under the due process clauses of the Fifth and Fourteenth Amendments of the US Constitution, the federal government and the states must have a compelling interest to override fundamental liberties. Privacy in the sense of liberty to educate children, to decide whether or not to use contraceptives, to decide whether or not to continue a pregnancy, and to decide whom to marry has been considered a fundamental constitutional right protected under this due process liberty.

In the 1960s and 1970s, US Supreme Court decisions about contraception and abortion saw privacy as part of a "penumbra" of First Amendment protections from government intrusion. Connecticut's prohibition on the use of contraceptives by married persons was held to violate this right to privacy: "We deal with a right of privacy older than the Bill of Rights—older than our political parties, older than our school system. Marriage is a coming together for better or for worse, hopefully enduring, and intimate to the degree of being sacred" (*Griswold v. Connecticut*, 381 U.S. 479, 483, 486 (1965)). *Griswold's* recognition of privacy was extended to cover the decision of whether or not to bear children in probably the most controversial Supreme Court decision of the last century, *Roe v. Wade* (410 U.S. 113, 153 (1973)), striking down Texas's prohibition of abortions. According to its many critics, this effort to delineate a constitutional right to privacy was not well defined (DeCew 2015).

More recently, the US Supreme Court has returned to the language of liberty, rather than privacy, to describe rights to make decisions about intimate personal matters. The transitional case was about whether the state may insist on a very high standard of evidence before allowing decision-makers for an incapacitated patient to authorize withdrawal of life-sustaining treatment (it may) (*Cruzan v. Director, Missouri Department of Health*, 497 U.S. 261 (1990)). In reaching its decision, the Court assumed for the sake of argument that patients have a fundamental liberty right—rather than a privacy right—to decline medical treatment. Subsequently, this liberty analysis has been applied to abortion (*Planned Parenthood of Southeastern Pa. v. Casey,* 505 U.S. 833 (1992)) and the right to same-sex marriage (*Obergefell v. Hodges,* 576 U.S. ___, 135 S.Ct. 2584 (2015)).

Even if privacy is not identified with liberty, privacy may be a very important means of protecting liberty. *Griswold* was concerned about the intrusions into the marital bedroom that would be needed to enforce a prohibition on the use of contraceptives by married couples. Protection from such spatial intrusion is important to foster marital and procreative liberty.

How is privacy related to confidentiality?

Protection of information—confidentiality—has also been called privacy. Confidentiality refers to your ability to choose with whom (or what) to share information about yourself. Many confidentiality protections are referred to as privacy protections in both popular discourse and law. In the United States, for example, the law protecting confidentiality of medical information is called the "HIPAA privacy rule." (HIPAA is the Health Insurance Portability and Accountability Act, the federal statute designed to streamline health insurance billing, which also included protection for the confidentiality of medical information.)

Strictly speaking, this identification of confidentiality with privacy is a mistake. Confidentiality is about control over information. This is just one of the aspects of privacy and is related to other aspects in complex ways. People may want to shield their bodies so that no information about their physical condition is ever collected. This may be undesirable—for example, if people stay away from doctors because they don't want to be tested for HIV because they fear the resulting information can't be kept confidential, HIV may spread (Francis 2008; ONC 2016). One recent survey reported that about 5% of Americans had not shared information with their physicians because they were concerned it could not be kept private (ONC 2016). On the other hand, people might want to protect confidentiality to protect other aspects of privacy, such as physical security that may be threatened if damaging information comes to light (Francis 2008).

How is privacy related to anonymity and de-identification?

Anonymity exists when characteristics cannot be attributed to an individual or thing at all—it is the complete dissociation of information from the entity to which it could otherwise apply (Ponesse 2014). For example, if someone posts an intimate description of a personal life on the Internet, but does not include any information about who the actual person is, so that no one knows or could know who is the subject of the life narrative, the narrative is anonymous. You can join some social media sites this way, but you are expected to give your name and other identifying information to join other such sites. When messages, letters to the editor in newspapers, campaign contributions, or votes are anonymous, it is because there is no way to link them to their sources. Anonymous surveys only collect answers to the survey questions, avoiding any questions that might link particular answers to the individuals who give them.

Controversies about whether anonymity should be protected are significant and are likely to increase. Facebook, for example, insists that people who sign up for accounts give their real identities, although people signing up could of course use pseudonyms. In 2014, Facebook launched an app, Facebook Rooms, where people could chat without revealing their identities. Although originally hailed as the future of the Internet (Alba 2014), Facebook Rooms closed in December 2015, along with several other apps (Beasley 2015). Facebook said that the features of the apps that had been popular had been incorporated into other aspects of its site, but still asks people for a name when they sign up for accounts because the general expectation is that Facebook users share their actual identities. Facebook's terms and conditions state that "Facebook users provide their real names and information, and we need your help to keep it that way" (Facebook 2016). Like many other aspects of privacy, anonymity has two sides; it can be the source of seminal ideas, Wikileaks, or terrorist threats that are magnified as they are transferred across the Internet. Anonymity understood as the initial absence of identifiers is different from information de-identification. De-identification starts with information that is linked to identified people and then removes any information that could be used to determine what information relates to each of these individuals. Many sets of what are called big data are made up of de-identified data in this way. Thus constructed, a de-identified data set is made up of information that originally came from individuals in identifiable form. The effort to extract likely identifiers is then only as good as the ability to guess what information might be used to re-identify people in the future.

In data regulations in the United States and Europe today, de-identified data are not included within the rules protecting the confidentiality of information because they are no longer considered to be personal information (Richardson, Milam & Chrysler 2015). This exclusion, however, is coming under serious criticism. It may be impossible to de-identify some types of information (e.g., a genetic sequence that is unique to a particular individual). Re-identification also may be more likely than many have thought when de-identified data are linked with public information that is identifiable, such as newspaper reports or voter rolls (Sweeney 2016). It may be difficult to predict in advance what information will turn out to be identifying in this way. Finally, some commentators believe that people have an interest in how de-identified information is used, as it may result in stigma or harm to groups, even when individuals have not been individually named (Fullerton and Lee 2011).

Anonymity and de-identification are also different from pseudo-anonymity, in which an individual's actual identifying information is replaced by a unique code. For example, health research involving patients who have been treated by multiple providers may need to link records of individual patients. If a common algorithm is used to generate a number from identifying information in each set of records, patients may be linked by the algorithm, but information that could actually identify the individual is not given to the researcher.

Is privacy the right to be forgotten?

In Europe especially, privacy has been seen to have a temporal aspect: the right at some point to be free of the past. European privacy law has recently come to recognize what is called the "right to be forgotten." Before the Internet, archives of court proceedings, newspapers, administrative decisions, or medical records would be at a fixed physical location; people who wanted to view the records would need to travel to visit them. If copies were allowed, they would be difficult to make: handwriting the information, or copying page by page. And copies were frequently forbidden; archives were to be examined, not transmitted. Photography, Xerox, and fax machines changed this somewhat, but still required initial physical contact with the document for duplication.

Today, records—from newspaper archives to court proceedings to medical histories—are maintained in electronic form. Many of these can be viewed, copied, downloaded, or transmitted, literally with the flick of a remote switch. And digitized records are rapidly searchable in a way that physical or photocopied records are not. Capacities for storage of digitized records have also been multiplying exponentially. The result is vast proliferation in the amount of information available about people and the ease with which it can be obtained. "Googling" is a common verb—and a common way of finding out about someone.

In 2014, the European Court of Justice ruled that Google Spain had violated European privacy law in continuing to maintain links between an individual, Mario Costeja González, and records of a forced sale of his property to satisfy a debt, which had been published in a Spanish newspaper (*Google Spain SL, Google Inc. v. Agencia Española de Protección de Datos (AEPD), Mario Costeja González*, no. C-131/12 [13 May], http://curia.europa. eu/juris/celex.jsf?celex=62012CJo131&lang1=en&type= TXT&ancre=). Links to the old record came up on Google searches for González, and he wanted them expunged. The European Court of Justice concluded that the continuing linkage violated both the European Privacy Directive (Directive 95/46/EC) and the Charter of Fundamental Rights of the European Union because the information was potentially embarrassing and of little or no contemporary value and because González was not a public figure. Since the ruling, this so-called "right to be forgotten" has been invoked in hundreds of thousands of requests to delink names from results in web searches. The new privacy regulation for the European Union adopted in April 2016 explicitly incorporates the right to erasure into European privacy law (EU General Data Protection Regulation Art. 17, http://ec.europa.eu/justice/data-protection/document/review2012/com_2012_11_en.pdf).

Stated broadly, the "right to be forgotten" encompasses several distinct possibilities. One is the right to "delisting"—to having a given Internet site not appear in a list of sites responsive to a search for a person using a particular search engine or search engines generally. A second is the right to end any further dissemination of information, as when a governmental record is deemed "private" and not accessible to inspection by anyone else, whether electronically or physically. A third is full erasure, where the information is no longer maintained at the source. Requests for delisting, such as that involved in the lawsuit against Google Spain, would not destroy the data at its origin; anyone who explored the archives of the newspaper could still view the record.

Not surprisingly, the "right to be forgotten" has generated intense controversy. Some argue that information should be widely available about everyone, once it has entered public space such as a website. It may be difficult to decide when information is sufficiently embarrassing, or when it has lost contemporary relevance, these critics of delisting say; information about Mario González's old debts might be very useful for someone contemplating offering him new credit. Critics are especially concerned that delisting decisions are made by private companies operating search engines, such as Google, which may have interests very different from those of the public in accessing information or those of individuals in protecting it. Such critics, who would prefer that the Internet facilitate the open flow of information, sometimes invoke the image of the Internet as a "Swiss cheese" full of holes (Powles 2015). In the United States, it is likely that attempts to assert the right to be forgotten would come into conflict with arguments for freedom of speech, including commercial speech (Timberg and Halzack 2014).

On the other side the argument is that erroneous or damaging information should not continue to be replicated across the Internet; even when it is corrected at its initial site, without a right of erasure it might continue to be transmitted from other sites to which it has been copied. People might quite rightly wish not to have libelous statements, errors about whether they have been convicted of crimes, gory details about accidents in which they have been victims, funerals of their loved ones, or reports of their having been raped, broadcast repeatedly in Internet searches about them (Bowcott and Wilshire 2014, Timberg and Halzack 2014). And arguably you should be able to outlive your youthful mistakes, which you cannot do if records such as expunged criminal convictions are republished and gain eternal life across the Internet.

How is privacy related to secrecy?

People exercising their right to privacy may choose secrecy, but privacy does not require secrecy. Secrecy is a special form of the exercise of control over the person, or intentional concealment (Bok 1983). It can be a hiding place, a fact about the person, something of commercial value, or important matters of state. The mythological rings of Sauron, Gyges, or Alberich that allow someone to disappear altogether portray a radical form of secrecy and the corrosive power it may bring. There are serious questions about whether the exercise of secrecy is psychologically or socially desirable. The message of the rings of myth is that secrecy detaches, corrupts, and ultimately deranges those who possess it. Commercial secrecy has also been criticized for the power it brings. Laws concerning trade secrets protect information discovered, collected, or possessed by a commercial entity that is of competitive economic value, as long as the entity takes reasonable steps to guarantee against its being revealed. The commercial advantages gained through trade secrets protection are controversial, as they may prevent others from benefiting from the information being exploited for profit. For example, certain US companies have lost patent protection for genetic tests and may now be secluding information about the significance of genetic variations they have identified, thus making their tests more valuable and more expensive (Cook-Deegan et al. 2013). At times, the stakes are higher. The UK Official Secrets Act protects information that the government believes would jeopardize national security if revealed to the public (Official Secrets Act 1989, http://www.legislation.gov.uk/ukpga/1989/6/contents). The scope of legitimate state secrets in contrast to governmental transparency is a perennial controversy about the proper role of government and democratic control over it.

What is "privacy in context"?

One of the reasons that the concept of privacy seems so elusive is that its requirements are often thought of in terms of expectations. Intrusions on personal space or publication of information may be judged to violate privacy if they are unexpected, unusual, offensive, or shocking, but not if they are part of the common fabric of daily life. Privacy reflects existing norms about the boundaries of the person. But it is not restricted to these norms; it may also press changes on those norms as they come to seem incongruent with how people might lead flourishing lives. Changes may be gradual, or may come in the form of a punctuated equilibrium—a series of radical shifts—brought by new technologies such as the Internet or social disruptions such as plagues, wars, or revolutions. The rapid development of the Internet and other forms of electronic communication may have brought just such a punctuated equilibrium in privacy norms. Some have argued that we have no privacy at all any more and we should just live with that fact; others contend that we need a new regime of complete protection.

The normative structure taken by any given social context is an empirical question. Helen Nissenbaum, a scholar of culture and technology, has developed a theoretical approach to studying privacy norms, "privacy in context." In this view, systems of social norms affect the flow of information in different social contexts (Nissenbaum 2010, p. 3). These context-relative social norms distribute power, protect relationships and interests, and allow people to interact without harm to one another. Stable privacy norms may allow intellectual freedom and democracy to flourish. Studying privacy requires understanding the norms in place at given points in time, how they fit together, and how they evolve—what Nissenbaum calls their "contextual integrity." People see their privacy as violated when information flows contrary to established norms, and experience the violation as especially troubling when the contextual integrity of the norms themselves is under challenge.

According to Nissenbaum, apparently paradoxical reactions about privacy are best explained in terms of contextual integrity. Consider as one example the idea of privacy in public. On the one hand, the possibility that you could have expectations of privacy when you are walking down a public street might seem paradoxical at best and ludicrous at worst. You are, after all, out in public. Peeking out of a window into the world is different from peeking into the window from the world. And "public" records are open to inspection for all to see (Nissenbaum 2010, p. 115). But we can recognize that what it means to be out in public may not be so simple by reflecting on whether you are similarly out in public when you enter what some call the "information superhighway" of the Internet. For the Internet brings heretofore unimagined possibilities of connectivity, of tracking the sites you visit and linking them together into a portrait of your interests, preferences, and personal characteristics. Similarly, surveillance cameras now can link up photographs of where you were throughout the day, describing exactly what you did to an unprecedented extent. The distinction between private space and the world outside, whether physical or virtual, does not capture the social norms in place that shape expectations about information flow, including how information may be assembled or may assume different significance depending on the context. Information collected when you pass by a single surveillance camera might not violate privacy norms, but assembling the information into a complete description of your daily life could.

Why protect privacy?

Privacy may be protected for its own sake, or as a means to the protection of other values. At the heart of arguments for privacy lies protection of the person, in multiple ways. Autonomy—in the sense of the ability to make authentic choices about central issues in life—is one core value urged in support of privacy. Autonomy is a direct argument for privacy as liberty. It is also offered in support of privacy as protection of personal space. Here, the idea is that unless people have space where they can think unobserved and on their own, they may fear that their thoughts are being monitored and may not feel free to choose as they wish. On the other hand, critics point out that cordoning off private spheres can allow oppression or exploitation to take place within them, as when women or children are forced into domestic servitude. Autonomy also argues for privacy as confidentiality, because choices with respect to information about the self are important in their own right and may also be needed to protect other kinds of choices. For example, the ability to keep information about sexual orientation confidential may be critical to maintaining intimacy with others or choosing where to work.

Liberty of conscience is a value that is closely related to autonomy. The relation is that people need the freedom to think for themselves in order to choose for themselves. If people think they lack freedom about what to think or believe, they may also be fearful about exercising choices in accord with their values. Liberty of conscience may evaporate if privacy—protected choices about what to think, protected space in which to think away from the prying eyes of unauthorized searchers, and protected information about what one is thinking—does not exist. Others argue that without privacy for thoughts, human creativity is less likely to develop (Garfinkel 2000; Rubel 2014).

The values of dignity and self-respect have also been connected with privacy. In 1948 the Universal Declaration of Human Rights, Article 12, declared, "No one shall be subjected to arbitrary interference with his privacy, family, home or correspondence, nor to attacks upon his honor and reputation." Human rights organizations such as Liberty in the United Kingdom often link their support for privacy with the preservation of human dignity: "The right to a private life is based on principles of human dignity and is inherently linked to many other rights such as equal treatment and free expression" (Liberty 2016). The Charter of Fundamental Rights of the European Union also draws the connection explicitly: Article 1 provides that "human dignity is inviolable. It must be respected and protected." Without privacy, people may be subject to intrusions that, because they are unwanted, are demeaning. Control of personal space may be part of what people need to have in order to develop a sense of themselves as individuals who are worthy. Control over information can save people from embarrassment or the use of information to demean or stigmatize. Privacy may be needed to protect people against discrimination. The inability to control sensitive information such as medical conditions, sexual orientation, or disability may subject people to loss of insurance, employment, or housing. Finally, protecting privacy may be critical to physical security. People may need the space of the home as a refuge from attack. If others gain unauthorized access to information, they may use that information to extort or threaten. Information about disease status, for example, has subjected people infected with leprosy, HIV, or other dreaded diseases to quarantine, isolation, or even being stoned to death.

In sum, autonomy, liberty of conscience, dignity and self-respect, non-discrimination, and security are all values that have been centrally linked to support privacy. Together, they suggest why one or more of the many facets of privacy matter a great deal for many people, but for different reasons.

It should not be forgotten that there is a dark side to privacy, however. Privacy protections may enable people to plan and hide acts of horror. Bodies are buried in sequestered basements, spouses and children are abused in the privacy of the home, and terrorist acts are plotted in secrecy.

Is privacy a modern idea?

Yes and no. Privacy is surely one of the defining issues of contemporary society; it may matter more today than at any time since World War II. Some deplore (and others celebrate) claims that privacy no longer exists. Still others advocate for a more expansive understanding of what privacy may embrace in the face of apparently omnipresent surveillance or threats of hacking. Privacy has a long history, but not as an experience known to most people in a real or sustained sense until relatively recently. Lives in crowded quarters or open spaces were not conducive to the protection of personal space. Past understandings of privacy, some developed in antiquity, continue to be influential on how people understand privacy today; however, new definitions have developed, with the result that our ideas about what privacy may require have expanded. Two historical developments are of particular contemporary significance.

First is the development of liberal theory in Britain from the seventeenth century onward. John Locke's defenses of the right to private property and freedom of association were premised on the idea of individuals having rights against a state with powers limited by consent (Locke, *Second Treatise*; Simmons 1992; Claeys 2008). Directly incorporated into the constitution of South Carolina, the Lockean picture of limited government was highly influential on American constitutionalism more generally. In *On Liberty*, John Stuart Mill wrote that the sole justification for social coercion was to prevent people from harming one another. This "harm principle," as it has become known, held that protecting people from harming themselves or requiring them to do what is moral could not be justified, at least for people who were capable of making their own decisions. In Mill's judgment,

> ... there is a sphere of action in which society, as distinguished from the individual, has, if any, only an indirect interest comprehending all that portion of a person's life and conduct which affects only himself, or if it also affects others, only with their free, voluntary, and undeceived consent and participation. When I say only himself, I mean directly, and in the first instance: for whatever affects himself, may affect others *through* himself; and the objection which may be grounded on this contingency, will receive consideration in the sequel. This, then, is the appropriate region of human liberty. It comprises, first, the inward domain of consciousness; demanding liberty of conscience, in the most comprehensive sense; liberty of

thought and feeling; absolute freedom of opinion and sentiment on all subjects, practical or speculative, scientific, moral, or theological. (*On Liberty*, Ch. 2, p. 15)

Mill's separation of actions into self-regarding ones that affect only individuals themselves and other-regarding ones that are the proper subject of social concern remains controversial. The second historical development is technological: the invention of photography. Photography made it possible to capture and reproduce representational images of persons and events. In 1890, Samuel Warren and later Supreme Court Justice Louis Brandeis published one of the most influential law review articles of all time in the *Harvard Law Review*: "The Right to Privacy." The article by Warren and Brandeis argued that technological change in the press and photography made a compelling case for privacy as a right. "... the next step which must be taken for the protection of the person, and for securing to the individual what Judge Cooley calls the right 'to be let alone.'" The right to be let alone was not a new right—Warren and Brandeis were quoting from an earlier treatise—but their article powerfully systematized what it claimed were developing trends in tort, intellectual property, contract, and other legal fields (Glancy 1979). One impetus for the article is reputed to have been Warren's annoyance at publication of the details of his family's social life in local newspapers.

Perhaps Warren and Brandeis's essay is so often cited because its argument remains modern. Warren and Brandeis defended private control over personal information in the context of the challenges posed by ever-changing communication technologies to potentially outmoded legal regimes governing personal information and its use. Technological change and its implications for privacy have been an important theme in privacy debates at least since the Warren and Brandeis article in 1890. Their concern was the adverse impact of the camera, taking pictures of people without their permission, and the rapid and wide distribution of newspaper articles that included the photographs. But concern over reproduction in newspapers was supplanted by other fears about privacy. A common image of 1930s movies was the telephone operator overhearing private conversations, or the neighbor listening in on conversations on a party line for his or her own delectation—a concern that was validated by the US Supreme Court's decision in 1928 that when operators could listen in, there was no Fourth Amendment requirement for a search warrant (*Olmstead v. United States*, 277 U.S. 438 (1928)). Today the controversy over the use of information available to telephone service providers has become the controversy over whether the government should collect information about the numbers called from telephones, the addresses to which emails are sent, or the geolocation of smartphones.

The scale of transmission of personal information and the ways it can be gathered and used by governmental agencies, groups, and organizations for their own purposes has grown astronomically. This scale and its expanding potential continue to offer us new ways to think about our expectations for privacy. Yet current debates continue to recognize the importance of the capability to insulate oneself in some areas of life from intrusion by others. Nonetheless, formal legal recognition of a right to privacy is relatively recent and incomplete in many jurisdictions. In many countries of the world today, the ability to escape the gaze of others may depend more on the disinterest of authorities than on effective formal prohibitions against such intrusions.

Is privacy a human right?

Privacy and related concepts are given clear articulation in many international human rights treaties and other documents. Some of these instruments have the force of law; for example, the Charter of Fundamental Rights of the European Union is law in all member states of the Union and is enforced by their courts and the European Court of Justice. Other such instruments do not have the force of law but of moral suasion. The power of all these documents, however, lies in their claim to protect rights that are of special importance because they are *human* rights. Indeed, in the aftermath of World War II, many Nazi officials were tried and convicted at Nuremberg for having committed crimes against humanity—even though much of what they had done was not specifically illegal under the laws of Nazi Germany.

But what is the special force of a human rights claim? It is that the right is one that is possessed in virtue of some special characteristic of human beings. To claim that a right is a human right is thus to claim that it is possessed by all and only human beings in virtue of some characteristic that is uniquely human. What that characteristic might be raises deeply controversial philosophical questions, however. Some argue that it is humanity itself; others claim that without further explanation of why "humanity" matters, this claim to human exceptionalism is "speciesist," privileging human beings over non-human animals without justification. Others locate the characteristic in dignity—indeed, many human rights instruments rest explicitly on dignity—in the sense of being the kind of entity that must be treated as an end in itself, never as only a means. Further explanations for why an entity should be treated as an end may rest in the idea that the entity has reason, the capacity for self-determination, or the capacity to make autonomous choices. Defenders of privacy as a human right then contend that it is either instrumentally necessary for the exercise of these capacities or intrinsic to their realization or value.

Locating the special characteristic(s) that ground human rights is not the only deep theoretical difficulty about human rights claims. Another is that some human beings may apparently lack the relevant characteristics, and some non-human animals or other beings (robots?) may apparently have the characteristics. Human beings with severe cognitive disabilities may never acquire capacities for reason or self-determination, for example. The consequence is that they are either left out of human rights claims, or some other basis for attributing rights to them must be located. The invocation of their humanity as a ground for their human rights then seems pushed back to simple privileging of the human. Nonetheless, something seems wrong about intruding on the body of a human being in a permanent vegetative state—even if the person is unaware of the intrusion and cannot object to it.

Privacy might also be viewed as a political or civil right, predicated on the structure of society, rather than on characteristics that are intrinsic to human beings. As a political right, privacy is joined either instrumentally or intrinsically to how democracy functions; privacy violations, it may be argued, threaten to undermine citizens' participation in government and their ability to exercise independent voice. As a civil right, it is seen as a needed way to protect people against discrimination and to further social inclusion on equal terms.

Are all individuals alike when it comes to privacy protections?

No, individuals are not all alike when it comes to privacy protection. In general, political or other public figures have less privacy protections than other people do. Politicians may expect that others will be interested in their financial transactions and their medical conditions or the content of their emails. Efforts to try to keep this information secret may meet with public criticism.

Emails played a controversial role in the 2016 US presidential election. Secretary Clinton was criticized for her use of a private server to send emails while she was Secretary of State; hacking of emails from the Democratic National Committee and members of the Clinton campaign proved politically damaging. It seems only prudent that anyone in a position of responsibility in any sort of organization, public or private, should not send an email that contains data or observations that they would regret having shared publicly. Privacy protection for emails sent by people who are in the public eye is at the time of this writing uneven. Perhaps the future of email transmission will be celebrated for its security for both the sender and the recipient. But for the time being the public disclosure of email content, long a staple in litigation, is now a component of electoral strategy and raises questions as to how best to realize private communication quickly and conveniently.

This does not mean that public figures shouldn't have some privacy. What it does mean is that difficult lines need to be drawn between the information that is justifiably public and that is appropriately kept out of the public eye. Some have drawn distinctions between the public persona of entertainers and their private lives; in March 2016, the high-profile professional wrestler Hulk Hogan won a $140 million verdict against the Internet gossip site Gawker for publishing a bootleg sex tape that he claimed concerned his private affairs. In another case distinguishing the public and the private for an otherwise public figure, the family of the Prince of Monaco won a judgment against publication of photographs of them on a skiing holiday—but not against publication of a photograph about the prince that might provide information of interest to the public about his health (*Von Hannover v. Germany* App. 40660/08 and 60641/08 (ECtHR 7 February 2012)). Accepted conventions may also affect what is published: in this respect, the United States presents a sharp contrast with France, where the convention governing personal lives of politicians until quite recently has been not to report on their private activities.

It also does not mean that individuals who have never been in the public eye are also well protected. Names of victims of crimes such as rape are typically withheld from the media. But if they are published by mistake, free speech law in the United States will protect media against suits for damages for breach of privacy (*Florida Star v. B.J.F.* 491 U.S. 524, 526 (1989)). Despite recognizing the right to be forgotten, European courts will still balance the contemporary relevance of information with its sensitivity to the individual in deciding whether it should remain available over the Internet.

What kinds of entities can assert rights to privacy?

Defining what kind of beings can assert rights to privacy depends on how privacy is conceptualized and justified. If privacy is justified as a human right, for example, it will attach directly only to human beings. Some might also argue that groups of humans linked relationally, such as families or tribes, have a human right to privacy. If privacy is seen as a political right, it may attach to those who are participants in political society. This might include individuals, groups such as families, clans, or tribes, or even artificial persons such as corporations. If it is a civil right, it will be viewed in terms of those who come under anti-discrimination mandates. Some aspects of privacy, such as protection of conscience or private thoughts, may be exercised only by certain kinds of beings, except perhaps by extension or analogy. Thus it may be thought that corporations or states cannot experience intellectual privacy—but could certainly claim that they wish to exercise control over information in their possession.

In debates over human rights, some have contended that non-human animals also have basic rights, such as to be free from pain or unjustified killing. These arguments rest on accounts of these animals' fundamental interests. If non-human animals have basic interests in seclusion or intimacy, on this reasoning it would likewise follow that they have certain aspects of privacy rights. A group called the Nonhuman Rights Project (http://www.nonhumanrightsproject.org/) has sought legal protections for primates who have been placed on exhibit or have been subjected to experimentation, so far without obtaining court agreement with their legal claims but with notable success in getting primates moved to sanctuaries. However, there is evidence that non-human primates behave in ways suggestive of privacy concerns. The renowned primatologist

Frans de Waal argues that chimpanzees have sufficient control over their sexual impulses "either to refrain from them or to arrange privacy first" (de Waal 2016, p. 224).

With respect to information protection, governments and corporations have obtained far more success than non-human animals in obtaining legal protection. In the United States, classified information is protected for national security purposes, law enforcement information can be secluded to allow investigations to proceed, and information collected for the US Census may be used for that purpose only. The federal Freedom of Information Act specifies limits to information that people may request from government agencies, and many states have similar laws as well.

Families and groups, too, may assert privacy rights. They may assert privacy either for the group or on behalf of individuals who are group members. Whether entities such as groups have an ontological status separate from their individual members is a deep philosophical problem. (Are groups "real"? Do they have minds or bodies? Can they think, believe, feel?) These ontological questions can be avoided, however, if the characteristics relevant to asserting privacy do not require assigning a special ontological status to groups, such as that they must be able to have emotions or thoughts in order to claim privacy. Such ontological questions are not raised by social norms that would protect group customs or rituals from wider discussion. Kukathas (2008), for example, argues that cultures should be able to determine what they will keep concealed as a way of limiting interference in their collective affairs. Ontological questions are not in play at all if groups assert privacy rights derivatively on behalf of their members, as Kukathas believes they do. Unpopular organizations in the United States have successfully asserted rights to keep their membership lists confidential in order to protect their members from reprisals (*NAACP v. Alabama*, 357 U.S. 449 (1958)).

Corporations also have been accorded privacy rights. US law regards corporations as artificial persons and has struggled with what this characterization means with respect to rights and responsibilities. Like groups, corporations are not physical persons that can be thrown into jail or physically silenced, but they are organizations with decision-making structures that can decide what messages to convey, what to pay for, and what to protect. The right to trade secrets—information of economic value that the organization has taken steps to protect—has long been recognized by the courts. These secrets were regarded as property and their violation as a form of unfair competition, and they are now given statutory protection. Recent, highly controversial legal developments have considered whether corporations can have rights such as free speech or conscience. In *Citizens United v. Federal Election Commission* (558 U.S. 310 (2010)), the Supreme Court struck down a prohibition on corporations and unions using general treasury funds to make contributions to political candidates, on the ground that it violated the corporations' right to political speech. In forbidding laws about political speech to distinguish between individual and corporate actors, the Court viewed corporate actors as having expression rights on a par with those of individuals. More recently, the Court has determined that closely held for-profit corporations have statutory rights of religious liberty to refuse to provide contraceptive coverage for their employees (*Burwell v. Hobby Lobby Stores, Inc.*, 134 S.Ct. 2751 (2014)). The extensive subsequent commentary has debated whether the Court's reasoning will be extended to constitutional protection for all for-profit corporations, rather than just those that are closely held, and thus might be thought of as alter-egos of their owners.

Privacy is thus a multifaceted idea that has drawn a great deal of attention over the ages. Most recently, with the ubiquitous reminders about hacking and identity theft, protection of personal information has been at the forefront in debates about privacy. The next chapter takes up many issues about personal information and privacy.

2

PROTECTING PERSONAL INFORMATION

BASIC ISSUES

Introduction

When you think about your privacy, you may care a great deal about your personal information. Notice the possessive pronoun: you may think about information about you as "yours," maybe even as your property. Some of you reading this may consider particular types of information especially personal and sensitive. But you may have very different ideas about which information is the most sensitive. Depending on your circumstances, you also may fear that information may be used against you. This chapter considers some general questions about personal information and how it is collected today. It also presents what is known about what people believe about information privacy and how they act, if at all, to protect privacy. The most common approach to protecting privacy today is what is called "notice and choice": the privacy notices you are given before you choose whether or not to share information. This chapter also considers whether this approach to information protection is a good fit with how people think and act. Later chapters take up questions about particularly sensitive types of information: health; education; financial, credit, and employment; information about law enforcement, crime victims, arrests, and convictions; and information on social media.

Before you read any further in this chapter, you might want to take stock of your own views on privacy so that you have some idea about how you would answer survey questions that others have been asked. Is privacy something you care a lot about? What kind of privacy matters the most to you? Do you sometimes think you are being asked to give up your privacy in order to get something you want, and does this bother you? Do you think you have control over information about yourself? Are there some uses of information from you that bother you more than others? Do you ever click on the "privacy policy" link on a web page—or even look for it? Do you read the privacy notices you are given when you get health care or the privacy policy that comes with your computer software? Could you say (without checking) what your privacy settings are on the social media sites you frequent?

What is personal information?

Personal information is information relating to an individual. When people have personal information about you, they don't have just general information; they have information that is specifically linked to you. That Cabrini-Green was public housing in Chicago, that it was believed by policymakers to be dilapidated and dangerous, and that it was ultimately demolished is general information; so is that many people flourished in Cabrini-Green and that the demolition was highly controversial. That a particular person grew up in Cabrini-Green is personal information—information that this person might very much wish to share to establish facts about his or her background, or information that he or she might not want to share at all. As time passes, people may change the personal information they want to share. As a person seeking a public career, you may want to reveal a great deal of personal information about yourself at the beginning—but you may find later that the glare of public attention is too intrusive and seek to delete as much information as you can.

In general, approaches to protecting informational privacy in use today focus on personal information. Information that is anonymous or de-identified is not included in privacy protections, even if it originally came from individuals. Nor is general information such as demographic statistics, socioeconomic statistics, public health information, or environmental information. As we shall see, however, individuals may have concerns about information that is not personal, especially if it might be used to make inferences about them that are objectionable or harmful. The limitation of privacy protections to personal information may be problematic.

Do you own your personal information?

Use of the possessive pronoun "your" to describe personal information suggests that it is something that you own, like your car or your sweater. People often refer to information in this way, as "theirs" or their "property."

Stories such as that in *The Immortal Life of Henrietta Lacks* (Skloot 2010) may reinforce this idea of information from yourself as property. Henrietta Lacks was a 31-year-old African-American charity patient at Johns Hopkins University with an incurable, aggressive form of cervical cancer. During her treatment, cells drawn from biopsy samples of her cancer tissue were recognized as having the ability to grow indefinitely. They became the HeLa cells in widespread use for medical research ever since—cells that have played a role in discoveries from the polio vaccine to tamoxifen as a treatment for cancer. Neither Lacks nor her family members were ever asked about the use of the tissue; people puzzled for decades over the cells' origin until journalist Rebecca Skloot told the history. Skloot's best-selling book raised questions about research ethics and justice for Lacks and her family—who had never known what had happened to the cells. After Skloot's book was widely read, there were calls for compensation for the family for the use of Lacks' tissue samples without consent, although there was no suggestion that her medical care had been compromised by their use. In 2013, researchers in Europe published a genetic sequence of a HeLa cell line, again without any consent from family members, although the publication noted the connection to Lacks. The publication was withdrawn after members of the family protested that their family's information had been released without consulting them (Callaway 2013). Johns Hopkins and the National Institutes of Health (NIH) reached an agreement with Lacks's family that further release of genome data from the cell line could occur on a restricted access basis for research only, vetted by a committee that includes members of the family (Callaway 2013).

If Lacks's cells and the genome sequence and other information drawn from them are the property of Lacks and her heirs, then they would have the powers over them that people generally have over personal property: the right to use it, exclude others from its use, destroy it, sell or rent it, pass it on to their heirs, and so on. The wrong they suffered would not only have been the lack of informed consent, but also the lost opportunity to realize economic gain from the tissues. They would also have had the right to make sure that the tissues were never used by others, by withdrawing them from the market or by destroying them. Of course, they could also have given away the tissues and the information for others to use.

What would an ownership model look like? If you had property rights to all of the information about you that goes out into the world, you could negotiate for its sale. You might try to insist on a nano-penny for each byte about you that websites have, perhaps accumulating a form of web-currency each time your information is collected and reused. No market like this has emerged, possibly because the costs of setting it up and managing all of the deals would overwhelm the value created. Or, perhaps no market has emerged because the data collectors have market power over the means of collection and individual data sources don't have any bargaining power. If individual data sources could band together and negotiate as a group, things might be different, but the transaction costs of getting data sources together might be far too high. Data sources are also so diverse that it might be difficult for them to find common ground. On the other hand, there is a great deal of money to be made from data drawn from individual sources; one estimate puts the market for big data analytics to be nearly $200 billion in 2019 (Dignan 2016).

One practical argument against applying an ownership model to information drawn from you is the inability to structure a market. There are theoretical objections as well. For example, if you—or anyone else—are able to withhold your data from use, very important knowledge may be lost. Developments in medicine, public health, social science, and many other areas depend on large, representative data sets. Decisions to withhold information—withholding it from the market or destroying it—may have deleterious consequences for these advancements (Contreras 2016). Relatedly, there is an important sense in which information is what economists call a "public good"—a good that benefits even those who don't pay for its use. Scientific developments from big data will benefit everyone, even those from whom no data are used.

There is a nagging tendency, though, to think about information in terms of property rights. The last sentence of the preceding paragraph could easily read like this: "Scientific developments from big data will benefit everyone, even those whose data are not used." Indeed, this way of writing the sentence seems less awkward, more familiar. So it's worth thinking further about whether there are moral insights captured in the possessory language. We think there are at least three.

The first is that personal information is monetized today. It just isn't monetized by the individuals from whom it is derived. Instead, it's monetized by many different types of information aggregators: pharmaceutical companies, firms analyzing the productivity of workers, firms predicting high-cost users of health care, firms creating analytics to predict poor credit risks, firms using data they have derived from genetic tests to determine whether particular gene variants are likely to be deleterious, firms predicting what ads to serve to consumers based on their Internet browsing habits, and many, many more. Some of these commercial uses benefit consumers, some do not, and some may be actively harmful—but one thing that is clear is that the aggregators believe the data are valuable to them, and they are often right. When privatized by aggregators, moreover, information is removed from what some see as a "data commons" that should benefit all of us. For example, the National Institutes of Health has recently set up a Genomic Data Commons as part of the efforts to use precision medicine to improve cancer care by tailoring treatment more closely to individual factors that are likely to affect its success (NIH 2016). And the 21st Century Cures Act, passed by Congress in the waning days of the Obama Administration, may allow more flexibility for use of information from electronic health records in research.

Second, the information does come from individuals, even when it has been de-identified. The sense in which it is theirs is that it comes from them in the first place. The pronoun describes the connection to the person; it's not a possessory "their" of ownership but rather a descriptive "their," as in "their date of birth" or "their country." Arguably, the fact that the information comes from someone and is about them gives them some kind of claim to how it is used, even if the claim is not one of ownership. In medical research, this claim has come to be understood as informed consent: that data about you should not be used without your consent. The settlement between NIH, Johns Hopkins, and the Lacks family reflects this idea: that the wrong done to Lacks and her family was not that she, and later they, did not get to profit directly from the sale of the immortal cell line, but that her tissues and the information drawn from them had been used without their knowing agreement. So did the court decision in an earlier and widely cited case involving the use of a patient's tissues to synthesize a treatment for his form of leukemia. The patient, John Moore, was treated at the University of California,

Los Angeles (UCLA), for hairy T-cell leukemia. His physician, David Golde, commercialized a cell line from his cancer tissues. Golde did this by perfecting the cell line involved and calling Moore back for later "tests" even though they were not needed for his medical care. Moore claimed that he should have shared in the profits from the cell line; the California Supreme Court determined that he did not have property rights in his body parts, although there might have been a failure of informed consent in how he was treated (*Moore v. Regents of the University of California*, 793 P.2d 479 (Cal. 1990)).

Even this idea of informed consent may be too strong for information, however. The informed consent model seems especially persuasive in the cases of Henrietta Lacks and John Moore because tissue samples were taken from their bodies for their health care and then were put to a different purpose. It would have been easy to ask them, at the time, whether their tissue could be used in later research. And it was tissue—something actually drawn from their physical bodies, even if cancerous—that was used to develop the cell lines. That tissue is a physical thing—not just a piece of information—may also be why property rights ideas seem to have traction in a case like Lacks's. But it is not so obvious that uses of tissue are the same as uses of information, even when the information is drawn from the tissues. The informed consent model applied to information gives you veto power over whether your information is used, even if you don't get to profit from its use. So it might still result in limiting the information that is available to science (Contreras 2016a).

A third moral insight can be gleaned from the idea that you should profit in some way, however: that there should be transparency about how data are being used and that there should be some social say over whether they are being used justly. This insight is captured by the concern in the story of Henrietta Lacks that her family never received any apparent benefit from the knowledge that was gained from their mother. If collections of information drawn from individuals are used only to give profits to others—like big pharmaceutical companies that price-gouge, so the criticism goes—there is an argument that this use is unjust. This isn't what actually happened in the Lacks case directly—the scientists who originally cultivated the cell line made it available to other scientists for free—but much of the subsequent use of the cells has been very profitable. What should be treated as a public good is redounding to significant private gain. This idea of justice may be captured in the data that suggest that people are much more concerned about commercial uses of their information than about other uses. In this view, the issue with the use of personal information is not that your property is being taken, or that you haven't given your informed consent, but that there is no thought—not even any public discussion—about whether the information is being used justly (Francis and Francis 2014).

What is "big data" and does it contain personal information?

"Big data" is a loose term used to refer to the vast data sets being collected by many different kinds of entities all over the world today. "Big data" may be collected by governments, law enforcement, corporations, insurance companies, data analytics firms, search engines, websites, and many, many other types of entities.

In general, data are called "big" when they are characterized by three "Vs": volume, variety, and velocity. That is, data sets are big when they have a lot of information, drawn from many different sources, and they are easily transferred and analyzed. Whether any particular big data contain personal information depends on the information within the data. Some sets of big data—for example, the data drawn from medical records and used by insurers to compare cost-effectiveness of treatments, or the population data used to assess incidence of disease—consist of de-identified data only. Other big data sets—for example, those drawn from web searches—may or may not contain identifiers such as Internet Protocol (IP) addresses. Even when data are de-identified, moreover, risks of re-identification will vary, depending on what data are combined in the big data set and what other kinds of data are available. In general, re-identification risks rise with the variety of the data because this may create mosaic effects in which there are very small numbers of people possessing a particular set of characteristics.

People are unlikely to be aware of whether information originating from themselves is included in big data sets, or in which data sets it might be included. The sheer volume and velocity of big data make this very unlikely. So does the fact that a great deal of the information that is in big data has at one point or another passed through a stage of being stripped of identifiers. If people are aware of data collection at all, it's likely to be at the initial point of contact, not as data are combined and recombined, transferred to others, or put to uses that might never have been anticipated at the time of original collection (Ohm 2014). Approaches to controlling or protecting what is done with big data that rely on individual notice, monitoring, and choice are thus unlikely to be effective, at least given current conditions of data collection, use, and regulation.

What ethical frameworks might be applied to big data?

Individual choice is unlikely to be effective in imposing ethical constraints on the use of big data. So, then, which values should be part of big data collection and use? A great deal of recent scholarly writing has been devoted to this topic. Let us take a look at a few possibilities.

One value that many writers agree on is transparency. There should be more openness about what data are collected, how they are used, and who uses them. Transparency helps people figure out how to do well in a networked world (Cohen 2012). Internet and financial companies in particular use algorithms for analyzing big data that are concealed (likely as trade secrets) but that may have deleterious effects, such as higher interest rates for consumers, without their knowledge (Pasquale 2015). Scoring methods are everywhere, from credit worthiness to employability, yet people don't know that they exist or how they work (Citrone and Pasquale 2014).

Quality is another problem with big data. Data gathered in the past may be less accurate or useful than data gathered later. Data matching may be imperfect. Efforts to scoop up large quantities of data may result in data sets that are simply a hodgepodge of what could be collected. Improving the matching and quality of data may require contextual information that makes it very difficult to scrub the data of identifiers.

Various ethical concerns surrounding the collection and use of big data relate to power imbalances. Information acquisition and control are sources of power, and we must be attentive that this power is leveraged fairly. For example, employers collect data about workers and consult data analytics firms to construct workplace rules and impose discipline on workers perceived as not meeting quality standards, but workers do not collect data or use it to constrain their employers in return. This imbalance seems unfair and unethical (Marx 2016). Similarly, how are we to control information collection and use in a democratic fashion? This question is especially urgent in the face of government surveillance (e.g., Balkin 2008; Haggerty and Samatas 2010). Some wonder whether it is even possible to maintain democracy in a world of mass surveillance (e.g., Scheer 2015). Chapter 10 is devoted to further exploration of these issues.

If individuals are ineluctably networked in the modern world, through big data and the myriad other forms of information technology, how can we re-conceptualize possibilities for human flourishing? At the core of the idea of privacy in context (see Chapter 1) is the idea that people need contexts of normative integrity in which to function—that is, they need to work within accepted privacy boundaries. These boundaries may be especially important when people construct identities through networks. Teenagers, for example, may be very willing to share social media with certain groups of friends but may be deeply distressed if others, such as teachers or parents, cross boundaries (boyd 2014). More generally, people may need to figure out how to function as networked selves, maintaining physical and psycho-social well-being (Cohen 2012). For this to occur, networked environments must not only be a source of knowledge that is operationally transparent, but a place in which boundaries of protection and access can be negotiated by individuals and communities. Networked geographies of accessibility—how one website can get information from another—are a critical factor. So is what Cohen (2012) calls "semantic discontinuity": the possibility that information flows can be separately structured in myriad ways that do not simply reflect protection of data pertaining to particular individuals. We address privacy in social networking further in Chapter 7.

Justice is another important aspect of the ethics of big data collection and use. We mentioned earlier that questions of justice are raised if information collected about some individuals is used in a way that benefits others, without consideration of whether the information might be used to benefit its original sources. There are also questions of justice within big data. If data collection or analytics are skewed by factors such as race or gender, resulting data uses may create further injustice. An example of this is the use of data analytics for policing: more policing in a given area may yield more crime data, but that doesn't show that an area in question has higher underlying crime rates. It may just reflect—and then entrench—unjust policing patterns (Ohm 2014). Using big data to profile possible types of offenders raises similar concerns.

Do people in the United States care about privacy in personal information?

Some people openly disavow the importance of privacy; John Halamka, a high-profile health system information officer, celebrated the open disclosure of his sequenced genome (Halamka

2015). But apparently, most people in the United States do care about privacy. At least, they say they do in surveys. Yet the history of privacy surveys in the United States makes answering this question difficult.

Beginning in the 1960s and for three decades thereafter, the political scientist and legal scholar Alan Westin produced a series of highly influential studies about attitudes toward privacy among people in the United States (Westin 1967; Hoofnagle and Urban 2014). Westin claimed that individuals fell into three groups: privacy fundamentalists, who rejected trading privacy for other benefits and wanted categorical protection (approximately 25% of the population); the privacy unconcerned, who were happy to share their information with others (approximately 20% of the population); and privacy pragmatists, who wanted to know the risks of trading information and assess them against any expected benefits (approximately 55% of the population). In Westin's view, these privacy pragmatists were at the core of the development of public policy—as he put it, "The policy struggle of the 1990s was (and remains today) a battle for the mind and hearts of the privacy pragmatists" (2003, p. 445). Westin testified frequently before policymaking bodies, including Congress, and his work was highly influential on the notice and choice structure of consumer privacy protection in the United States today.

Westin died in 2013, and his way of dividing people into privacy pragmatists, privacy fundamentalists, and privacy unconcerned has come under considerable recent criticism. Hoofnagle and Urban, scholars at the Berkeley Center for Law and the Internet, have conducted a series of recent surveys including not only Westin's questions but also questions about how much respondents know about privacy and questions about their attitudes toward specific contemporary privacy choices such as the use of cookies to track Internet browsing (https://www.law.berkeley.edu/research/bclt/research/privacy-at-bclt/berkeley-consumer-privacy-survey/). Westin asked consumers how strongly they agreed with these statements: "(1) consumers have lost all control over how personal information is collected and used by companies; (2) most businesses handle the personal information they collect about consumers in a proper and confidential way; and (3) existing laws and organizational practices provide a reasonable level of protection for consumer privacy today." Westin classified those who strongly agreed with (1) as privacy fundamentalists and those who disagreed with (1) but agreed with (2) and (3) as the privacy unconcerned; the remainder he classified as pragmatists. But, as others have pointed out, this categorization confuses consumers' levels of knowledge about privacy protections and the extent to which they care about these protections. People might know a lot and care little—or care a lot and know little. Indeed, people who care a lot and don't know very much might very well disagree with (1), believing they have more control than they actually do, and agree with (2) and (3), believing that they are better protected than they actually are. At least up until 2013, consumers overwhelmingly misunderstood privacy protections (Hoofnagle and Urban 2014). Consumers were very likely to believe that if a website has a privacy policy, that means that their privacy is protected—when the fact is that website privacy policies only tell consumers what they will do with information, including sharing it widely. Somewhat surprisingly (as they have grown up with the Internet), young adults were less well informed than older adults about the law implementing privacy protections (Hoofnagle et al. 2010). Westin's "unconcerned," therefore, may only lack knowledge. And so-called privacy pragmatists may be woefully inaccurate about whether the trade-offs they make reflect their actual preferences.

The Pew Research Center has also collected extensive data about privacy attitudes in the United States. In survey work conducted after Edward Snowden's revelation of surveillance activities by the US government, Pew found that 91% of Americans believe that consumers have lost control of their personal information online. Most are not confident that their records will remain private or secure, no matter the type of organization collecting the information. Nearly three-quarters say it is "very important" to be in control of who can get information about them, and about two-thirds say it is "very important" to control what information can be obtained (Rainie 2016). The Pew data also indicate that Americans report feeling confused about what information is being collected and how it is being used. Perhaps orthogonally to the data of Hoofnagle and his coauthors, the Pew survey indicates that younger adults are generally more proactive about privacy, have experienced more privacy problems, and have taken more steps to protect privacy than older adults have (Rainie 2016).

According to the Pew Research Center data, the privacy decisions of US consumers reflect trade-offs. People are generally willing to share information when they believe doing so will have some value for them. Retail loyalty cards, for example, are acceptable to about half the population, even though they are unacceptable to about a third. People are willing to have their physicians place information on a health information website to make it easier to access the information and schedule appointments, if they are assured that the website is secure (52% acceptable, 26% not acceptable, 20% "it depends"). People are also willing to permit surveillance that they believe will be protective, such as allowing employers to install monitoring cameras after workplace thefts (54% acceptable, 24% unacceptable, 21% "it depends"). But they are far less willing to allow their insurance company to install equipment to monitor their driving habits to assess eligibility for discounts (37% acceptable, 45% unacceptable, 16% "it depends"), or to allow a site arranging a high school reunion to create a personalized profile to send advertising (33% acceptable, 51% unacceptable, and 15% "it depends"). They are even more unwilling to allow a thermostat sensor to be installed in their home that would help them save on energy bills if it also tracks their basic movements around their home (27% acceptable, 55% unacceptable, 17% "it depends") (Rainie and Duggan 2016).

On the other side of the trade-off, privacy attitudes also reflect the sensitivity of the information to consumers. People regard their Social Security numbers as very sensitive (90%), followed by health information (55% very sensitive, 26% somewhat sensitive), telephone conversations (54% very sensitive, 27% somewhat sensitive), and the content of their email messages (52% very sensitive, 25% somewhat sensitive). People also are particularly concerned about locational data from the perspective of what it reveals (Rainie and Duggan 2016). Media preferences (9% very sensitive, 22% somewhat sensitive) and basic purchasing habits (8% very sensitive, 33% somewhat sensitive) are viewed with significantly less concern (Rainie 2016). Pew data collected before the Snowden revelations also indicate that people are likely to have tried to use the Internet in a way that avoids hackers or criminals (33%) or advertisers (28%) and are least likely to have tried to avoid the companies whose websites they visit (6%), companies who might want payment for downloaded files (6%), the government (5%), and law enforcement (4%) (Rainie 2016).

In another recent study, scholars at the University of Illinois examined the intersection between knowledge and opinions about online privacy (Kesan, Hayes, and Bashir 2016). Their study concluded that consumers frequently want more privacy options than they are given by the market; they submit information online because they want a service and do not think they have alternatives. This study also indicated that people in the United States care more about protecting their privacy from the government than they care about protecting their privacy from other individuals or businesses.

Thus people do apparently care very much about privacy. How they balance privacy against the benefits of revealing information may depend on the context, the benefits of disclosure, and the sensitivity of the information. Unfortunately, people may know far less about how to try to realize their privacy preferences in practice.

Do Europeans think any differently about privacy?

With Nazism, fascism, communism, and the East German Stasi in particular, Europeans have had more immediate experiences of state intrusions on privacy than have most residents of the United States—or at least their parents have had these experiences. A common claim about contemporary attitudes, however, is that Europeans are more suspicious of privacy intrusions from private-sector actors, such as corporations, than they are of state intrusions. Data bear this out.

The Eurobarometer surveys are large population surveys conducted periodically by researchers on behalf of the European Union. The most recent available survey on attitudes toward data protection indicates that only 15% of EU residents believe they have complete control over what happens to information about them on the Internet, while 31% believe they have no control at all and 50% believe they have partial control. (The rest either don't know or believe it depends on the Internet site.) A large majority (71%) say that providing personal information has become necessary to obtaining services, but over half (57%) disagree that this is not a big issue for them. Nearly a third (29%) mind providing personal information in exchange for free services over the Internet. Data repurposing is one of the most serious privacy concerns for Europeans, with 69% wanting to give new consent for new data uses. Nearly two-thirds trust their national governments, just over half trust EU institutions, but only a third trust Internet service providers, and only a quarter trust online social networks, search engines, or email services (European Commission 2015). These figures have moved slightly toward greater privacy concerns than those reported in a more comprehensive study in 2011 (European Commission 2011).

Although these surveys ask different questions and thus can't be directly compared, several themes do appear in common. People on both sides of the Atlantic say that privacy is a significant concern and believe that they do not have control of information on the Internet. Europeans may be more concerned than Americans about commercial uses of data, especially when data gathered for one purpose are put to another use. People in the United States may be more concerned about surveillance by the government (Kesan, Hayes, and Bashir 2016). If US laws are a reflection of attitudes, people in the United States are more worried than people in the European Union about government access to information. These laws, however, may be more reflective of general US distrust of government than of views about the government as less trustworthy than the private sector when it has information (Hoofnagle 2016a).

What is the "privacy paradox"?

The so-called privacy paradox is that, although people say they care very much about privacy, they behave as if they did not. People allegedly express worries about their privacy and state that they are committed to its protection, while blithely using frequent shopper cards that collect data about their purchases, communicating intimate details of their lives on social media sites such as Facebook, clicking "I agree" to un-protective privacy policies without even reading them, and searching the Internet for highly sensitive forms of information without setting controls to restrict capture of their browsing history. If you say that you care a lot about privacy, but then can't remember what your social media privacy settings are, you might be an illustration of the privacy paradox.

Why this paradox, if indeed it exists? Some commentators point to the inevitability of access to data: in the words of Scott McNealy, then CEO of Sun Microsystems, "You have zero privacy anyway. Get over it" (Polly Sprenger 1999). Perhaps some, despite still saying they care about privacy, evidence in their behavior that they really have gotten over it. Or perhaps the convenience of Internet use—the world of information at the touch of a key—and its immediate gratification overwhelm any longer-term prudential commitment to privacy. Or perhaps reading privacy policies that are long, complex, and composed of unreadable legal boilerplate seems too daunting or a waste of time. Another explanation may be that many people are simply misinformed, believing that their privacy is far better protected than it really is by privacy policies (Hoofnagle et al. 2010)—although this rosy optimism may be evaporating in light of the revelations about US government surveillance by Edward Snowden and the seeming ubiquity of reports of hacking, spyware, and data breaches (Rainie 2016).

Moreover, this account of the "privacy paradox" as a disconnection between attitudes and behavior may be too simple. Irrational cognitive biases in decision-making may give rise to other, subtler paradoxes about individuals' attitudes and information-sharing behavior. Readers should be aware that there is a great deal of evidence that humans' ways of thinking distort their decisions in predictable ways—and decisions about privacy are no exception.

For example, Brandimarte, Acquisti, and Loewenstein (2013) present data to the effect that increasing perceived control over the publication of private information increases the willingness to disclose, even when that leaves people more vulnerable to others accessing the information. At the same time, decreasing perceived control has just the opposite effect, even when the result is that people are more protected. This is a paradox of perceived control and risky behavior: the greater the perceived control, the greater the likelihood of risk-taking, with the perverse result of worse outcomes. A further complexity, drawn from behavioral decision research, is that differences in perceived relative risk—how much greater the risk of one alternative is in comparison to another—may be more influential on individual behavior in actual circumstances than differences in absolute risk (Adjerid, Peer, and Acquisti 2016); that is, a change decreasing the level of protection in a privacy policy may be more impactful on individual privacy behavior than a policy that fails to protect privacy in the first place. Think about this: Are you more likely to distrust a social media site if it changes its privacy policy than you would be if it didn't have a published policy at all? That's irrational, as companies without a policy might not protect privacy at all. Another illustration of this irrationality is the status quo bias and default settings: consumers are much less likely to change default privacy settings, even when the settings do not reflect their actual preferences. Consumers may be especially prone to cognitive biases when they encounter new technologies such as the smart devices making up the Internet of things (Bailey 2016; see Chapter 9). Policymakers are beginning to consider how to take these factors into account in designs of websites and their privacy policies, as a recent conference at the US Federal Trade Commission called PrivacyCon illustrates.

What types of data are being collected by governments and what is being done with the data?

The short answer is that a great deal of data, of many types, can be acquired by any government with the capacity for collection. Protections for official secrets, national security, and law enforcement in particular make it difficult to know the exact contours of what is being collected. There are frequent calls for increased transparency so that citizens may be able to monitor and oversee the actions of their governments. The reply from governments is that they may need "deep secrets"—the very existence of which is even secret (Pozen 2010).

The revelations by Edward Snowden of US government surveillance sent shock waves around the globe. Snowden released records showing that the US National Security Agency (NSA) collected vast amounts of "metadata": data about data, such as records of addresses to which email messages were sent and of phone numbers called or texted from cell phones. These records were obtained from service providers such as cell phone companies. Although they do not reveal the contents of the conversations, the metadata may be very revealing, indicating anything from calls to a psychiatrist, a suicide prevention hotline, a call girl service, a takeout restaurant, or members of a known terrorist cell. This mass collection was approved by the US Foreign Intelligence Surveillance Court and was kept secret; in the view of the federal government, the collection was justified for national security purposes without the showing of probable cause that would have been required for a warrant under the Fourth Amendment. In 2015, the United States cut back the surveillance program to include only data collected about calls or messages sent to or received from locations outside the United States. We discuss these programs and how they worked further in Chapter 9.

Among government agencies, police departments also collect a vast amount of information. Video surveillance via closed circuit television (CCTV) systems is ubiquitous, especially in the United Kingdom. In the United States, it is used to monitor traffic, public events, transportation systems, and activity in public places. Police also use license-plate-recognition technology to monitor automobile movement. Some police departments are also using big data drawn from diverse sources including social media, property and arrest records, and commercial databases to analyze individuals' "threat scores" and levels of crime activities in specific locations (Jouvenal 2016). Commentators express concern about the ways in which surveillance may increase inequality if it is targeted to vulnerable populations (Franks 2016). State and local governments vary, however, in the extent of their willingness to surveil. San Francisco is a city of great wealth, a favored tourist destination, and a community that celebrates diversity and privacy. But it is also a city of rising housing values and limited housing stock; as a result, housing is unavailable to the less well-off, and San Francisco now has the highest property theft rate of the largest American 50 cities. It is also a city that bars the installation of surveillance cameras found in most other US cities (Fuller 2016).

Many governments play a significant role in the delivery of health care. Even in the United States, where much health care is provided in the private sector, Medicare and Medicaid are major payers for care. As payers, they accumulate a great deal of information about both providers and patients that can be used to analyze disease trends, cost trends, practice patterns, and the efficacy and quality of care. Public health systems also collect extensive amounts of health information, from immunization registries, tumor registries, and birth defect registries to reports of contagious diseases, reports of potential bioterrorist incidents, and blood samples obtained in newborn screening. These data may be collected by state and local public health departments and are often shared with the federal Centers for Disease Control and Prevention and potentially even with the World Health Organization.

Finally, there are many allegations of efforts by governments to obtain data illicitly. Countries such as China, North Korea, and Russia have been accused of data hacking attempts against both the US government and private sector entities. In one high-profile theft, the North Korean government was accused of hacking personal information from Sony Pictures in order to demand that Sony cancel the release of its film *The Interview*, about a plot to assassinate North Korean leader Kim Jong-un. Sony altered plans for release of the film and eventually settled for over $8 million in compensation for its employees whose data were stolen. In other very controversial examples, there is evidence that the Russian government was behind the hacking of the Democratic National Committee in the 2016 US election and the German Parliament in 2015.

What types of data are being collected in the private sector? How ubiquitous is tracking?

The short answer is that private sector data collection is expanding exponentially and shows no signs of declining. Collection mechanisms, data types, data actors, and storage technologies have continued to change rapidly. People concerned about the data that others might hold about them should simply assume that most information is out there somewhere; the really important questions are who has the information, what they can do with it, and how it is protected. Much information collection involves only de-identified data, but removal of identifiers does not mean a guarantee against re-identifying individuals or drawing inferences about characteristics of members of small groups. To illustrate the scope of current data collection, we sketch four examples briefly: Internet tracking, health information, geolocation information from cell phones, and the data collected from the "Internet of things." The use of individual cell phones to take pictures and videos has become ubiquitous as well, although there is a sense in which this data collection is more democratized, as anyone can do it.

Internet tracking is perhaps the most long-standing and best known of data collection methods. Web search engines gather data about searches conducted from devices such as computers or smartphones unless individuals set their browsers to restrict this practice. The data thus gathered can be linked with data from social networking and other forms of data to produce quite extensive portraits of individuals. Some uses may be beneficial to either the individual or society: the ability to predict serious individual disease (such as possibly pancreatic cancer before it is diagnosed) or to identify incipient outbreaks of disease. Other benefits may concern far less serious matters—food, shopping, or vacation preferences— but may nonetheless be welcomed by individuals. Other uses of tracking may produce less welcomed results: not only advertising but also price discrimination, adverse credit decisions, revelation of sensitive information such as sexual orientation or pregnancy, or algorithms that make decisions about where to advertise opportunities in a manner that has a disparate impact by race (FTC 2016). Some Internet providers give users "do not track" features modeled on the very popular "do not call" system. A proposal by Federal Trade Commission staff for a comprehensive "do not track" system has not gone forward.

Health information drawn from patient records has been assembled in huge data sets by provider organizations, payers, and data analytics firms. Data from electronic health records, electronic prescribing, personal health records, Internet apps that record data, and wearable devices such as Fitbits can be combined into data sets that are used to analyze costs and quality of care, predict high-cost patients, compare treatment effectiveness, identify rare side effects of drugs, or provide valuable information for public health. These data may also be used by pharmaceutical companies to identify providers to target for participating in clinical trials or product marketing. Much of this information is de-identified, but some is not, such as information used to identify patients who may have unusually high health-care expenses. This information may be used to try to figure out how to manage care for these individuals so that their health improves and their treatment costs less. Analytics firms such as Explorys, spun off from the Cleveland Clinic, or Blue Health Intelligence, from Blue Cross Blue Shield plans, may have data about more than 50 million or even 100 million individuals.

Cell phones, unless they are turned off, emit locational information continually so that the phones can be picked up by the nearest transmission tower. Companies such as AirSage use de-identified locational data to analyze traffic patterns, shopping patterns, and population locations in emergencies (http://www.airsage.com/Technology/How-it-works/). Locational data are central to services such as Uber driving or Google maps. Locational data are also used by police to determine whether suspects were present near crime scenes.

The so-called Internet of things is made up of smart devices—devices that are connected to the Internet and can send and receive information through it. From large machines such as automobiles to appliances such as stoves and thermostats, Internet connections are increasingly built into everyday objects. These have great advantages: turning up the heat or turning on the stove on the way home from work, car sensors that can trigger automatic braking, or medical devices that can report real-time information about patients' conditions. But as the Pew data discussed earlier in this chapter reveal, people are increasingly uncomfortable with the extent to which their every movement can be observed and transmitted.

What are fair information practices (FIPs)?

Although what are called fair information practices (FIPs) are widely admired, the extent and means by which they are implemented vary widely. The effectiveness of the notice-and-choice system they employ has also come under question.

FIPs were first crystallized in a report for the US Department of Health, Education, and Welfare published in 1973 (Gellman 2015). The report, "Records, Computers and the Rights of Citizens" (https://epic.org/privacy/hew1973report/default.html), stated these five basic principles for data protection:

- "There must be no personal data record keeping systems whose very existence is secret.
- There must be a way for an individual to find out what information about him is in a record and how it is used.
- There must be a way for an individual to prevent information about him that was obtained for one purpose from being used or made available for other purposes without his consent.
- There must be a way for an individual to correct or amend a record of identifiable information about him.
- Any organization creating, maintaining, using, or disseminating records of identifiable personal data must assure the reliability of the data for their intended use and must take precautions to prevent misuse of the data."

These principles echo themes sounded by Westin in his privacy surveys and publications. They emphasize notice about what information is being collected. They state that people should be able to choose how information about them is subsequently used. And they accord people the right to correct erroneous records about themselves. These FIPs are found in many variations across the globe and are the basis for approaches to privacy worldwide (see Gellman 2015 for an excellent history of FIPs). The extent to which they are actually implemented, however, remains variable.

FIPs have also been criticized for their reliance on notice and choice. This approach places the responsibility for making decisions about personal information on individuals themselves. There are advantages and disadvantages to this general approach. On the one hand, it lets individuals make different choices about how information is to be collected and used. It also lets individuals make different choices about how much it matters to them to take the time to scrutinize privacy policies and make privacy choices.

On the other hand, there are many problems with leaving information protection just to individuals (Cate 2010). It takes a great deal of time to read privacy policies carefully—time that individuals simply do not have if they are confronted with different privacy policies almost daily. Most people just click "I agree" buttons without reading the dense material they are given. But if individuals ignore or do not read notices carefully, they may be surprised by how information about themselves is shared or used. In many cases, this may not matter, because the information use is benign or even beneficial. But many notice and choice architectures are difficult or confusing for consumers to find, understand, and use; the choices they make may be shaped by these structures and might be quite different in other settings. Irrationalities built into human decision-making, such as the status quo bias that leads people to stick with default settings, mean that decisions may not reflect preferences very accurately.

Notice and choice, moreover, take place at the original point of contact with the information subject. You may be told, when you visit a website, that it has a privacy policy, and you may be asked to agree with the policy before you share information. But there may never be follow-up about what happens to the information afterward, particularly if data sets are de-identified or merged (Ohm 2014). When information is originally collected, the collector may have certain plans for the use of the information—but these plans might change as new opportunities become available (Hoofnagle 2016b). Syndromic surveillance—noticing a pattern, the significance of which was not anticipated antecedently—may reveal insights that no one could have anticipated in advance (Francis et al. 2009). The use of notice and choice assumes a data world that is frozen in time. European privacy law insists that re-consent is necessary if data are repurposed—but, like US privacy law, this does not apply to de-identified data. Highly general descriptions of the purposes of data use may be so vague as to preclude genuinely informed consent ("we may use your data for research . . ."). It may be difficult if not impossible to contact people for re-consent—so in the United States, at least, waivers are readily granted for uses of information from large sets of patient records for later research, provided researchers say that confidentiality will be protected and a review committee doesn't think the research is so sensitive that it cannot be conducted without new consent.

The notice and choice approach presents collective action problems as well—that is, lots of choices made by different people may add up in ways that no one wants. Individual choices about data collection and use may result in disparities in the information that is available for valuable social purposes, such as public health or medical research. Individuals may want alternatives that are only available if others make similar choices—but they are not in a position to communicate with or to influence others in making their decisions about what data to share. Problems of cybersecurity, hacking attacks, and data theft further fuel concerns that reliance on individual choices to protect privacy is insufficient. An alternative to individual notice and choice might be uniform information collection, coupled with stringent requirements governing transparency about what is being done, permissible uses of the information, and required practices for information security.

What ethical obligations do professionals have to protect personal information?

The approach to confidentiality obligations in the professions has been quite different from the notice and choice approaches found in data protection structures that follow FIPs. Professional confidentiality obligations are typically prescriptive obligations grounded in trust relationships. Individuals visit professionals for services that they cannot provide for themselves. The services may be too time-consuming, may require special training or expertise, or may require special licenses. When individuals need professional services, they may be in quite vulnerable positions: under arrest, sick, or in spiritual crisis. They may have little or no ability to choose the information they wish to share. Professions, especially the learned professions such as theology, medicine, or law, have developed stringent ethical obligations to keep information confidential. Where licensing is required, some of these ethical obligations may be legally enforced. For the most part, these ethical obligations developed before the current notice and choice approach. Individuals may in some cases consent to having information revealed by professionals and are of course typically free to reveal the information themselves outside of the professional relationship, but this is the exception rather than the rule.

The most stringent ethical obligation of confidentiality is that of Catholic priests and the confessional. The obligation to keep confessions secret is a "sacred trust" and is absolute, even if the priest's own life is at stake. The penalty for violating this trust is excommunication of the priest. Priests who have concerns about what they are told in confession may ask the penitent for permission to discuss the issue outside of the confessional. If the penitent refuses, the priest's ethical obligation is to take the information with him to the grave (Saunders 2000, Clergy in other faiths may have quite different confidentiality obligations, especially when congregations set rules for their faith communities or when there are lay clergy (e.g., Audette 1998). State laws requiring reports of child abuse pose particularly difficult issues for clergy. Many states exempt clergy in faiths requiring confession from these requirements; indeed, such exemptions may be required by constitutional protection for the free exercise of religion. In the United States, rules of evidence also permit individuals to exercise the clergy–penitent privilege to prevent their religious authorities from testifying about confidential communications.

From ancient Greek times, physicians have been charged with obligations of confidentiality. The Hippocratic Oath, in its classic version, provided that "what I may see or hear in the course of the treatment or even outside of the treatment in regard to the life of men, which on no account one must spread abroad, I will keep to myself, holding such things shameful to be spoken about" (copy from NOVA, http://www.pbs.org/wgbh/nova/body/hippocratic-oath-today.html). This stricture may be more about the secrets of the guild of physicians than about those of patients, but obligations of confidentiality are widespread in the health professions. The AMA Principles of Medical Ethics provide that "[a] physician shall respect the rights of patients, colleagues, and other health professionals, and shall safeguard patient confidences and privacy within the constraints of the law" (AMA Principle IV, http://www.ama-assn.org/ama/pub/physician-resources/medical-ethics/code-medical-ethics/principles-medical-ethics.page). The American Nurses Association Code of Ethics states that "[t]he nurse has a duty to maintain confidentiality of all patient information, both personal and clinical in the work setting and off duty in all venues ..." (ANA Code 3.1, http://nursingworld.org/DocumentVault/Ethics-1/Code-of-Ethics-for-Nurses.html). Serious violations of these requirements may be grounds for the state to revoke a professional's license.

As we shall see in the next chapter, which will focus on health information, physicians may be subject to a variety of reporting requirements. Legal requirements include reporting suspected bioterrorism, reporting knife or gunshot wounds, reporting abuse of children or vulnerable adults, and reporting contagious conditions. Physicians may also be encouraged or required to report information with implications for safety, such as conditions that might impair driving. They may also have a duty to warn about patients who are a risk to themselves or to others. As with clergy, patients may invoke a variety of evidentiary privileges to prevent their physicians from testifying against them in court. They may also be sued for damages in court for violations of confidentiality; in one case, a physician gave an adoptee the identity of her birth mother so she could make contact. The birth mother was "not pleased" and recovered damages for the breach (*Humphers v. First Interstate Bank of Oregon*, 696 P.2d 527 (en banc) (1985)).

Lawyers, the third of the historical learned professions, also have stringent obligations of confidentiality. The idea behind this obligation is that clients will not give their lawyers the full information they need for adequate representation if they cannot trust that the lawyer will maintain their secrets. There are exceptions to protect both lawyers and society; in the United States, lawyers may reveal information as required by law, to avert crimes that threaten serious bodily harm, or as needed to defend themselves. Their clients may also invoke the privilege to prevent their lawyers from testifying in court. Lawyers have an obligation not to lie to courts or commit fraud on behalf of their clients, but otherwise are obligated not to reveal any other information about bad things their clients might have done. In one very well-known case, lawyers appointed by the court to defend Robert Garrow in a murder case followed their client's directions as to where he had buried the bodies of other victims. The lawyers were investigating the possibility of an insanity defense and needed to know whether Garrow's confession to the other crimes was correct. Parents of the victims knew the lawyers were defending Garrow and suspected him of the additional murders. When the parents called the lawyers to ask if they knew anything about the victims, the lawyers did not tell them anything. When the information later came out in court, the case horrified many, but the lawyers' decision was a correct understanding of their professional obligations (Hansen 2007; *People v. Belge*, 372 N.Y.S.2d 798(1975)). The privilege that clients can assert to prevent their lawyers from testifying takes different forms in different legal systems; for example, lawyers in France do not have the privilege for advice provided as in-house counsel, and across jurisdictions there are significant variations in the range of legal advice covered by the privilege.

Other professions where public safety is involved may balance obligations to protect the confidentiality of their clients with the need to protect the public. Architects' clients pay them to design buildings, but the buildings will be used by many others and thus the architect's job has public safety aspects as well. The American Institute of Architects' Code of Ethics and Professional Conduct requires its members to advise clients against decisions that violate laws or regulations and materially affect public safety, to refuse to consent to these decisions, and to report the decisions to local enforcement authorities unless the situation can be resolved in some other way. Thus if a client insists on installing stairs that violate the building code and is going ahead despite the architect's objection, the architect has a duty to report the situation to the building inspector (2012 Code, Rule 2.105, http://www.aia.org/aiaucmp/groups/aia/documents/pdf/aiapo74122.pdf). Engineers are like architects in having dual responsibilities to their clients and to the public. The Code of Ethics of the National Society of Professional Engineers provides that engineers should "hold paramount the safety, health, and welfare of the public"; under this general rule, the Code also says that engineers should not reveal information without their client's consent unless required by the Code (Code of Ethics II.1.c, https://www.nspe.org/ resources/ethics/code-ethics).

People in many other occupations—some traditionally considered professions and others not—may possess a great deal of information about their clients that the clients believe is confidential. Think about what your plumber, your beautician or barber, or your auto body mechanic might be able to figure out about your health status. Your plumber might observe the general cleanliness or condition of your dwelling or signs of bathroom overuse; your hairdresser might see that you have head lice; and your auto body mechanic might notice many scratches on your car that are indicative of diminishing capacity to drive safely. Other than requirements in their licensing laws and any applicable state or federal laws prohibiting unfair trade practices, these professionals do not have obligations to keep this information confidential. They may have little guidance about what to do with this information as well. According to the Register of Beauty Professionals, beauty, spa, and nail professionals should responsibly demonstrate "[d]iscretion in dealing with confidential client disclosures" (Code of Ethical Conduct, Principle 2, http://www.registerofbeauty professionals.co.uk/resources/code-of-ethical-conduct). The Automotive Service Association, a voluntary association of owners and managers of automobile service businesses, has a code of ethics, but it does not include a provision about confidentiality. The National Institute for Automotive Service Excellence, a voluntary organization that certifies mechanics' skills, has a code that likewise does not have a principle about protecting information about clients (https://www .palmbeachstate.edu/programs/Diesel/Documents/ASE%20 Code%20of%20Ethics.pdf). The American Society of Plumbing Engineers, also a voluntary society, has a code prohibiting its members from misusing client information and requiring them to report any knowledge of actual or suspected violations of building codes.

In sum, professions differ greatly in the ethical obligations they expect of their members in dealing with clients' information. Some, such as Catholic clergy, must guard it to the death.

Others apparently may discuss information more freely and may have reporting obligations that override confidentiality. The general starting point for professionals is confidentiality, however, with exceptions for the public interest and individual choice. Professional confidentiality thus places responsibilities on professionals in the first place, rather than on individuals, to make decisions about how information is to be protected.

3

PRIVACY AND HEALTH INFORMATION

Introduction

In addition to being regarded as particularly sensitive by many people, health information has several characteristics that make privacy particularly salient. Health care is very important to people's prospects in life—so much so that it may be regarded as a fundamental good. People do not have a great deal of choice about accessing health care—they may stay away from health care only at significant costs to themselves—so it is not easy to avoid having a medical record. In addition, people do not control what is entered into their medical records: the records are created by health-care providers. Information in these records may be required for many purposes—jobs, professional licenses, housing, insurance, to name just a few—and may last for a lifetime. Many of these records are assembled about children and raise the questions about privacy within families that are considered in Chapter 7.

What is health information?

Health information is any information relevant to your physical or mental health. So far, so good, but what is "health"? The World Health Organization (WHO) construes "health" very broadly: "Health is a state of complete physical, mental and social well-being and not merely the absence of disease or infirmity" (WHO, http://www.who.int/about/definition/ en/print.html). This definition, which has never been changed since it was adopted in 1948, has been criticized for medicalizing society and for labeling people with chronic conditions or disabilities as "unhealthy" (Huber et al. 2011). Alternative definitions are also very broad, for example, the ability of a human organism to adapt and self-manage (Huber et al. 2011).

For purposes of this discussion, we can think about health information as any information relating to how an individual is doing either physically or mentally. Understood in this way, "health" is not a normative concept; different modes of functioning are not necessarily "unhealthy" or bad—they are just different. But information about these differences will be regarded as information about health. So if you enter into your Facebook newsfeed that you just went for the longest run of your life, that you are upset about gaining weight, or that you are feeling down, you have entered health information. Information in your medical records may include a great deal beyond how you are doing physically or mentally: your address and phone numbers, Social Security number, employment status, billing information, and information about your social or family circumstances. Under US law, this is considered health information if it is in your medical record, even though it may not concern your physical or mental well-being at all. That's actually why health information is a particularly juicy target for identity thieves—it has everything they need to know about you—and it can't be readily changed, either, unlike your credit card or PIN.

What privacy concerns are raised by health information?

Health information is considered sensitive or very sensitive by over three-quarters of people in the United States (Rainie 2016). People just may not want others to know about their health; or, they may fear the consequences if others are aware that they have diseases or disabilities.

Why might people want to keep their health information from others? Health conditions may be important to individuals' identity and their sense of who they are. People may not want others to see them as ill or injured. They might fear that if others have information about an illness or disability, they will perceive them differently: as weak, flawed, damaged, or as objects of pity (The Body Project 2016). Psychologically, they may fear that they will see themselves differently once information about their health is out to others. They might be more inclined to play a sick role, especially if this is what others expect them to do.

Sharing information about current health or health histories also may be a way for people to establish intimacy with one another—or keep their distance (IOM 2009). Health may relate to other matters that people feel very protective about: the condition or appearance of their bodies, their sexuality, or their basic bodily functions such as excretion. Just knowing that others have some information about such things may be embarrassing or emotionally troubling, even though no use of the information will be made at all. Thinking about how you would feel if you knew your neighbor had read your medical records in comparison to how you would feel if she had read your grocery list might give you a sense of whether you regard medical information as especially sensitive.

Protecting health information may also be important for instrumental reasons. Despite prohibitions on disability discrimination, employers may be less likely to hire or to promote people when they know about their health conditions. Employers may worry about the expense of unhealthy employees, not only because of health insurance costs (a concern addressed in the Affordable Care Act to some extent), but also because of the costs of absences, disability insurance, and workers' compensation. Employers may also consider the economic advantages or disadvantages of training or advancing particular employees; if an employee is likely to become ill, drop out of the workforce after starting a family, or die prematurely, investing substantially in her improvement may not seem productive over the longer term.

Employers may also want to use health information at the level of the workforce in ways that might be problematic for workers. Employers are investing in wellness programs to improve worker health, provide employees with care recommendations, and reduce the costs of illness and injury among members of the workforce. These programs have both benefits and risks for workers. Employers are using data analytics firms such as Castlight to try to predict and address likely health-care needs of their workers based on aggregate data from wellness programs and employee health insurance claims. Employers are not supposed to be able to gain access to individually identifiable health information about their workers through these programs. However, they can be provided with analyses using de-identified information to predict answers to questions such as how many employees are likely to get pregnant or to need back surgery during the upcoming year. One way to predict pregnancy is to track the percentages of covered employees who have ceased to fill prescriptions for birth control medication; with de-identified data, this could still give employers information about their workforce in particular regions or employment sectors (Silverman 2016). Even though this information does not single out particular individuals, it may lead employers to adopt policies that disadvantage workers considering pregnancy: more careful monitoring of sick leave, rigorous checking to make sure employees arrive at their assigned times, or reduced flexibility in shift assignments, for example (Zarya 2016).

The availability of health information may also affect your ability to obtain insurance or credit. The Affordable Care Act (ACA) in the United States did address one major fear about health insurance by prohibiting health insurers from turning people down for coverage because of preexisting conditions. The ACA also prohibits insurers from "experience rating"—that is, charging you more for insurance if you have a past history of costing more. (It does allow premiums to rise with age, up to a ratio of 1 to 3, and to be as much as 1.5 times higher for people who smoke. It also allows for premium adjustment based on participation in wellness plans. For example, you might have to pay up to 30% more for your health insurance if you are obese and don't attend a weight loss program.) But the ACA only concerns health insurance; you can still be turned down for disability insurance, long-term care insurance, mortgage insurance, or life insurance, based on your health information. And as of this writing (in late 2016), it is uncertain how long these ACA provisions will remain in effect.

Credit scores may be impacted directly by reports of failure to pay medical bills (see Chapter 5). These reports may take place while consumers are still sorting out what their insurance companies are going to pay for their care and what portion of the bill is their responsibility (Rosenthal 2014). Moreover, credit scores may not be the only information used to make business decisions, such as whether to enter into a contract or grant a loan. Increasingly, data-mining companies are using predictive algorithms to make suggestions about individuals' risk levels. The algorithmic analytics are largely secret, but may include information that is directly or indirectly related to health. For example, the presence of medical debt, an abrupt change in eating out as indicated in credit card purchasing patterns, or abandonment of a regularly used fitness app may suggest a major change in your health status. This may in turn lead a data analytics firm to suggest that you have become a poor risk for a loan, with the result that you are either charged more or are turned down (Executive Office of the President 2016).

Should privacy in health information be protected?

Information about the health of a population and the individuals within it may be important for national security, public health, improvement in the quality of health care, identification of harmful side effects of medication or devices, the development of precision medicine, and medical research more generally. If information is available but not all of it is shared with the parties that may have important uses for it, particularly if it is significantly limited about particular population subgroups, these benefits may be realized incompletely or inadequately at best. Some privacy advocates have argued that individual preferences about data use should be taken into account in the availability and use of individually identifiable health information, even if overall benefits are reduced. Some also contend that the concerns are overblown (Rothstein and Shoben 2013).

Bioterrorism is a major national security concern. Intermittent threats of the release of toxic agents such as ricin or deadly infections such as anthrax have led to required reporting of suspected incidents of bioterrorism in the United States. The European Union has a coordinated system for reporting health emergencies of this kind (http://ec.europa.eu/health/ph_threats/com/preparedness/docs/HEOF_en.pdf). Medical information may be critical to the detection of bioterrorist emergencies. For example, people may present to emergency rooms with unusual symptoms; if these symptoms are reported to state or local health departments, to the US Centers for Disease Control and Prevention, or to the EU Early Warning and Response System, patterns may be identified more quickly than would otherwise be the case. Reported information may need to contain patient identifiers, to allow for verification of its accuracy, to prevent double-counting, and to allow for interventions if needed to prevent or reduce disease spread.

Public health depends on data to identify disease incidence and prevalence, current population health, and health trends. This information can be highly valuable to communities for identifying areas where they are doing well and areas where they need improvement. For these purposes, the health information does not need to identify particular individuals. Many counties across the United States, for example, are publishing dashboards of health information such as percentages of uninsured residents, percentages of residents who have seen primary care providers or dentists within the past year, and percentages of residents who are overweight or obese. Information in these dashboards may enlighten community residents about community medical needs. Information about disease patterns may also identify previously unrecognized environmental hazards such as radon levels. Unfortunately, they may also contain unfavorable information about particular geographical areas or community subgroups. Members of these groups understandably might not want to participate in the assembly of information that might be regarded as stigmatizing to them—for example, the report that the percentage of HIV infection in poor African-American women who are residents of Washington, D.C., was over 12% in 2012. On the other hand, without this information the seriousness of the risks to this demographic group might not be apparent.

Traditional public health surveillance also uses infection reporting and contact tracing to reduce the transmission of infectious disease. This surveillance requires identifiable patient information if patients are to be interviewed and counseled about the importance of treatment and monitored for adherence. Public health officials also need to know the identities of possible contacts if they are to be checked and possibly treated for infection. It is typical for states to require reporting of contagious conditions such as sexually transmitted diseases or tuberculosis. If information about the Ebola outbreak's movement from rural to urban areas in West Africa in 2013 had been transmitted more quickly and if its international significance had been recognized earlier, much of the spread might have been averted.

The ability to use data to evaluate and improve the quality of care is an important factor in the design of the electronic medical records in use today. Many large health-care systems and data analytics firms use data from electronic records to identify whether care benchmarks are being met, whether particular providers are outliers, whether some providers or patients tend to receive more or more expensive care than might be necessary, or whether there are problematic variations in care patterns by practice group or region. Analytics can also be used for health-care systems to compare their performance with that of other systems—although because many systems consider their patient data to be proprietary information, these comparisons may be less than fully systematic. Apart from care quality, the federal government and other health-care payers use data analytics to identify patterns that may reveal health-care fraud. In theory, these data analytics could also be available to patients, so that they could see patterns in the practices of the doctors they visit, the insurance plans paying for their care, or the hospitals in their vicinity. Information about care quality thus may benefit patients in many ways. Nonetheless, there could be downsides to the use of this information, for example if hospitals or physicians serving impoverished patients are dropped from plans for quality reasons without receiving needed support for improvements, or if providers serving especially challenging groups of patients are labeled as having inferior outcomes and therefore do not receive payment incentives based on measures of care quality.

Another benefit from the collection and use of health information is the identification of infrequent side effects from medical treatment. Approval of drugs or devices for marketing is based on evidence of safety and efficacy in clinical trials on limited numbers of patients. When these interventions come into more widespread use in the general population, evidence may surface about infrequent side effects, risks, or benefits in certain subpopulations, or interactions with other treatments. The United States now maintains a "sentinel" program using patient information to try to identify adverse outcomes that are due to medical treatment. This program was implemented after a pattern of reports of serious side effects, such as heart attacks and strokes, in patients using the pain killer Vioxx.

In his 2015 State of the Union Address, President Obama announced a precision medicine initiative. The initiative is to gather information about a voluntary national research cohort of over a million volunteers. It will use this and other patient information to ascertain variations in genotypes and other individual variations that may enable medical treatments to be more directly tailored to individual patients. With targeting, only patients who will benefit can be offered treatment; others will avoid the costs, inconvenience, and risks of interventions that do not work for them. Hopes for precision medicine are especially high in cancer treatment, where risky and very expensive novel forms of therapy are available or are under development. Yet there are major gaps in the information available about particular patient groups. Genotypic information and its phenotypic relevance are particularly lacking among African Americans, Native Americans, and Arab Americans, for example (Chouchane 2015; Reardon 2015). There are also many questions about the role of socioeconomic factors in the interplay between genotype and phenotype. Much of the research on the role of genetic variants in cancer has been conducted in largely white, upper-income, urban areas, leaving obvious information gaps (Reardon 2015). There will be less knowledge to use in tailoring treatment in the patient populations that do not participate in such research. Another problem may emerge if insurance companies begin to insist on high levels of evidence to authorize payment for expensive precision medicines and there are insufficient data to meet this standard for certain subpopulations of patients. Comprehensive sets of patient information will be needed to address these disparities.

Similar concerns are apparent for medical research more generally. The patient populations who volunteer for clinical trials for cancer are disproportionately likely to be well off and white. This may be in part the result of their treatment in high-level cancer care centers, their access to medical care, and the stage at which their disease is diagnosed. It may also be because African Americans are reluctant to participate in research; memories linger of the notorious Tuskegee syphilis study in which the US Public Health Service withheld effective treatment from African-American males in rural Alabama so they could continue to study the natural history of syphilis. Or it may result from problematic assumptions on the part of physicians about attitudes or ability to comply with treatment regimens (Smedley, Stith, and Nelson 2002; Matthew 2015). In sum, the benefits of comprehensive data sets of medical information are clear. Risks are clear, too: information may be used or disclosed in ways that might prove objectionable, emotionally painful, or harmful. Several approaches to these dilemmas are possible. Different approaches might be justifiable for different purposes, depending on the benefits and risks of the data use in question.

One approach is to continue with the notice and choice framework that is in use today for the privacy of medical records (see the discussion of HIPAA later in this chapter) and to encourage more people to allow information from them to be used. This solution respects choice but risks limiting the availability of information. It does not work if data are needed to detect medical emergencies such as incipient epidemics or bioterrorism. Another problem is that it may compound health disparities because information is unavailable about certain patient groups but not others.

Another approach is to allow all information to be used as long as some or all identifiers are removed. The idea here is to protect against instrumental harm: if people cannot be identified, information cannot be used against them. This solution does not fully eliminate the risks of re-identification, however. With current data management techniques, it reduces the risk to levels estimated at below 1%; re-identification risks may be higher or lower depending on the method of de-identification used and the public availability of other types of information (Benitez and Malin 2010). Some may judge a tenth of a percent chance of re-identification as acceptably low; others would regard any risk as too high, depending on what they have to lose. De-identification also does not respect patients' desires that information drawn from them not be used at all, or not be used in particular ways. De-identification also does not protect against information that is unfavorable or stigmatizing to members of a group. In a notorious case, researchers from Arizona State University used de-identified blood samples drawn from members of the Havasupai tribe for studies of schizophrenia and tribal migration patterns. The samples had originally been obtained with consent for the study of diabetes, a major health issue for the tribe. Members of the tribe found these new uses highly offensive, even though the information used was not identifiable; the university ultimately settled a lawsuit with them. Complete or partial de-identification also may limit the utility of information when identifiers are needed, such as for linking data sets, for following up to verify outcomes, for correcting outdated records, or for connecting individuals to one another or to locations.

De-identification also does not solve the concerns people might have about certain uses of information. Some are unhappy about commercial uses of information even when they are willing to share their information for efforts to improve health. For example, several states passed laws prohibiting pharmacies and pharmacy benefit management companies from selling de-identified patient data to drug companies. The drug companies used this information to follow the prescribing behavior of physicians and to identify physicians who might be willing to participate in enrolling their patients in clinical trials. The states were concerned that drug company advertising targeted to physicians might increase health-care costs. The Supreme Court held that the statutes were an unconstitutional violation of commercial free speech (*Sorrell v. IMS Health, Inc.*, 131 S.Ct. 2653 (2011)).

Still another approach is to mandate when data must be collected or protected from collection. When data collection is required, it would be subject to stringent controls on data use and security. Required data collection might be part of getting certain kinds of care. This is the public health approach to gathering information about some conditions; for example, all states have tumor registries that contain information reported about every tumor diagnosis and treatment in the state. Patients treated for benign tumors or cancers are likely not even aware that these registries exist. The registries are a very valuable source to ascertain disease incidence; for example, they can reveal the possibility of cancer clusters suggestive of toxic exposures in a given location. Mandatory data collection from people taking particular drugs might also be a good way of identifying side effects or seeing whether the drugs are effective; it could save people from serious side effects and insurers from paying for drugs that are very expensive but risky or ineffective. On the other hand, mandatory collection fails to respect individuals' desires for choice and, depending on the controls imposed, might include data from some individuals for uses to which they would object. To guard against questionable disclosures or uses, this approach requires strong transparency and oversight. It is most justifiable for uses where there are urgent issues of health, public safety, or justice.

What ethical obligations of confidentiality do doctors have?

Physicians belong to one of the professions historically considered to have very strong confidentiality obligations. These obligations date from the early development of scientific medicine. They are based on the importance of trust for people who seek expert services in situations of profound vulnerability (Majumder and Guerrini 2016).

As noted in Chapter 2, in ancient Greece, physicians pledged the Hippocratic Oath: "What I may see or hear in the course of the treatment or even outside of the treatment in regard to the life of men, which on no account one must spread abroad, I will keep to myself, holding such things shameful to be spoken about" (NOVA translation of classical version, http://www.pbs.org/wgbh/nova/body/hippocratic-oath-today.html). The reference to shame raises a further dimension to the justification for confidentiality: that either physicians or their patients might look bad in the eyes of others if they reveal information about disease or treatment.

Medical students today make a commitment to modernized versions of the Oath. The American Medical Association Code of Ethics Principle IV provides: "A physician shall respect the rights of patients, colleagues, and other health professionals, and shall safeguard patient confidences and privacy within the constraints of the law." The AMA Ethics Opinion 5.05 (http://www.ama-assn.org/ama/pub/physician-resources/medical-ethics/code-medical-ethics/opinion505.page?) states that patient information must be kept confidential so that patients feel free to make the full disclosures needed for treatment.

Opinion 5.05 lists two exceptions to the obligation of confidentiality. The first is when a patient threatens to inflict serious physical harm on another and there is a reasonable probability that the threat will be carried out; in this case, physicians should take reasonable precautions for the victim, including notifying law enforcement. The second is when disclosure is required by law or court order; here, physicians should notify the patient, disclose only the minimum necessary information, and advocate for confidentiality, including seeking changes in the law. These exceptions were tightened up in an amendment in 2006 emphasizing the importance of confidentiality. For contemporary physicians in the United States, legally required disclosures are primarily reporting requirements. Physicians are required to report gunshot or knife wounds, suspected bioterrorism, many contagious diseases, and suspected abuse of children or vulnerable adults.

When HIV first became prominent, physicians were deeply conflicted about confidentiality. In some situations, physicians treating both members of a couple knew that one member was HIV positive and that they were having active sexual relations in a way that put the other at risk of what was then a fatal disease. Physicians felt conflicting loyalties between keeping the confidences of the one patient and protecting the health of the other. Some took the view that physicians should warn the at-risk partner, but only after extensive efforts to counsel the patient to avoid risky sex, to encourage patients to make the disclosures themselves, and to tell the patient that the physician does plan to share the information to the extent needed to prevent the risks of harm (e.g., Brennan 1989). Others argued that despite the compelling moral reason to protect partners, it was overridingly important to keep confidentiality to protect patient trust and encourage treatment (e.g., Gillon 1987). Reporting requirements in a sense took physicians off the ethical hook; they could tell their patients before testing that there was simply no choice about whether to report a positive test result.

Email and electronic medical records pose new challenges of confidentiality for physicians. Communicating with patients via email is convenient but risky if the communication is not secure. Electronic medical records are easy to copy, transmit, and share—but with this ease comes risks to both data security and to privacy. The electronic medical records systems in use today, moreover, do not contain mechanisms to segregate types of information that may need special ethical or legal protections, such as mental health information, information about abortions or other reproductive matters, information about sexually transmitted diseases, and genetic information. When these records are shared, there is access to the entire record, rather than to the parts of it that might be relevant to the care in question.

In response to the development of electronic records and forms of electronic communication, the AMA has issued several ethics opinions. About email, Opinion 5.026 (http://www .ama-assn.org/ama/pub/physician-resources/medical-ethics/ code-medical-ethics/opinion5026.page?) adopts the notice and choice model, cautioning that physicians should give their patients notice about privacy and security risks and an opportunity to accept these risks. The AMA encourages the use of electronic medical records and urges physicians to put their patients' interests first in notifying them of any breaches (Opinion 5.10, http://www.ama-assn.org/ama/pub/physician-resources/ medical-ethics/code-medical-ethics/opinion510.page?).

What if patients want to keep health information from themselves?

Confidentiality usually applies to keeping information from others, but some patients also may wish information to be withheld from themselves—to experience a kind of self-privacy. Until recently—and possibly even to some extent today—physicians withheld information from patients about cancer diagnoses. Some raise the concern that information may be damaging to patients who are already anxious (Zaleski 2015). One approach that is recommended to take account of differences among individual patients and patients with different cultural backgrounds is for physicians to discuss with their patients what they do and do not want to know before significant health issues emerge. This approach respects individual choice if it is done carefully. One area of current controversy is sharing laboratory test results with patients. Many physicians would like to disclose this information to their patients themselves so that they can explain its significance and counsel patients about what to do; they are especially worried about patients learning or believing on their own that they are seriously ill. However, it is now legally required that federally certified laboratories give test results directly to patients on request (http://www.hhs.gov/about/news/2014/02/03/hhs-strengthens-patients-right-to-access-lab-test-reports.html).

A related major area of controversy concerns genetic tests. Suppose you are a patient with breast cancer and have been tested for whether your cancer is associated with a mutation of the *BRCA-1* gene. You may get three kinds of results: that you have a gene variation known to be associated with the disease, that you have a variation that to the best of present evidence is not known to be associated with the disease, and that you have a variant of "unknown significance." The variant may be very rare, so that there is not enough evidence to know whether there are established correlations between the variant and breast cancer. (Your data may, of course, play a role in ongoing efforts to determine whether there is a correlation.)

You could just be given the information that you have a variation known to be associated with cancer or that you do not. Or, you could be given the more fine-grained information. Some commentators argue that you should just be told whether you have the known deleterious variant because you may misunderstand or be worried about the more extensive information. Others argue that you should be told everything if that's what you want.

Another complication brought by genetic information is that you may be tested for a variation in one gene (like *BRCA-1*), but the testing may reveal that you have a variation in a completely different gene that wasn't being looked for at all. This sometimes happens with imaging studies, too: you have a CT scan for a broken rib and it reveals a small lung nodule that may be cancerous. These are called "secondary" or "incidental" findings; writers in medical ethics disagree about how much you should be told about them, especially when there's nothing medically to be done. The situation is even more complex in research, where participants are often told that because this is research, they may or may not learn anything that will be beneficial to them—but the participants may be under the misconception that they are getting treatment and the researchers may have knowledge that might be very important for them (Richardson 2012). There is also evidence that most patients want to know about secondary findings even when they might be anxious and there is nothing to be done (Phillips et al. 2015). One approach in bioethics is the notice and choice model: that you should be told before you have a test about the possibility of secondary findings and should be offered a choice about what you want to be told (Presidential Commission 2013). Radiologists are more circumspect about what patients should be told and have developed guidelines about what patients should be told based on the likely clinical significance of the findings (Berland et al. 2010). The American College of Medical Genetics originally stated that certain secondary findings should be reported regardless of patient choice; these were findings (such as those concerning *BRCA-1*) that involved serious diseases with known interventions (Green et al. 2013). This recommendation was later changed to a notice and choice approach, allowing patients to opt out of receiving the findings if they so wished (https://www.acmg .net/docs/Release_ACMGUpdatesRecommendations_final .pdf). These choices about genetic information may also have implications for family members, which are discussed further in Chapter 7.

Do psychiatrists have special obligations of confidentiality to their patients?

The American Psychiatric Association (APA) has created a special annotated version of the AMA code of ethics for psychiatrists (APA 2013). The APA regards confidentiality as especially important to psychiatry, "based in the special nature of psychiatric therapy." It views the advent of computerization, duplication, and data banks as an "increasing hazard" because of the highly sensitive nature of mental health information. Psychiatrists may reveal information only with patient authorization or legal compulsion; disclosures must be limited to only what is relevant. The annotations state explicitly that information such as sexual orientation or fantasies is usually not necessary to disclose. In cases of doubt, psychiatrists should give priority to patient confidentiality and test in court the legal need for disclosure.

Mental health providers face especially complex issues about revealing information that their patients might be dangerous. In the highly influential *Tarasoff* case decided in 1976, the California Supreme Court held that psychiatrists have a reasonable duty to warn. Prosenjit Poddar, a patient of a psychologist at a University of California hospital, told his therapist that he was planning to kill a woman identifiable as Tarasoff when she returned home from a summer abroad. His therapist recommended commitment, a recommendation countermanded by the head of the department. The therapist also notified the campus police, who did not detain Poddar because he seemed to be acting rationally. Poddar killed Tarasoff, and her parents brought suit for damages for the failure to warn her of the impending danger. The California court held that there is a reasonable duty to warn foreseeable third parties in danger from their patients and thus it was a question of fact whether the mental health providers had lived up to this duty (*Tarasoff v. Regents of the University of California*, 551 P. 2d 334 (Cal. 1976)). This reasoning was the basis for the AMA's first exception to the duty of confidentiality in Opinion 5.05 that permits physicians to reveal information needed to protect victims from serious physical harm.

What about information that could be life-saving?

The "duty to warn" cases involve patients who are potentially dangerous to others. There are also cases in which patients are not the danger, but information about them could be life-saving to others. Some have argued that any duties of disclosure rest with the patient; others have argued that the physician has a duty to disclose information about one patient that could save the life of another. Some of these cases have involved exposure to infectious disease, where the illness of one person indicates the likelihood that another person has also been exposed. For example, in *Bradshaw v. Daniel*, 854 S.W.2d 865 (Tenn. 1993), the court said that there could be a duty to warn a non-patient that she also had likely been exposed to Rocky Mountain spotted fever. Several cases have reached divergent conclusions about whether physicians or family members have the duty to warn other family members of the possibility of serious genetic diseases, a situation considered in more detail in the discussion of privacy within families in Chapter 7 (*Pate v. Threlkel*, 661 So.2d 278 (Fla. 1995); *Safer v. Estate of Pack*, 677 A.2d 1188 (N.J. Super. 1996)).

In a case in which there was no connection between the person with life-saving information and the person seeking the information, a court held that the information was confidential

(*Head v. Colloton*, 331 N.W. 2d 870 (Iowa 1983)). Head had leukemia, at that point treatable only by a bone marrow transplant. The hospital had a registry of the results of tissue typing tests, and Head found out that there was someone in the registry who would be a match for him. His match did not want the information revealed; she had the tissue typing performed because she was willing to help a family member. Head sued to get the information but the court held it was properly kept confidential.

What legal protections are there for health information in the United States?

In the United States, protection of health information depends on where it is held and how it is being used. The most important differences concern whether the information is in a medical record located within the health-care system and whether it is being used for research or for public health. The starting place in understanding health information in the United States is HIPAA, the Health Insurance Portability and Accountability Act. This section explains HIPAA and the protections it gives for information in medical records located within the health-care system. HIPAA is largely based on the notice and choice approach of FIPs.

HIPAA was enacted in 1996 to allow for the easy transfer of medical information among providers and payers. Privacy was not its primary goal, although Congress recognized the need for privacy protections to facilitate data transfers. (Many people are confused about this because of the "P" in the HIPAA acronym, which suggests it might have been about privacy.) HIPAA governs individually identifiable health information held by nearly all health-care providers and payers in the United States today. The exceptions are providers who do not maintain any information in electronic form, such as some mental health-care providers. HIPAA also applies to the "business associates" of these covered entities: data analytics firms, law firms, business services, software providers, cloud storage providers, and other entities that have access to individually identifiable health information. HIPAA does not, however, apply to entities beyond the realm of covered health-care entities and their business associates. Obviously, a great deal of individually identifiable health information is not covered by HIPAA. This includes information that individuals enter into the extraordinary variety of apps for smart devices available today. It includes devices that provide biometric measurements for the individual but that are not part of the medical record, such as Fitbits—even if the patient's doctor recommends their use. Contrary to many people's expectations, it also includes information downloaded from the patient's medical record and stored somewhere else, such as on a home computer. The use of mechanisms such as the "Blue Button" provided to Medicare or Veterans Administration patients to download their medical information transfers that information out of the realm of HIPAA. Many patients may not realize this, since the download comes from their doctor's record and contains exactly the same information.

HIPAA divides information uses and disclosures into three levels of protection. Some information uses do not require patient authorization. Some information uses require that the patient be given the opportunity to object. Finally, some uses require patient authorization. The actual classifications are very complex and we just hit a few major highlights here. Without patient authorization

- information may be disclosed to patients when they request it (45 C.F.R. § 164.524)
- information may be used for treatment, payment, or health-care operations such as quality assurance; this means that information may be shared among members of the treatment team, with other physicians involved in the patient's care, with insurance companies, or with care managers (45 C.F.R. § 164.506)

- information may be transferred for public health as required by law (45 C.F.R. § 164.512(b))
- information may be disclosed if needed to report victims of abuse; victims must be informed about these disclosures, however, unless being told about the report would risk harming them (45 C.F.R. § 164.512(c))
- information may be transferred in response to court orders or subpoenas, although for the latter, efforts are required to notify the individual to allow for objections (45 C.F.R. § 512(e))
- information may be disclosed to protect against serious threats to health or safety (45 C.F.R. § 164.512(j)).

Outside of disclosures to the individual, for treatment, payment, and health-care operations, and for public health, other disclosures permitted without authorization must be limited to the minimum necessary information.

In the course of receiving medical care, individuals may want to allow others who care about them to have information without their formal authorization. For this reason, HIPAA allows some disclosures when the patient has an opportunity to object and does not (45 C.F.R. § 164.510). Information in hospital directories—whether the person is a patient, the level of seriousness of their condition but without any actual medical details (e.g., "doing well" or "critical"), and religious preferences to religious officials—may be disclosed in this way to callers asking for the individual by name. Providers may also disclose information to persons involved in the patient's care: spouses picking up prescriptions for each other, family members invited to be present in the examining room, or loved ones involved in the care of patients in intensive care.

All other uses and disclosures require patient authorization. Specific real-time authorization is required for the use of information for marketing (45 C.F.R. § 164.508(a)(3)). The idea here is that patients don't want their medical information used by drug companies to contact them directly. Similarly, the disclosure of "psychotherapy notes," progress notes about therapy maintained separately, require special and separate authorization (45 C.F.R. § 164.508(a)(2)). The idea here is that mental health information is particularly sensitive for patients. At many points in time, patients may need to have others act for them. To determine how to handle these situations, HIPAA defers to state laws. States may decide what authority parents have to access medical information about their children, and what information children may access, with the exception of special provisions for reproductive information. States may determine the identification and authority of personal representatives such as guardians or individuals named in patients' advance directives.

HIPAA also requires that patients be given privacy notices by their providers (45 C.F.R. § 520). Patients also have the right to get copies of their records and to request correction of any errors in them. Patients must be notified if there are breaches of their HIPAA-protected information. If breaches involve 500 or more people, they must also be reported to the US Department of Health and Human Services Office of Civil Rights (OCR). Individuals may also file complaints with OCR about how their health information has been used or disclosed. OCR investigates breaches and complaints and may assess monetary penalties and seek corrective action against those found wanting. At present, no provisions have been developed to share monetary penalties with individuals who have been harmed by health information breaches, although Congress in 2010 directed this to happen within three years. HIPAA violations may also be state torts, such as the public disclosure of private facts; for example, a patient recovered damages from Walgreen's Pharmacy when an employee disclosed to the employee's boyfriend that his ex-girlfriend had herpes and had ceased to fill her birth control prescriptions before she became pregnant with his child (*Walgreen Co. v. Hinchy*, 21 N.E. 3d 99 (Ind. App. 2014)).

In 2010, Congress added breach notification requirements for a group of entities called "personal health record" (PHR) ıdors and related entities. PHRs are electronic records of identifiable health information that may be gathered from many sources and that is managed, shared, and controlled primarily for the individual. Entities such as medication management apps that access information in a PHR are also covered by breach notification. Websites that just allow individuals to enter information such as weekly weights are not PHR vendors and do not have the breach notification requirement.

Another addition to HIPAA in 2010 was a special privacy provision when individuals pay out of pocket for their treatment. The HIPAA privacy rule says that covered entities must allow individuals to request that their records not be shared for treatment, payment, or health-care operations—but that these requests do not need to be accepted (45 C.F.R. § 164.522(a)). However, in 2010 Congress said that these requests must be honored for care that individuals pay for out of pocket (42 U.S.C. § 17935(a)(2)). So, for example, people may want to pay out of pocket for services such as STD testing or a visit to a mental health professional and request that this information not be shared. In reality, medical records typically do not include information about how patients pay for their care, and this provision may not turn out to be very effective.

The myriad other entities outside of HIPAA, including PHR vendors, fitness apps, and social media sites, do not have HIPAA protections, even though they may contain health information at least as sensitive as that in doctor's records. Other than the requirement of breach notification for PHR vendors, the only federal standards that apply to these entities are the prohibitions on unfair or deceptive trade practices enforced by the Federal Trade Commission (FTC). States may have more stringent protections and some, such as California, do.

What about information used in research?

In the United States, two different sets of federal rules apply to the collection and use of information in research. One is the

HIPAA privacy rule requirement for authorization that applies to information covered by HIPAA. For most research with identifiable patient information in existing patient records, HIPAA authorization is required. No notice or authorization is required, however, if the information is de-identified to a set of standards set out in HIPAA (if properly de-identified, information is no longer within HIPAA) or made into a "limited data set" that is stripped of most identifiers but may have more fine-grained information about the patient's location, age, and date of treatment (45 C.F.R. § 164.514). The authorization requirement for use of identifiable information in research may be waived if the research is approved by an appropriate review board, confidentiality is adequately protected, and the research could not practicably be carried out if authorization were required (45 C.F.R. § 164.512(i)). Waivers for research use are quite common, especially for studies involving retrospective review comparing outcomes for patients receiving different treatments for the same condition. Waivers may be especially important for research on large groups of patients, or for research going back many years. People or their representatives may be difficult to contact over time, and the HIPAA authorization requirement applies for 50 years after a person has died.

The other set of rules applying to the use of health information in research consists of the federal rules governing research with human subjects. These rules apply to any federally funded research or research that will be used to get approval for new drugs or medical devices. Many large research universities also apply the federal regulations to all the research they conduct, whether or not it is federally funded, although this has become somewhat less common because the requirements are thought to be cumbersome. The regulations apply when research involves identifiable living persons. They require informed consent, a process that includes explaining the risks and benefits of participating in research. For research using health information, risks include that the information might be embarrassing or troubling or that the researchers might need to report certain findings such as abuse. Risks also include security breaches, although researchers are cautioned to take precautions to keep data segregated and in locked files.

Because the federal rules governing research with human subjects are cumbersome and are not always consistent with HIPAA, the federal government engaged in a long process of studying revisions to them. New rules were proposed in 2015 to ease the restrictions on research involving information only (in contrast to research involving actual interventions). These proposals would allow use of patient information in research, as long as patients are given general notice that this might happen and that no identifiable information is disclosed by the researchers. Different rules, including broad consent, would apply to biospecimens, such as those drawn from Henrietta Lacks or John Moore, and to whole genome sequencing (see Chapter 2). These proposals have been critiqued as both too limiting and under-protective (IOM Committee 2016). They were issued in final form as this volume went to press (82 FR 7149). The 21st Century Cures Act, enacted in December 2016, requires HHS to study possibilities for streamlining HIPAA authorization for participation in research.

What about information used for public health?

HIPAA allows medical information to be given to public health as required by law. When health information is given to the federal government, including for public health, it is governed by the federal Privacy Act. This Act incorporates the purpose limitation requirement of FIPs: with certain exceptions, identifiable information given to the federal government for one purpose—for example, payment by Medicare or study of a disease outbreak by the Centers for Disease Control and Prevention—cannot be used in identifiable form for another purpose without the individual's consent. It also cannot be disclosed in a way that would allow the individual to be identified (5 U.S.C. § 552a). This limited the data that were available in the Obama administration's efforts to "liberate" data through healthdata.gov. Many public health law requirements are at the level of the individual states. When health information is transferred to public health authorities, it will then be governed by whatever state law protections apply to public health information. Some states have protections for health information that are even more restrictive than the federal government protections. Other states may give greater weight to the freedom of information. One example is a state court decision in Illinois involving efforts by a local newspaper to gain information from the state tumor registry for an investigation of suspicions that environmental hazards had caused an increase in cancer rates. Illinois ruled that the newspaper had a right to obtain de-identified patient data from the state's tumor registry—even though the small numbers of patients with the cancers in question meant that it was likely that individuals could be identified from the data (*Southern Illinoisan v. Illinois Department of Public Health*, 218 Ill. 2d 390, 844 N.E.2d 1 (Ill. 2006)).

Are there special legal protections for mental health and substance abuse information?

Mental health and substance abuse treatment information may be especially sensitive and potentially damaging. Patients may be deterred from getting needed treatment if they fear that this information may not be kept confidential. Because of the many deleterious social effects of these conditions—homelessness, inability to work, crime associated with drug use—there are also social interests in encouraging people to receive treatment, so there are risks to the general public when privacy concerns obstruct treatment, as well as risks to patients.

Under federal law, there are special protections for certain records of treatment for drug or alcohol abuse (45 C.F.R. part 2). If patients are treated in facilities that describe themselves as providing substance or alcohol abuse treatment and that receive federal funding, federal authorization, or federal assistance, their treatment records receive these protections. Patients must give special written permission for these records to be disclosed. This requirement also applies to any subsequent re-disclosures of the records. Records may not be used to start criminal proceedings unless there is an order from the court to do so.

These regulations were put into place in 1975 in response to patient concerns that substance abuse treatment information would be used to prosecute them as part of the US war on drugs announced by President Nixon in 1971. This was well before changes in patient care models were developed to encourage integrated forms of care delivery. The regulations may make it difficult for patients' primary care physicians to know about substance abuse treatment and thus for this treatment to be integrated with other aspects of patients' care. In February 2016, the US Department of Health and Human Services published a notice of proposed rule-making to make significant changes in these regulations. A primary change is to allow patients to make a more general designation of "to whom" information may be shared so that consent is not necessary each time the information is shared within a care organization. In addition, the 21st Century Cures Act will require HHS to issue guidance concerning the circumstances under which caregivers may have access to the health information of people with serious mental illnesses in order to provide support for decisions about treatment.

Many states also have special protections for mental health treatment information or for information about treatment for substance abuse.

Are there special legal protections for genetic information?

Many people regard genetic information as particularly sensitive, although others are critical of "genetic exceptionalism."

Genetic information may seem different from other health information because it allows inferences to be drawn about family members. Genetic information may also seem different because it is thought to be more determinative of likely health outcomes than, for the most part, it really is (e.g., Tabery 2014). In 2008, Congress enacted the Genetic Information Nondiscrimination Act (GINA). GINA protects genetic information, which is defined to include the results of genetic tests, genetic tests of family members, and manifestation of diseases or disorders in family members. "Genetic tests" include not only gene sequencing but also measurements of proteins or metabolites that reveal information about genotypes or chromosomal changes. "Genetic information" does not include information about actually manifested disease in a person. Thus GINA protections would apply to the information that an individual has tested positive for the *BRCA-1* gene or had a sister with breast cancer, but it would not apply to the information that the individual herself has had breast cancer.

The basic principles of GINA are that employers, labor organizations, and health insurers may not discriminate on the basis of genetic information or request individuals to provide genetic information. For employers, there are important exceptions: the GINA prohibition does not apply to information obtained when employees seek health services from the employer, when they provide information in connection with applications for family or medical leave, or when the employer uses the information to monitor the biological effects of toxic substances in the workplace. Even in the case of the exemptions, however, information must be kept in separate files, and treated as a confidential medical record. Employers also do not violate GINA if they obtain the information inadvertently, as when an employer overhears an employee discussing the health information of a family member in the break room.

Like employers, health insurance companies offering group plans may not discriminate in premiums or request genetic information. These plans may not raise employers' premiums based on genetic information about a group member, may not require or purchase genetic information for underwriting purposes, and may not limit who may enroll in a group plan based on genetic information. To some extent, the impact of this aspect of GINA has been superseded by the ACA's prohibitions on coverage denials.

Because GINA prohibits covered employers and insurers from requesting or obtaining genetic information, it may function more effectively than other civil rights statutes. Here's why. Suppose you have been fired from your job. You may not know why; you may not even be suspicious that the reason you lost your job was that your employer had learned about a family member's recent diagnosis with a very expensive illness. Maybe you are just told by your employer that revenue is down, you were the last hired, and they needed to let someone go. You might have your suspicions, but there is no hard proof of anything. The burden will then be on you to sue for employment discrimination, claiming that your employer's adverse action was based on disability, or sex, or race, or some other protected category. Your employer may reply that there was a legitimate non-discriminatory reason you were fired—the downturn in revenue, or maybe some slippage in your performance, or the fact that you were late to work more than the employer's rules permitted. This will make it very difficult for you to carry any burden of persuasion that it was discrimination that led to your dismissal. The actual structure of how things will go depends on the employment discrimination statute under which you are suing, but the point here is that if employers can't—and don't—have the information in the first place, they can't use it to discriminate at all. So, unlike other civil rights statutes, GINA tries to head off discrimination before it can occur.

Many states also have laws giving special protection for genetic information. Four states declare genetic information to be the individual's personal property and place special constraints on its use: Alaska, Colorado, Florida, and Georgia.

Are there special legal protections for information about disabilities?

Under the Americans with Disabilities Act (ADA), people with disabilities do have some special protection for information about their disabilities. Title I of the ADA, the section prohibiting disability discrimination in employment, provides that employers may not ask job applicants whether they have a disability, although they can ask employees about their abilities to perform essential job functions (42 U.S.C. § 12112(d)(2)). Once an offer is made, employers may require a physical examination, if the employer requires the exam for all new employees and if it is job related and consistent with business necessity (42 U.S.C. § 12112(d)(3)). Employers may also require fitness for duty examinations. Except if supervisors need medical information for necessary accommodations, or if the information is needed because the disability might require emergency treatment, any medical information must be kept in separate medical files and treated as a confidential medical record.

The result of these ADA requirements is that many employees with hidden disabilities—mental health issues, intermittently symptomatic conditions such as multiple sclerosis, or cancer in remission—may be able to keep their employers from knowing about them. However, these employees may face difficult choices if it seems likely that they will require accommodations, such as time off for medical appointments or treatment. The ADA provides that it is discriminatory to fail to make reasonable accommodations "to the known physical or mental limitations of an otherwise qualified individual" (42 U.S.C. § 12112(b)(5)). Coupled with the prohibition on employers asking outright whether employees have disabilities, this means that the onus is on employees to make their disabilities known if they need to seek accommodations. Employees may see themselves as between a rock and a hard place: on the one hand, not wanting their employer to know they have a disability because they are worried about the consequences, and on the other hand, having difficulty performing their jobs without accommodations and thus risking giving employers ammunition to use against them.

What about recording medical encounters?

Both health-care providers and their patients may want to record medical encounters. Health-care facilities may also install surveillance cameras for safety reasons. Any recording without consent raises questions of privacy because of the information the recording might reveal. These questions are especially acute when recording reveals information about other patients that may violate their privacy.

Health-care providers may want to record encounters with their patients as part of patient care. An example would be filming the gait of a patient with a neuromuscular condition in order to allow for later comparisons. Such films are part of the patient's medical records and are protected by HIPAA, just as are any other medical records. Providers may also want to record patients for education or research. Recordings may be used for education and training within institutions as part of health-care operations without patient authorization. The same recordings may not be used in research or presented externally without authorization. According to the AMA, physicians may present films of patients to the public for educational purposes. Also according to the AMA, except in very unusual circumstances, patients should not be filmed for public presentation unless they are able to give their own informed consent, and they should be able to revoke that consent at any point in time.

Occasionally, cases occur in which physicians suspect caregivers of abuse and wish to record their interactions with patients without telling the patients they are doing so. There is a condition called "Munchausen's by proxy" in which parents make their children sick. (Munchausen's disease is a condition in which patients make themselves sick, apparently from the need for attention or to play the sick role. Munchausen's parents are thought to want to play the role of nurturing parent to an ill child.) Parents may appear to be loving caregivers of children who are inexplicably ill. When the children are hospitalized, surreptitious surveillance cameras are installed in their rooms; whether this is ethical is disputed among bioethicists. Some argue that it is permissible to protect children, others that it should be specially approved perhaps on the analogy to research, and still others that it is a violation of the rights of parents (e.g., Evans 1995; Lahey 2014).

Hospitals and other health-care facilities may be sites of violence. This concern is especially strong in emergency departments, where patients may be brought who are victims or perpetrators of crimes. Surveillance cameras have become standard in these facilities. Also, when police enter health-care facilities, they may be equipped with body cameras that are turned on. These recording devices collect the information that is within their scope. Many are concerned that the recording is an unethical violation of the privacy of patients. Health-care facilities have responded by implementing policies about recording that are posted for the public. Health-care facilities also are struggling to work out what to do about police recording on their premises. It is fair to say that the controversy over police use of body cameras is continuing to evolve, and hospital practices may do so as well. On the one hand, arguably these cameras are important for public safety, to document police behavior for the public, and for the police to protect themselves. On the other hand, these cameras may record highly sensitive information about patients or their caregivers. Chapter 6 on law enforcement discusses these issues in more detail.

There are also concerns that recording in health-care facilities violates the HIPAA rule if conducted without patient authorization. Use or disclosure of the information for law enforcement purposes is permissible under HIPAA in specific circumstances, limited to the minimum necessary information. These circumstances include responses to subpoenas or administrative requests, information needed to identify or locate suspects, information such as gunshot wounds required by law, evidence of a crime committed at the health-care facility, and evidence needed to prevent or lessen a serious and imminent violation of the health or safety of individuals or the public.

State laws may also protect patient privacy from recordings. For example, after volunteer first responders posted pictures on Facebook of Cathy Bates, a victim of a fatal accident, before members of her family were located, New Jersey passed a statute forbidding such publication without consent. Connecticut has a similar law (Varone 2012).

On the other side, patients may wish to record their encounters with health-care providers. One justification is that patients may want to consult recordings afterward to remember or understand what their providers have said. Or, patients may want to share the encounter with family or friends who can help them process it or support their understanding. When patients want to record for these reasons, it should not be difficult to obtain their providers' consent for the recording. Writers in ethics have suggested that physicians should encourage recording for these purposes (Klugman 2015; Rodriguez, Morrow, and Seifi 2015).

More cynically, patients may be suspicious that physicians are behaving disrespectfully or giving them substandard care and may wish to record surreptitiously. Recording may alter the nature of the physician–patient relationship and may be a manifestation of mistrust of the health-care system or of particular physicians. Physicians have been advised to be aware that recording may be occurring and to behave as respectfully and thoughtfully as they can with their patients. When recording is suspected, one suggestion is to seek transparency in the effort to improve patient trust (Rodriguez, Morrow, and Seifi 2015). In one damaging case, a patient's smartphone recording of his colonoscopy captured viciously insulting comments by the anesthesiologist. The patient had recorded the procedure to be sure that he understood the instructions for follow-up that he would receive. But the insults on the recording led him to sue for defamation and malpractice, and he was awarded $500,000 in damages (Jackman 2015). A few states such as California have laws that prohibit private recordings without the consent of the person being recorded, but in many states, recording statutes only require the consent of one party to the recording—which can be the person doing the recording. Patient advocates and plaintiffs' malpractice attorneys have been lobbying for recording consent statutes to be amended to permit the procedure in states where it is now illegal (Bailey 2015). On the other side, patients have been criticized for playing "gotcha" and running what are essentially sting operations on their health-care providers (Klugman 2016).

Patients who record care encounters sometimes post these recordings on social media sites or want to share them with the media. For example, parents of children who have received life-saving care may wish to make their heartwarming stories public. Even when these stories heap praise on caregivers, there are concerns that they may violate the privacy of health-care workers or other patients if they are published without consent. In states that only require one party's consent to recording, there likely are no legal restrictions on patients making or sharing recordings of their health care. As smartphone video capabilities only continue to grow, conflicts about recordings and their publication are likely to grow more frequent. Just imagine if the birth of your first child was on YouTube.

Does surveillance enhance independence for people with cognitive impairments, and if so, is it justifiable?

Recording and other methods of surveillance, such as ankle bracelets, have also been proposed for patients with cognitive impairments. Family members of patients in care facilities may wish to record their treatment because they fear neglect or abuse of their loved ones who are unable to protect themselves

(Hoffman 2013). Surveillance cameras at exits may be a way of monitoring whether people with dementia wander and watching them when they do, giving them more freedom within and beyond where they live. Tracking devices—from implanted chips to external bracelets—may allow people with impairments to be about in the world or within where they live while assuring others that they are protected.

Some may object that these surveillance devices are unjustified paternalism and an invasion of privacy (Klugman 2014). Others may argue that they are permissible with advance consent of patients themselves, given while they still had decision-making capacity, or possibly by their surrogate decision-makers. Writers in bioethics have questioned whether it is possible for surrogate decision-makers to understand how surveillance is experienced by people with cognitive disabilities, however (Ho, Silvers, and Stainton 2014). These writers also argue that surveillance raises questions of justice, such as whether it is primarily for the benefit of those being surveilled or those responsible for caring for them.

Do famous people—politicians, sports stars, movie stars—have privacy in their health records? Should they?

With respect to the ethical standards and laws governing health information, famous people are just like anyone else: obligations of confidentiality apply. Nonetheless, famous people may be pressured into revealing health information or may find it advantageous (or disadvantageous) to do so. And they may be the object of paparazzi, prying eyes, gossip columns, or information theft. Sometimes, information about their health conditions may be important to public decisions about the responsibilities they should have, to public support, or even to betting, such as on the outcomes of sporting events.

Historically, political leaders were able to keep information about their health away from the public. Despite what is now believed to be mental illness (Garrard and Peters 2012),

King George III for a period of time was treated outside of the public eye. Grover Cleveland's surgery for oral cancer, Woodrow Wilson's stroke, and Franklin Roosevelt's level of disability from polio were effectively masked (LaMotte 2015). Winston Churchill's heart attack after his famous victory speech before Congress in 1941 was kept secret by his doctor— at a crucial moment of leadership as the United States was entering World War II (Maier 2014). John F. Kennedy, for all his apparent youth and robust health, had Addison disease (a form of adrenal insufficiency) and was treated with steroids— a condition that was effectively obscured (Mandel 2009).

Today, the situation is quite different. The public may believe that it has the right to know information about the health of people running for office or people holding office (Brody 2011). This information may be important to judgments about the person's competence or decision-making ability. Interest in the health of public figures has occurred in countries across the globe. The European Court of Human Rights, a court with strong privacy commitments, thought that the public had an interest in seeing photographs of Prince Rainier III of Monaco that saw him walking in a way that suggested he was in good health—but not in seeing photographs of the royal family on vacation (*Von Hannover v. Germany*, App. no. 40660/08 and no. 60641/08 (ECtHR 7 February 2012)). People might argue that any signs of incipient Alzheimer's disease in President Reagan during his term in office (Berisha et al. 2015) should have been revealed to the public, or that President Kennedy's steroid treatment was relevant to his judgment. It might be important to assumptions about the length of time people are likely to be able to serve in office. For example, Paul Tsongas made information about his treatment for lymphoma and his prognosis public when he was running for president; he died from the disease five years later, at age 55 (DeWitt 1997). Sometimes, health information can ruin the career of a politician, even when it is of questionable relevance to performance: Thomas Eagleton was dropped from the Democratic ticket as George McGovern's vice presidential candidate when news surfaced that he had been hospitalized for depression and had received electroshock treatment a number of years earlier. Some might argue that health histories are relevant if politicians have taken positions about controversial medical topics such as abortion or Medicaid expansion; voters might want to know whether candidates or their partners had abortions, used contraceptives, or were at some point on Medicaid. Current presidential candidates are expected to reveal their health information, as both Hillary Clinton and Donald Trump did during the 2016 election cycle (LaMotte 2015). Chapter 10 on privacy and democracy explores these questions more fully.

Some sports stars may be under contractual obligations to allow their health information to be shared with their teams or by their teams. Collective bargaining agreements in major sports in the United States (the NBA, NFL, and MLB) all require athletes to submit to medical examinations and to disclose medical information about themselves (McChrystal 2015). Also, the rules of their professional organizations may require information to be shared as a condition of entering a competition; drug testing and testing for biological sex are examples. There may be significant conflicts of interest in the exercise of privacy choices: athletes may wish to conceal their medical conditions from teams or competitions so that they get to play or are not disqualified. They may be taking drugs forbidden by their sport (even though legal) to gain a competitive advantage. Teams may have interests in concealing information about the health of their players to keep the opposition guessing about their tactics and whether their big star will be in the lineup. They may also wish for information to be limited when they are seeking to trade players. Odds in sports betting may shift depending on the health of key players, and there are opportunities for unfair insider trading if some people have information about players' conditions that is not generally available to others. Sports competitions may also have entry rules that require testing and disclosure of results, including results of drug tests and analyses of biological sex. HIPAA does not prohibit any of these contractual arrangements that require athletes to authorize release of their medical information. Arguments for release of medical information about entertainment stars are arguably less compelling. One argument is that people admire these figures and sometimes pay considerable amounts of money to see them; people might wish to direct their admiration elsewhere if they knew certain facts about their health conditions or treatment they had undergone. A star of a well-known police TV series in Germany sought to suppress publication of information that he had been arrested and convicted for cocaine possession—exactly the kind of offense that might have been the target of the police superintendent he played. He also claimed that the arrest and conviction pertained solely to his private life, which he had kept separate from his life as an actor. The European Court of Human Rights held that the interest in freedom of expression overrode his interests in individual privacy (*Axel Springer v. Germany*, app. No. 39954/08). Other celebrities might publicize information about their health conditions to encourage people to undergo needed health screenings or treatments; Angelina Jolie has been very public about her prophylactic double mastectomy and later removal of her ovaries and fallopian tubes because she has tested positive for the *BRCA-1* gene (Jolie Pitt 2015). Still other celebrities, however, might want to keep health information entirely private in situations in which it bears no relationship to their celebrity; writers Jackie Collins and Nora Ephron, for example, each kept a breast cancer diagnosis secret for many years (Hart 2015). In the United States, HIPAA protections apply to celebrities in the same way they do to anyone else; some of the first criminal prosecutions for intentional violations of the HIPAA regulations involved attempts to sell information about stars such as Farrah Fawcett, Maria Shriver, and Britney Spears to the media (Ornstein 2008; Hennessy-Fiske 2011).

How can you make decisions about your health information?

In making decisions about your own health information, the most important thing to know is how widely protections vary. HIPAA applies only to information within the health-care system. Because there have been many reports of security breaches of health-care systems, people may think that information with their doctors is not very safe. But to some extent this is misleading: because of the breach notification requirements, we know more about these breaches than about what might be occurring with health information elsewhere. There are breach notification requirements for personal health record vendors. But other than the FTC Act prohibition on unfair and deceptive trade practices and various state laws (see Online Appendix), health information available elsewhere does not receive any special privacy protection.

You also should know that you have a right to find out the information in your medical records that is covered by HIPAA. People can request copies of the information and ask to have it corrected if it is inaccurate. This is important, as inaccuracies can be life-threatening. Electronic medical records are only as accurate as the people entering the information in them. It is not unusual for data entry to be wrong, or for the wrong patient's information to get in another person's chart; medical identity theft is becoming increasingly common.

As a patient, you can also be an intelligent user of your physician's electronic system. Portals that allow you to view some of their records are increasingly common; these require usernames and passwords. You should know that it is risky to share your log-on information with others, even if it seems convenient. If patients want to give others access to their records so they can be helped with care—such as elderly parents with their children—they should see whether their doctor's system allows them to establish separate log-in credentials.

You should also be aware that physicians are allowed to share information in many ways. Most important, information may be shared for treatment, payment, public health, and law enforcement without patients being aware that this is happening. If you enter into medical research, you should keep records of the study and, if you wish, follow up with your physicians about what has happened to the information in the study and whether any results from the study have been published. If studies involve registries of patient information—there are registries for many diseases, from genetic conditions such as cystic fibrosis to many cancers to Alzheimer's disease (see https://www.nih.gov/health-information/nih-clinical-research-trials-you/list-registries)—you should know whether you are in the registry and whether information from your medical records is being shared with the registry on an ongoing basis. Parents may be asked to enter their children into registries; if they agree, they should be aware of what information is being shared about their children and whether their children should know about the registry when they become adults.

Finally, you should be aware that outside of the realm of HIPAA, there is really very little protection for medical information. Entering health information into interactive websites—many exercise sites, weight loss sites, and health log sites allow information to be shared with Facebook or with friends on the site—may result in information becoming more public than you would ever expect. Surfing the web for medical information, while potentially informative, is also potentially revealing. If you want to keep health information or inferences about your health private, you should understand and be careful about your privacy settings.

4

PRIVACY AND EDUCATIONAL INFORMATION

Introduction

Like health care, education raises complex privacy issues. Education is very important to people's prospects in life. In the United States and in Europe, people do not have a great deal of choice about accessing education, at least before they become adults. In addition, people do not control what is entered into their educational records: the records are created by their teachers, administrators, or schools. Information in educational records may be required for many purposes—jobs and professional licenses, for example—and may last for a lifetime. Grades don't change, although they may be supplemented by later academic records. Many educational records are assembled about children and raise the questions about privacy within families that are considered in Chapter 7. Schools and universities may use web-based services as teaching tools or to manage records in ways that raise questions of privacy. Outside of schools, services may also be available to manage applications or testing. In addition, for reasons of safety, schools have become major sites for surveillance that may reveal information about students, teachers, and others within them. Such surveillance also opens the door to very real threats to intellectual freedom.

Educational institutions are important locations for developing ideas and the exercise of intellectual freedom. John

Dewey saw public education as critical to the diversity of perspectives and ideas that help democracy flourish. Protecting intellectual privacy may be critical to the process of democratic education. Today's educational institutions are also an important place for generating new knowledge, and they need the protection of privacy for academic freedom. Like schools, colleges, and universities, libraries also have been at the forefront of protecting intellectual privacy.

What is educational information and how is it being collected?

Concerns about privacy in educational information are raised by the contents of educational records, by collection of data to assess school performance, by surveillance in schools, and by the many services allied with or supporting education. People may be worried about how information in these materials will look to others or how it may be used against them. Think about your own school records: there may be copies in your drawers or your parents' closets, but the originals will remain at all of the institutions you have attended.

Educational information as discussed in this chapter includes, first, any information in educational records: school transcripts, test results, graduation records, attendance records, disciplinary issues, health information, letters of recommendation, and much more. Second, it includes information transferred from these records to other sources, such as those for managing applications for admission. A third kind of educational information is information gathered within schools, such as that filmed by surveillance cameras, but also recordings that may be made by students or others on smart devices. Fourth, schools may require their students to use the web and Internet-based materials; assignments, grades, and communication between teachers and families may take place over the Internet. Information gleaned from these uses may be very revealing about what individuals know and are thinking about. Finally, libraries may have information about patrons' uses of computers and about the books or other materials they have looked at or checked out.

In educational records, universities and colleges, secondary schools, primary schools, and even preschools collect and store a great deal of information about individuals as students. These records may contain information not only about educational performance, but also about medical needs, behavior and mental health, disciplinary actions, disabilities, and family circumstances. Educational records will, of course, include assignments and assessments of academic performance. Medical information in the records may indicate proof of required immunizations or insurance; it may also include any documentation supporting requests for accommodations for disability. Records of student behavioral issues and disciplinary processes could prove devastating for later prospects; for example, many states require applicants for admission to the bar as a lawyer to provide any information about academic misconduct and may deny candidates on the basis of matters such as plagiarism. Educational records also may include information about family economic circumstances that is needed to demonstrate eligibility for free lunches, fee waivers, or financial aid for tuition. Law enforcement records, such as arrest records for thefts or vandalism on school property, are not considered educational records and are maintained as criminal justice system records.

Much of this information in educational records may be quite sensitive. In addition, much is collected about children too young to give meaningful consent. The information may concern not only the students themselves but also their family members, friends, or neighbors, from whom consent is not sought and may not be available.

In the effort to counter educational disparities and to improve overall educational quality, public schools have been encouraged or required to implement curricular standards and to assess student performance. Led by the federal Department of Education, these efforts have sparked intense controversy. One target of criticism has been the collection of data from testing that is used to generate report cards on schools. Some critics object that the data stigmatize students in schools that are labeled as "failing" and may risk being identified with particular students or small groups of students. Other critics object to any kind of centralized database containing student information. Such objections are not limited to data collection by the federal government; inBloom was a private foundation funded by the Gates Foundation and the Carnegie Foundation to collect and store student performance data and make it available for performance evaluation analytics. The foundation drew heated controversy because it collected this data about students and was forced to shut down several years after opening (Herold 2014). Other management platforms remain that permit data analytics, such as PowerSchool or Clever.

Schools today are increasingly sites for surveillance. CCTV systems are in use all over the world for school security. Security is, of course, important for education to take place and to protect those engaged in it. Yet surveillance systems also enable information to be used to monitor students' behavior or to assess the competence of teachers. Technologically, they allow video from classrooms, halls, bathrooms, or other locations on school grounds to be streamed to law enforcement, parents, or other sites away from the school itself. Understandably, concerns about the privacy of both students and teachers have intensified with the ubiquity of these devices (see Data Protection in Schools, http://www.dataprotectionschools.ie/en/; Perry-Hazen and Birnhack 2016).

School surveillance may also include the monitoring of Internet use by individuals using computers through campus networks. Monitoring may be aimed at preventing the use of sites that might be damaging to children, such as child pornography sites. Monitoring may also be used to protect campus networks from outside security breaches. After a security breach involving patient data at the University of California at Los Angeles Medical Center, the University of California system implemented a program to monitor unusual traffic on its network wherever that traffic occurred. Members of the faculty at the University of California at Berkeley protested that this monitoring could involve personal information and could chill academic freedom in research on controversial topics (Lohr 2016).

Many school systems in the United States have turned to commercial firms to provide classroom technology, to manage communication between schools and parents, to provide students with assignments that can be submitted electronically, and to maintain educational records. These systems create individualized learning management tools and thus acquire a great deal of individually identifiable information. PowerSchool and Clever are two examples of firms selling software for school districts to use as learning management tools; these platforms can be connected to many different learning apps. Google sells inexpensive Chromebook laptops that are loaded not only with its web search capability but with many other software programs; Google educational programs are reportedly used by over 50 million students worldwide (Peterson 2015; Google for Education, https://www.google .com/edu/products/productivity-tools/classroom/). Google promises not to make any commercial use of information provided by students using its core services (e.g., Google Docs, Gmail, Calendar). But Google considers many other services that students may use frequently to be outside of the core suite (e.g., Search, YouTube, or Maps), and privacy advocates are concerned that information about individual students using these sites may be collected for commercial purposes (Peterson 2015). Several commercial firms offer lecture capture software that allows everything that happens in a classroom to be recorded. This technology is becoming popular as a way for universities to place more learning content online, to accommodate disabilities, or to allow students to replay difficult material, but its use may impinge on the privacy of both faculty and students attending the classes that are recorded. Students may also want to record classes using their computers or smart devices; many universities now have policies that require instructor permission for recording and permission from any students who are recorded.

Students may need to use their educational records as they apply for additional educational programs, licenses, or jobs. Private firms such as Parchment offer services to manage educational records, such as transcripts (http://www.parchment .com/solutions/organizations) or financial aid applications. These education information management systems make it simpler for students to submit their transcripts for college applications or financial information for financial aid. But they may raise significant privacy concerns, depending on how the services share students' information. Parchment's privacy policy explicitly states that it will share "certain information" (unspecified) with schools and colleges from which transcripts have been obtained, with other companies performing support functions, and (ironically under a section entitled "protection of rights") to comply with legal process or respond to claims that information on the site violates the rights of third parties or—most important—to protect the rights, property, or personal safety of anyone (http://www.parchment.com/ privacy-policy/). In another recent example, a proposed sale in bankruptcy of the assets of a career and college planning site, ConnectEDU, drew objections from the Federal Trade Commission when it did not propose to allow the site's users to delete their data before the sale (Chmielewski 2015). Services such as Interfolio are also available that manage dossiers for job seekers and contain information drawn from educational records, confidential letters of reference, and materials created by applicants themselves.

Why protect educational information?

A number of strong reasons support individual control over educational information. These reasons in favor of individual control are especially compelling when the information is in the student's records, but they apply to other information as well.

First is the importance of education itself. Education plays a critical role in individual life prospects, and an educated citizenry fosters democracy. If students believe that schools will use information about them to their detriment, they may clam up or stop attending. Parents may also keep their children home if they want to keep information about their children out of the hands of authorities they believe might misuse it. An example is concern about immigration status; although undocumented students have a constitutional right to attend school (*Plyler v. Doe*, 457 U.S. 202 (1982)), parents may be afraid that attendance may reveal their children's or their own undocumented status. Undocumented students may be afraid to enter college because they wish to protect information about their status or their families' status (Gonzales 2009). While physical safety is generally used as an argument for monitoring what is occurring in schools, lack of privacy may also lead students to feel unsafe. If students believe that the information collected about them will be used against them—by other students bullying them, by teachers disliking them, or by authorities seeking to suppress them—school will not be a welcoming place for them to learn or to think.

Defenders of students' rights argue that privacy is especially important to the ability to try out novel ideas and form identities (boyd 2014). Others argue that privacy is critical to the formation of ideas needed for the progress of knowledge and robust democratic debate. Schools and universities have historically been incubators for novel ideas that may be threatening to established centers of power. Access to records may be used to discredit students who are challenging authority, to root out dissenters under the guise that they are merely troublemakers, or to threaten students with sanctions if they think or act boldly to challenge wrongs against themselves, their fellow students, or others in society. Surveillance cameras especially may chill freedom of inquiry and expression in schools. Repressive regimes across the globe have targeted academics for expressing views that they believe to be subversive. Human rights organizations such as Human Rights Watch and Amnesty International regularly report arrests and detentions of academics as human rights violations. In the United States, conservative groups have taped classroom sessions to document what they consider to be biased teaching; reported threats against these teachers have resulted in some cases. That surreptitious recordings are easy to make and reproduce is seen by many as a potent threat to intellectual freedom.

Educational information also may significantly affect long-term prospects. Applications for further education typically require submission of transcripts from all educational institutions attended. Licensure in many professions may require submission of educational materials and recommendations from institutions attended. Many job applications require educational information as well. For these reasons, maintaining the integrity of educational records and protecting individual choices about when to reveal them are especially important.

In addition, people do not have control over the information that is included in their educational records. Up to a certain age, school attendance is mandatory. For the most part, students do not generate the records and cannot pick and choose what is in their records; educational authorities do. Children may be too young to consent in any informed way to record-keeping about them. Without such control, students have to rely on privacy policies, rather than their own actions, for their protection.

Homeschooling has become a way for some families to limit the information that is available to others. In 2016, an estimated 2.3 million students were being homeschooled in the United States. Homeschooling is popular for many reasons: the ability of parents to be involved in their children's education, the ability to tailor education to the needs of individual children, the flexibility it provides, and the ability to avoid schools that are of poor quality. Advocates for homeschooling object to efforts to collect data about student performance on standardized measures (e.g., HSLDA 2014). Critics of homeschooling worry especially about quality control, the lack of challenges from diverse ideas or perspectives, and the risk that widespread homeschooling will undermine the democracy-promoting aspects of public schools (West 2009). For these critics, it would be unfortunate if parents felt driven to homeschool their children because of concerns about privacy. Even with homeschooling, however, there may be concerns about the privacy of records. For students who are homeschooled, state laws govern the records that must be kept. In some states, records are kept within the home and may be quite minimal. Other states have a variety of reporting requirements. Even when state laws do not require significant record-keeping, records may be necessary for the child in the future if he or she plans to apply to college or for jobs. There are record-keeping companies that will provide services for homeschooling; the privacy policies of these sites vary, and in some cases may permit the use of information for advertising purposes (e.g., http://homeschoolmanager.com/privacy-policy/). These homeschool records and reports are not protected by the federal FERPA statute described in the following section.

Finally, much of the information in educational records may be very sensitive. Children may not want others to know their grades, their medical conditions, their home situations, or their level of economic insecurity. Disciplinary records may lead to law enforcement and, as described earlier, some families are worried about the information about their immigration status being shared. Information observed in schools may also be sensitive; students may want to try out unpopular ideas without necessarily agreeing with them, or may be shy about testing their skills in front of others. They may wish to visit Internet sites without others knowing their interests in the material they have seen.

When, if ever, should educational information be revealed? Why?

On the other side, individuals may wish to share their educational information. At times, they may lose out on opportunities if they do not share information. It is important to make sure that demands for information are not unreasonable and that the information is justified in terms of the purpose for which it is sought, however. Otherwise, individuals may be put in a position in which they have to share sensitive information in circumstances where it bears no or very little relevance to the legitimate interests of the seeker of the information but which could be very damaging. School disciplinary proceedings are a good example of the need for relevance: a substantiated plagiarism charge during law school might be very relevant to a state bar's decision whether or not someone is likely to be trustworthy as a lawyer, whereas a student's troubles in elementary school might not.

There also may be important reasons for some educational information to be shared without the individual's consent. Educational institutions may need to share information internally if they are to provide good education to their students. If students transfer schools, new schools may need to know about their prior performance and any problems with it. For example, information about prior episodes of cheating might be relevant to new schools—but with the important caution that this information should not turn into a lifetime of stigmatization. A general problem with sharing information when students transfer is that students may wish to leave schools because they have been subjected to ill-treatment or discrimination; having labels follow them may unjustifiably re-create the attitudes they were seeking to escape.

Degrees conferred by public institutions are public acts; some might argue that this information should be publicly available. Many might think this information is not sensitive and that people should be able to verify the supposed educational achievements of others. Some might also argue that what goes on in public education—what is taught, how it is taught, whether teaching reflects diverse or ideological perspectives—ought to be open to the public, even if this might require observing individual students as they participate in the process. Some argue that classroom recordings should be shared without permission as a way to improve the quality of teaching. Many students would like to be able to demonstrate that professors present material in systematically biased ways, or that students have been targeted for their views or otherwise have been discriminated against. Quality, fairness, and non-discrimination are surely important educational values. In many circumstances, however, there may be ways to encourage and assess achievement of these values without surreptitious recording, including policies that require openness and agreement to recording.

Safety is one of the most compelling but complex reasons for sharing educational information without consent. Schools should be safe environments for students to learn in and protected spaces for academic freedom. Tragedies such as the mass shooting at Connecticut's Sandy Hook Elementary School, in which 20 students and six staff members were killed, are a terrible reminder of the need for school safety. At times, students themselves may be the threat; at Virginia Tech University, a student killed 27 other students and five faculty members. If sharing educational information with law enforcement is necessary to keep schools safe, arguably it should be shared.

But very difficult judgment calls are required in determining when sharing information is necessary for safety. Student mental health information poses significantly challenging problems in this regard. On the one hand, students with mental health issues may be unfairly stigmatized or inappropriately judged to present a danger—with seriously damaging results for them. On the other hand, educational institutions that are unaware of students' mental health issues will be unable to provide supports or accommodations that they may need and to respond in the very rare cases of genuine danger.

Risk assessments in psychiatry are methodologically complex; current methods lack specificity, especially for low frequency events, thus significantly over-identifying people who are supposed to be at risk (Buchanan et al. 2012). As discussed in the preceding chapter on health information, mental health professionals have especially strong obligations of confidentiality in order to encourage people to trust and seek treatment. The detailed report for Virginia's then-governor Tim Kaine, prepared after the Virginia Tech shootings, reveals these tensions (Review Panel 2007). The student who committed the shootings had received extensive counseling and accommodation for anxiety and selective mutism while in high school, but these records were not transferred with his transcript. Under federal law, universities may not make pre-admission inquiries about disability status; students wishing accommodations must request them, and the student did not do so. At Virginia Tech, the concerns had included a report by an English professor about violent writing and a refusal to stop taking pictures of classmates that led to removal from the class, a report of harassment against a woman student, other reports of strange emails from the student, a mental health prescreening that judged him a danger to self or others, and several other instances of inappropriate or violent writing assignments. The psychiatrist conducting the prescreening for commitment relied only on his interview of the student and did not collect collateral information, apparently because of limited resources and privacy concerns. Among the explanations were inaccurate beliefs about privacy laws and inconsistencies between the privacy laws governing educational information and those governing health information. There were also judgments that the various situations in which the student had been involved had each been taken care of, and so the information about them was not reported further within the decentralized structure of Virginia Tech. None of the information was given to the student's parents, either, although they had been very involved earlier in helping him get needed mental health treatment.

An additional complication about student privacy is the role of parents (or others who serve in the position of parents). Parents may make decisions about whether to share the information of their underage students. But as students get older, they may legitimately wish to have control over their own lives and some levels of privacy from their parents (see, e.g., boyd 2014). Resolving conflicts in such cases may be difficult. On the one hand, parents have strong interests in protecting and guiding their children. They may be expected to act for their children's best interests and will need good information about them in order to do so. On the other hand, students may care very deeply about keeping some information to themselves. Moreover, there may be circumstances in which students legitimately fear that their parents will act abusively if they are given certain information, such as about sexual orientation or reproductive decisions. These dilemmas are especially pressing for school counselors, who may need to respect students' wishes for confidentiality but have legal obligations to report information to parents (or guardians) or others, particularly when underage students are engaging in behavior that is risky to themselves or others. The American School Counselor Association recommends that counselors clarify in advance any possible limits to confidentiality (ASCA 2014), a recommendation that may chill candor in counseling. We discuss these issues about parents and children further in Chapter 7.

There may be a variety of both good and bad reasons for these conflicting approaches to educational privacy. Perhaps one explanation for surveillance and the availability of records in primary and secondary schools is that children are thought to have lesser privacy rights than adults, either because of their need for protection or because of the rights and duties of others, such as their parents, to be involved in their lives. Another explanation may be that societies deem the protection of safety especially important in places of education that children are required to attend and where free inquiry may raise troubling ideas. Still another explanation may be that schools are believed to be sites of particular vulnerability and need for protection; in the United States, schools and universities have been targets of gang violence and of some of the most devastating mass shootings. Less favorably, critics allege that school surveillance is used to pry into students' lives and impose behavioral standards on them; one elite school in the United Kingdom came under fire for having 500 surveillance cameras that students alleged were used to catch them kissing or engaging in trivial misbehavior, such as cutting into lines (Bingham 2015). A still darker explanation may also be that schools and universities have been particular sites for political activity and protest and have drawn repressive surveillance in many countries around the globe as a result.

In sum, important reasons support confidentiality in educational records. The interests of students and school safety weigh heavily on the other side. Academic freedom can be undercut if educational proceedings are recorded to monitor what is said and to threaten unpopular ideas. There may be conflicts between students and their parents about access to information. That there are delicate balances between these considerations suggests that information should be shared without individual consent only with strong justification of the need for the information that is to be shared.

What legal protections does the US FERPA statute provide?

In the United States, the Family Educational Rights and Privacy Act (FERPA) (20 U.S.C. § 1232g; 34 CFR Part 99) protects student education records. It applies to all schools receiving funding from the federal government under applicable programs of the US Department of Education. FERPA governs "education records"—which are defined broadly to include any record, file, document, or other material maintained by the educational institution that contains information directly related to a student (20 U.S.C. § 1232g(a)(4)(A)). FERPA does not apply to some private schools or other educational settings not receiving federal funding. It also does not apply to materials gathered in schools that are not "educational records" as defined, such as teachers' own notes or perceptions, personal recordings made by students or others, or surveillance by designated law enforcement personnel within schools.

FERPA gives parents and eligible students the right to review records and request correction of inaccuracies. "Eligible" students are those who have become 18 or have entered postsecondary institutions at any age. That is, FERPA draws the line for parents to access information at the time when a student turns 18 or enters postsecondary schooling, whichever comes first. However, parents of postsecondary students may receive records if their students are dependents for tax purposes, if there is a health or safety emergency, or if a student is under 21 and has violated laws or policies concerning alcohol or controlled substance use. And school officials may share personal observations or knowledge with parents. Under these provisions, Virginia Tech could have shared their concerns about the student with his parents if they had determined a health or safety emergency; professors also could have shared their personal concerns.

Under FERPA, parents or eligible students must consent in writing to most disclosures of information from educational records. Consent is not required when records are disclosed to school officials with legitimate educational interests or schools to which a student is transferring. It is not required when records are used for program audits or evaluation, school accreditation, or certain research on behalf of the school. Nor is it required for appropriate disclosures in connection with financial aid applications. Importantly, consent is not required when records are disclosed to comply with judicial orders, to deal with health or safety emergencies, to juvenile justice pursuant to state law, or pursuant to several other legal requirements.

Instead of consent, FERPA provides an "opt out" option for what it terms "directory information," which includes name, address, and other contact information; degrees, honors, and awards; participation on athletic teams; and dates of attendance. Current students or their parents must be given an annual opportunity to opt out of the listing of this information. For past students, additional notice is not required, but the school must continue to honor any opt out requests made while the student was in school. This means that members of the public can verify directory information without notice to or consent of students who have not opted out. Services that verify educational credentials, however, may not use additional information such as Social Security numbers to verify identity, without obtaining the individual's consent.

After the shootings at Virginia Tech, the US Department of Education's Family Policy Compliance Office issued a guidance document on FERPA and campus emergencies (FPCO 2011). The guidance states that identifiable information from education records may be disclosed as necessary to address emergencies without written consent. This exception is limited to the period of the emergency and the information necessary to address the emergency. It does not include disclosures made for disaster or emergency planning in advance—only disclosures "in connection with" an actual or impending emergency. The guidance also noted that FERPA only covers educational records that are maintained by the educational institution; personal observations of teachers or students are thus not educational records and thus may be disclosed.

Although FERPA appears highly protective, it has been amended numerous times since its original enactment in 1974, and there are significant areas of ongoing controversy. On one side, critics contend that educational institutions have used FERPA inappropriately to protect their own interests. Universities may, for example, invoke FERPA to shield unfavorable information about student behavior or performance, although one FERPA amendment exempted campus crime logs from FERPA protection. Postsecondary institutions also are required to release to the alleged victim of any crime of violence or non-forcible sex offense the final result of a disciplinary proceeding by the institution against the alleged perpetrator. Elementary or secondary schools may use FERPA to avoid some forms of disclosure of concerns about test results or school safety. Advocates of increasing transparency about school performance believe that more information should be revealed than is currently available.

On the other side, FERPA allegedly underprotects records as well. A 2002 amendment to FERPA in the USA PATRIOT Act passed in response to 9/11 allowed disclosures in connection with terrorism investigations without notice to students (20 U.S.C. § 1232g(j)). (We'll have a lot more to say about the USA PATRIOT Act in Chapter 9.) Foreign students attending educational institutions under an F-1 visa must sign a form authorizing disclosure of any information needed by the Immigration and Naturalization Service to determine non-immigrant status. And regulations adopted in 2011 allow a variety of service providers to schools to receive records as authorized representatives of the schools they serve. These providers may include services such as PowerSchool, Clever, Google Apps for Education, and the inexpensive Chromebook laptops sold to many schools running Google software. Although Google Apps promises not to target advertising to students in primary or secondary schools or in their core services, states that they are FERPA compliant, and promises to require parental consent for children under the age of 13 in compliance with the Children's Online Privacy Protection Act (COPPA), privacy advocates remain critical of the implications of this and other educational service providers, especially when schools use services beyond the Google core (Chmielewski 2015; Peterson 2015). One concern is that under COPPA, schools may approve use of education programs without parental consent, so long as these programs are limited to the educational context and are not used commercially.

Another confusion created by the fact that the United States doesn't have a comprehensive privacy law lies between FERPA and HIPAA, the statute protecting health information and described in the preceding chapter. HIPAA was enacted after FERPA and specifically provides that information protected by FERPA does not fall within HIPAA (45 C.F.R. § 160.103 (2016)).

This means that for schools that are subject to FERPA, any records relating to their students will be under FERPA, including immunization records, school nurse records, counseling records, or records maintained on services received by students under the Individuals with Disabilities Education Act. Schools that do not receive federal funding (many religious and private schools particularly) are not subject to FERPA, however; if they provide medical or psychological care for students that otherwise fits the HIPAA requirements, it will be protected under that statute. FERPA also contains a specific exception for students over 18 or postsecondary students receiving medical and psychological treatment records at the institutions they attend (20 U.S.C. § 1232g(a)(4)(B)(iv)). These records are not under FERPA but may be under HIPAA and require authorization for release. Under this provision, any medical or psychological treatment received by the Virginia Tech student would not have been under FERPA; it would have come under the HIPAA protections.

What protections are there regarding surveillance cameras or other recording devices in schools?

Surveillance cameras in schools, on school grounds, or in school facilities such as buses are an area of FERPA controversy. These cameras are installed for safety reasons, and they record what is within their line of capture. The recordings thus may contain information about many students and school personnel as they interact. Parents of students who are bullied or who are in fights at school or on school buses have sought to have the videos released. Members of the public, including journalists, have also requested recordings of reported school incidents. Schools have contended that these are educational records covered by FERPA, so they cannot release any video or audio recording without getting the consent of the individual students recorded or redacting the information of students who do not consent. People seeking the recordings claim that they are not educational records because they do not concern educational performance. Some legal decisions have agreed that these surveillance camera recordings are FERPA protected, reasoning that they are maintained by the school and are directly related to the students identifiable in the video (e.g., *Bryner v. Canyons School District*, 351 P.3d 852 (Utah App. 2015)).

However, not all school surveillance videos are educational records under FERPA. The US Department of Education Family Compliance Office guide for elementary and secondary schools notes that security videotapes obtained by designated law enforcement units within schools are not educational records. Videos designated as law enforcement may be released even if they contain identifiable images of other students (DOE 2016). The Department of Education has not issued further guidance about surveillance cameras, despite requests, so this remains an area of open controversy.

Educational institutions increasingly are relying on lecture capture technologies to record class sessions. If the recordings are maintained by the school, they are educational records under FERPA. They thus require consent by any student recorded if they are to be disclosed. Any identifiable information about students who do not consent must be redacted before the recording is disclosed.

With the ubiquity of smart devices, individuals themselves may record events within schools. Such recordings do not come within FERPA as they are not maintained by the school. Any restrictions on private recordings or their use depend on state laws or the policies of the educational institutions themselves.

In other countries, the legal status of surveillance cameras in schools may also be unclear. One recent study in Israel of decisions to install these devices learned that principals generally believed that the law protected the privacy of these recordings when any protections were at best ambiguous (Perry-Hazan and Birnhack 2016). The authors of this study concluded that principals were operating with a legal imaginary, a set of unverified assumptions about the law, rooted in thoughts about what the law should be. In the European Union, information collected by schools and universities is governed by the general data protection regime. Law enforcement, however, is outside the scope of EU competence, and CCTVs installed for this purpose may come under this exclusion.

What about information possessed by testing services?

Many testing services are used for admission to private schools, postsecondary educational institutions, and professional licensing. Testing services may also provide employers with test instruments tailored to their needs. Students using these services must provide them with certain personal information. Students from outside the United States who wish to take US-based tests are warned that their information may be transferred to the United States and will be subject to US privacy rules (for ETS, see https://www.ets.org/legal/privacy; for ACT, see http://www.act.org/content/act/en/privacy-policy.html). The US College Board in its privacy policy warns students that use of the service involves consenting to cross-border transfer of data to the United States, which may have less protective privacy standards than their home countries (https://www.collegeboard.org/privacy-policy).

These testing services promise not to share your student information except as you direct. They tell you how to request correction of information and how to close an account. Closing an account does not mean that scores will be deleted, however (e.g., http://www.act.org/content/act/en/privacy-policy.html). The sites also indicate that scores may be shared with schools. They also monitor third-party sites such as Facebook to see what ads for the services have been accessed by students using the services.

Student rights with respect to testing services are limited to personal data. Students have sought to compel disclosure of materials such as examiner's notes that might explain why they received the grade that they did. In *Nowak v. The Data Protection Commissioner*, [2016] IESC 18 (28 April), the Irish high court referred the question of whether examination scripts and examiner's notes are personal data to the European Court of Justice (ECJ). The Irish Institute of Chartered Accountants took the position that these materials from the test to become a chartered accountant were not personal data because they could not be used to identify the individual. Nowak took the position that the handwriting in the scripts was biometric information and thus identifiable. He also contended that because the results of an exam are personal data, the raw material by which that result is arrived at is also personal data. According to the Irish court, no other national courts have decided this issue. Because the Irish court then found that the matter was unclear, it submitted it for judgment to the ECJ.

Are letters of recommendation confidential?

Letters of recommendation may be confidential, depending on the circumstances in which they are requested and whether or not rights of access are waived. Letters of recommendation that are part of students' educational records are protected under FERPA. That means that students would normally have a right to see them, and that they would only be available to others with their consent. FERPA, however, allows students to waive their rights to see letters, and many students do. Students are often advised to waive their rights so that letters seem more reliable to those who receive them. The disadvantage of waivers, however, is that students may never know whether inaccurate or damaging information was included in a letter. Letter writers unfortunately may be oblivious to how comments may be taken by others and may say things that are unintentionally negative. Some letter writers may agree to write letters without warning students that the letters will not be strong; many academics consider this practice to be unethical, but no mechanisms are in place to prevent it.

Letters of recommendation that are not educational records may or may not be confidential, depending on the circumstances. Plaintiffs claiming employment discrimination, for example, have succeeded in getting access to letters of recommendation needed to demonstrate their case (e.g., *Dixon v. Rutgers University*, 521 A.2d 1315 (N.J. Super. 1987)). The US Supreme Court has held that First Amendment academic freedom does not bar the Equal Employment Opportunity Commission from access to these materials to investigate discrimination claims (*University of Pennsylvania v. EEOC*, 493 U.S. 182 (1990)).

If you need to take tests with accommodations, can you keep this information from being shared?

Students taking the standardized tests used for admissions to schools, colleges, or universities and students taking licensing examinations have the legal right to reasonable accommodations under the US Americans with Disabilities Act. Many students take these tests with accommodations such as extra time, reading devices, scribes, or quiet settings. Test services are required to report scores of tests taken under accommodations in the same way that they report other scores. In the past, some services, notably the service offering the law school admissions test, "flagged" scores to indicate that the tests were taken with accommodations. The US Department of Justice opposed the practice, claiming that it suggested that the scores were not valid and that it discouraged test takers from requesting accommodations out of the fear that they would be discriminated against (DOJ 2014).

Test takers in California brought suit against the Law School Admission Council (LSAC), claiming that its practice of flagging test scores (among many other practices) violated the Americans with Disabilities Act. The Department of Justice intervened on behalf of the test takers. The LSAC settled the case in 2014 and agreed to stop routine flagging of test scores (DOJ 2014a). Test takers requesting accommodations can now be reassured that this information will remain private unless they choose to reveal it because they wish to seek accommodations at schools they attend.

What privacy protections are there for people using libraries?

Libraries are a location of lifelong learning for many people, have a long-standing tradition of protecting the privacy of their patrons, and raise many of the same policy concerns that are raised about educational records.

Since 1939, the Code of Ethics of the American Library Association (ALA) has affirmed the right to privacy for library patrons (ALA Council 2002). During the anti-communism crusades of the 1950s, librarians proclaimed the "freedom to read" materials others might consider subversive (Johnson 1989). The ALA bases its commitment to privacy in the importance of reading and "uninhibited access to information" (ALA 2016). People must be able to select materials without damage to reputation, ostracism from the community, or criminal penalties (ALA 2016). To honor this commitment, libraries collect as little information about their patrons as possible and insist on proper legal justification for any subpoenas seeking access to the information they do possess.

Despite these commitments, libraries are placed under pressures to reveal information about their patrons' interests. Johnson (1989) describes how the reporters Bernstein and Woodward got access to White House requests for material from the Library of Congress as they were investigating the Watergate scandals. The Library of Congress has since adopted policies stringently protecting the confidentiality of reader requests for use of the collection. Most states have laws protecting library records, although the force of these statutes varies. In the late 1960s, a time of political protests, the federal agency responsible for investigating explosives sought library records of patrons who had accessed material on making bombs. The ALA urged its members to resist any fishing expeditions into library records (Johnson 1989). There have also been periodic pressures against libraries owning books some consider obscene and keeping the circulation records for these books confidential.

Law enforcement has also sought library records in connection with criminal investigations. In *Brown v. Johnston*, 328 N.W. 2d 510 (Iowa 1983), the police were investigating a series of local cattle mutilations. With a subpoena, they sought the library records of people who had checked out books on witchcraft and related topics. The library board and a library patron sought to enjoin the library from disclosing the materials. The court ordered enforcement of the subpoena, reasoning that any privilege of confidentiality was overridden by the societal need for the information.

The USA PATRIOT Act, enacted in the wake of the 9/11 terrorist attacks, gave intelligence agencies new powers to access library records. Under § 215 of the Act, records could be accessed based on submissions to the secret FISA court (see Chapter 9). They could also get these records with a National Security Letter (NSL), an administrative subpoena that does not require a court order. Recipients of these letters are not permitted to disclose even that they exist, so they are very difficult to monitor. Four Connecticut librarians, members of a public library cooperative called the Library Connection, challenged an NSL; they were permitted to break their silence only after a court's revocation of the non-disclosure order (Cowan 2006). A 2006 amendment provided that libraries were not subject to NSLs under the Stored Communications Act, 18 U.S.C. § 2709(g). In 2007, however, the Internet Archive, a nonprofit library of free books, movies, software, websites, and other materials, received an NSL. With the help of the Electronic Frontier Foundation and the American Civil Liberties Union, the Archive challenged both the letter and the prohibition on disclosure, claiming that it fell within the exception for libraries. The government settled the case and dropped both the NSL and the gag order about it (EFF 2016). Because of the secrecy, it remains unclear how frequently libraries have been subject to records access under these USA PATRIOT provisions. Recently, government efforts to get other records such as telephone metadata have received far more publicity, but the importance of privacy for library users should not be underestimated (Elliott 2013).

How can you protect your educational information?

To protect your educational information, the most important thing you can do is know what is in your records and where these records are located. You might be surprised to know what is actually there. You should check the records for accuracy and request any needed corrections.

You should also read the notices of FERPA rights that you are given. You should make careful decisions about whether you want to opt out of having directory information be public. You should also think carefully about any decision to allow access to your records and about whether you wish to waive your own right to see letters of recommendation. It is particularly important to know what is in your records before consenting to disclosure. Finally, you should be aware that many service providers are in use both within and outside educational institutions. If you are concerned about privacy, you should seek information about the service providers in use at educational institutions that you or your family members attend, including their privacy policies.

5

FINANCIAL INFORMATION, CREDIT INFORMATION, AND INFORMATION FOR EMPLOYERS

Introduction

This chapter considers privacy for you as you participate in economic life. Should you be able to keep information about your finances, your creditworthiness, or your tax payments confidential? Because engagement in economic life has impacts on others, including possibilities for power and influence, perhaps it is never entirely self-regarding. Taxes, especially, support overall levels of public spending; for this reason alone, the public has an interest in knowing what everyone pays. Lenders may need to know whether their potential borrowers are likely to repay in order to set interest rates or decide whether to lend at all. And employers surely at least have some good reasons for needing to know about the backgrounds and activities of their workers. On the other hand, many people want to keep information about their finances, their borrowing, or their taxes, to themselves. This information can be used to discredit them, deny them opportunities, or otherwise disadvantage them. And employers may overreach, peeking into desk drawers or cell phones, or seeking to control what employees do when they are not at work—activities that employees may think they are doing "in private."

What is financial information?

Financial information is all the information about your finances: how much money you have, where you keep it, how you have it invested, and how you spend it. It includes the information in bank records, records of investments, and records of credit card expenditures. Federal and state statutes protecting information falling under this general description likely have more limited definitions of the information they cover. Consumer credit information assembled to determine whether individuals are good risks for loans or other similar transactions are protected by a different set of laws in the United States and are discussed later in this chapter.

Should privacy in financial information be protected? Why or why not?

As with other kinds of personally identifiable information, people may have both non-instrumental and instrumental reasons for protecting the privacy of financial information. Some people simply believe that others should not be able to know their incomes or how much money they have. These people may refuse to answer survey questions asking their level of family income, for example. People may also believe that the amounts they have earned or saved over a lifetime are their own business; stories are familiar of unassuming people who managed through thrift or cleverness to save up fortunes or leave valuable art collections to their communities. Some believe that it is a matter of identity to be able to keep financial information secret: to appear to the world as they would like to be seen, whether as rich or as poor, without being called out as hypocrites because their public persona does not match private reality. People also believe that how they spend their money is up to them: that as long as they pay their bills, they should be able to be misers or spendthrifts, and spend their money wisely or frivolously, without being subject to prying eyes, disapproval, or shame.

Financial information can be used against people in many ways. Theft and identity theft are the most obvious ways that information such as account numbers or PINs can be used against people. So are scams or fraud, especially against people who are perceived as vulnerable. High-pressure sales tactics may be used to induce them to spend money in ways they would otherwise never think of doing. Charities, churches, or alma maters may send solicitations that range from the merely annoying to the more directly predatory. Levels of wealth or expenditures may be used to damage reputations of financial acumen or probity, legends of having risen from poverty, or admiration for having been charitable or self-sacrificing. Organizations may not want to employ people who are perceived as too rich (will they really want to work hard if they don't need this job?) or too poor (are they likely to embezzle or pilfer if they are tempted?).

Knowledge about people's expenditures may also be used against them. Credit card bills can demonstrate cheating on a spouse or an expense account. Expenditures may be read by family members to suggest that older relatives are cognitively impaired and in need of protection. Or, they may indicate that people are engaging in activities that are controversial or are judged to merit disapproval. Knowledge about expenditures may create conflicts within families, if children realize that their parents are spending their expected inheritance on travel or charitable donations or just squandering it—or, if parents think their children are not saving wisely for their own futures. Changes in spending habits reportedly have been used to suggest changes in health status that might make people poor risks for mortgages or insurance.

Information about finances can also be used to attack unpopular groups. If groups are required to disclose their contribution lists, some contributors may be deterred from giving. Efforts to identify contributors to groups such as the Communist Party, the Irish Republican Army, the NAACP, the Jewish Defense League, or more recently certain Islamic organizations have been perceived as improper threats against legitimate differences of opinion and freedom of association. Many people want their donations to charities to be listed as anonymous so others do not know they have given. Their reasons may range from feeling threatened by public knowledge of the contribution to simply not wanting others to be aware of their generosity.

On the other hand, financial information may be very important to legitimate investigations of crimes such as bribery, fraud, insider trading, pyramid schemes, human trafficking, drug trafficking, or money laundering. It may be critical to investigations of tax evasion through efforts to hide money offshore or in shell corporations. National governments seek financial information as a way to identify supporters of terrorist groups or to assess their strength.

Furthermore, without estimates of individuals' financial information, it may be difficult to ascertain the extent of their influence. We may not know where they are contributing money to charitable or political organizations. We may not know whether they are giving to universities in hopes of influencing the views of scholars otherwise thought to be impartial. Individuals with strong political views and interests may seek to keep their contributions secret so the public does not understand the power they are wielding. Recently, the Americans for Prosperity Foundation, a foundation controlled by the Koch brothers, was granted a court order against efforts to require release of its list of donors (*Americans for Prosperity Foundation v. Harris*, no. CV 14-9448-% (C.D. Calif. 2016), https://v6mx3476r2b25580w4eit4uv-wpengine.netdna-ssl.com/wp content/uploads/2016/04/Docket184.pdf). The foundation claimed that their donors had been subject to threats and the court found their evidence persuasive on this point, but critics believe they are trying to hide where their money goes (Dunbar 2016). Relatedly, there may be serious issues of injustice in societies that are not open and transparent about how money talks within them—or even about their levels of income inequality or concentrations of wealth. We will return to these issues in the discussion of privacy and democracy in Chapter 10.

People involved in personal disputes also may want to hide their financial assets. Spouses in divorce proceedings may try to sequester some of their assets from being considered by the court in dividing marital property or making awards of alimony or child support. People applying for bankruptcy may seek to hide assets from their creditors. People hoping to avoid the requirement to spend down assets to become eligible for Medicaid may try to conceal or transfer assets so that they can be passed on to the next generation rather than being used to pay for nursing home care. These behaviors are not legal, but financial information may be needed to uncover them.

What legal protections are there for financial information in the United States?

In *U.S. v. Miller*, 425 U.S. 435 (1976), the US Supreme Court held that the Fourth Amendment's prohibition on unreasonable searches and seizures did not extend to records in the possession of banks. The Court reasoned that people did not have an expectation of privacy in these records because they had shared them with a third party, the bank. (This is called the "third party doctrine" and is discussed in the Online Appendix.) It was thus not an unreasonable search for federal investigators to gain access to these records without a search warrant or other legitimating legal means. In a parallel decision that same term, the Court held that people do not have Fourth Amendment privacy expectations in records shared with their accountants (*Fisher v. U.S.*, 425 U.S. 391 (1976)). In response to these decisions, Congress enacted the Right to Financial Privacy Act (RFPA) of 1978. This Act created statutory rights in financial information that are similar to but weaker than Fourth Amendment rights would have been.

One important limit of RFPA is that it applies its protections only to private individuals or partnerships of five or fewer individuals (12 U.S.C. § 3401(4)). Corporations, trusts, estates, unions and other associations, and larger partnerships are not covered by the statutory right to privacy that RFPA creates. Another limit is that RFPA defines the financial institutions it covers: banks, savings banks, card issuers, industrial loan companies, trust companies, savings associations, building and loan companies, homestead associations, credit unions, and consumer finance institutions that are located within the United States or its territories. RFPA does not apply to institutions located elsewhere, such as the Swiss banks famous for keeping their customers secret (12 U.S.C. § 3401(1)). Perhaps most important, RFPA applies only to requests for information from federal government agencies; it does not apply to requests from state or local governments or private individuals (12 U.S.C. § 3401(3)). Some states have similar statutes protecting the privacy of financial records more generally; others do not.

RFPA grants those it covers the right not to have their records disclosed to federal agencies without notice and their authorization or other legal justification. Other justifications can be legal search warrants, judicial subpoenas, administrative subpoenas, or formal written requests authorized by regulations and sought in a legitimate law enforcement inquiry (12 U.S.C. §§ 3402, 3408). Notice may be delayed by a court order if there is reason to believe it would result in danger to others, flight, destruction of evidence, witness intimidation, or other interferences that might seriously jeopardize an investigation to the same extent (12 U.S.C. § 3409). A significant exception to the protection of RFPA is that it explicitly permits financial institutions or their employees to whistle-blow: to notify government authorities that they have information that may be relevant to a possible violation of any statute or regulation (12 U.S.C. § 3403(c)). So a bank employee might notify the government of unusually large deposits and withdrawals from a particular account. Whistle-blowers are immune from liability for making the report, as well as for not informing the customer that the report has been made. Other exceptions to

RFPA protection include financial institutions collecting on debts or processing government-guaranteed loans (12 U.S.C. § 3403(d)). There are many other exceptions relevant to government enforcement activities and a special exception for counterterrorism or intelligence activities (12 U.S.C. § 3414). RFPA is one of the many federal statutes protecting privacy that has been weakened by amendments that make it easier to investigate crimes such as trafficking or terrorism.

The Gramm-Leach-Bliley Act (GLBA), passed in 1999 to modernize financial institutions and updated by the Dodd-Frank Wall Street reforms in 2010, includes provisions requiring financial institutions to safeguard the confidentiality of customer information. Its protections are broader than those in RFPA because it is not limited to inquiries from the federal government. Its basic approach is the notice and choice approach of FIPs (see Chapter 2), requiring financial institutions to provide their customers with annual notices of their privacy policies (15 U.S.C. § 6803). There is a model form specifying the information that must be included in these disclosures (15 U.S.C. S 6803(e)). Customers must be given the right to opt out of any planned disclosures (15 U.S.C. § 6802). However, many disclosures are exempt from the opt-out requirement, including joint marketing agreements with other financial institutions. Financial institutions also are obligated to establish appropriate security provisions and to protect against threats, hazards, or unauthorized access to financial information (15 U.S.C. § 6801). The GLBA privacy protections have the same exceptions for law enforcement and national security that are found in the RFPA.

Should public employees, politicians, or other particular groups of people be able to keep their financial information private?

In many states, the salaries of public employees are openly available. The justification is that members of the public have the right to know how their money is being spent. Public employees may also be required to make disclosures of other outside income or gifts to allow conflicts of interest to be monitored or discouraged. Requirements to disclose investments, income, or gifts may also extend to members of the public official's immediate family or household members. Arguments for disclosure are especially compelling when public officials are in positions that demand impartiality or the appearance of impartiality. Judges, for example, arguably should disclose any of their financial interests, including any gifts or outside income and earnings from investments, so that people appearing before them may be reassured that they are not unfairly influenced by their economic interests.

Elected officials may also be required to make disclosures of their financial information, depending on their position. Although not required, the practice of most presidential candidates has been to reveal at least some of their financial information for public scrutiny. During the 2016 election, Donald Trump's refusal to make his tax returns public was a controversial subject. Some argued that the information should be public so that voters could determine the accuracy of his claims to business acumen, or whether he might have financial interests that could affect his judgment in office. We discuss questions about privacy for political candidates more fully in Chapter 10, on privacy and democracy.

In light of concerns about conflicts of interest, payments by pharmaceutical companies to doctors are now made public. Curious patients can find out whether their doctors are accepting payments for speaking, consulting, or entering patients into drug trials by going to OpenPaymentsData.cms.gov. These disclosures also may help reduce drug expenditures if they lead physicians to reconsider prescribing expensive brand name drugs or patients to inquire about any concerns they have.

In the wake of the Supreme Court's decision about free expression and campaign contributions, there have been increasing calls for transparency as a way to monitor influence on elections. We discuss the issues raised by privacy in political contributions in Chapter 10 on privacy and democracy.

How can you protect your financial information?

The short answer to how to protect your financial information is to read the privacy notices your financial institutions send out to you every year. They look long and boring and filled with legalese—and they probably are—but they state what these institutions will do with financial information. They also tell you how to opt out of disclosures. You may want to pay particular attention to disclosures that the institution plans to make to outside entities offering various services if you want to opt out of these. You can't opt out of uses of information needed for normal business operations, joint marketing arrangements, fraud investigations, or other legally permitted or required disclosures, however. The Federal Deposit Insurance Corporation has a useful set of instructions for consumers (https://www.fdic.gov/consumers/privacy/yourrights/) that you might also want to read.

What is credit information?

Credit information is information designed to reveal whether people can be relied on to repay debts or otherwise meet contractual obligations. Today, it is collected by large companies maintaining and analyzing records of over 200 million people in the United States and producing reports about them (CFPB 2012). Similar companies also do background checking that includes criminal history, educational history, and employment history, among other information. The reports compiled by these organizations are called credit reports, and they receive special statutory protection in the United States.

What are credit reports and what information may be in them?

In more naive times, people would lend each other money or enter into contracts with a handshake or other expression of trust. If further assurance was needed, they might turn to a formal guarantor who would back up the promises made. We live in less trusting times, however, and people want information in order to judge the levels of risk that others present to them. In the background lies a problem economists term the "asymmetry of information": people seeking loans have personal access to information about their circumstances that lenders do not have. Solving this problem helps encourage lending, allows lenders to adjust interest rates to the level of anticipated risk, and reduces the frequency of default. In response to the problem of asymmetry, lenders created structures to share information among themselves; early credit reporting agencies emerged at the beginning of the nineteenth century in the United States (Olegario n.d.). As they developed, these were largely groups of merchants in a given locality who shared all kinds of information about creditors' reputations, from whether they had paid their bills to whether they had recently been married (Furletti 2002). The creation of revolving credit accounts at stores and the emergence of bank credit cards in the 1970s were a major stimulus to the development of the credit reporting industry.

The contemporary credit reporting industry is largely a creature of the period after World War II. By the 1970s, with the advent of electronic data processing systems, the credit reporting industry had evolved to a consolidated group of three primary credit reporting agencies—TransUnion, Equifax, and Experian—collecting and sharing information across a variety of industries nationwide. In the United States today, these three major credit reporting agencies maintain information on over 200 million people and provide credit information in response to requests for it (FTC 2012, p. 2).

The Fair Credit Reporting Act (FCRA), enacted in 1970 in response to consumer concerns, set rules for the credit agencies. It covers reports from credit reporting agencies as well as from agencies compiling information for the background checks that are in widespread use today. Under the FCRA, a "consumer report" is "any written, oral, or other communication of any information by a consumer reporting agency bearing on a consumer's credit worthiness, credit standing, credit capacity, character, general reputation, personal characteristics, or mode of living which is used or expected to be used or collected ... for the purpose of serving as a factor in establishing the consumer's eligibility for ..." credit or insurance for household purposes, employment, or one of a list of other authorized purposes (15 U.S.C. § 1681a(c)). Clearly these reports can, and do, contain many different kinds of information.

On a monthly basis, credit reporting agencies receive information from over 10,000 data sources. Credit card companies and brand name credit cards account for over 60% of the data (CFPB 2012). The information in a credit report will include individual identifiers such as name, present and former addresses, Social Security number, and date of birth. It will include "trade lines": information from specific creditors such as credit card companies or mortgage companies. Trade line information will include balances, account history, and credit limits. Credit reports will also include public record data such as bankruptcies, court judgments, or tax liens. The major credit reporting agency reports do not include arrest or conviction records, but other consumer reporting agencies, such as those providing background checks for employers, may include this information. Credit reports will also include collection items and any fraud or security alerts placed by the consumer. Finally, the reports will include a list of all the inquiries to the account for the preceding two years—so someone receiving the report will know whether prospective employers, lenders, landlords, insurers, or others, have been given recent access (CFPB 2012). An access report can help a lender know whether someone has applied for many jobs or has sought credit from other sources.

Credit agencies match data with individuals through data architectures they have developed; because there is no independent verification, matching accuracy is a significant problem. About a fifth of consumers get copies of their credit reports in any given year; 8 million file inquiries or disputes. About 40% of the disputes concern reports from collection agencies.

Credit scores are an additional form of information that may be provided with credit reports. These scores are designed to assess the relative risk that the consumer will default. They are generated by models used by the credit reporting agencies; the first such models were created in the 1980s to predict bankruptcy risks. The Fair Isaac Corporation (FICO) developed data models in the early 1990s that are in common use for generic scoring. Companies also develop scores for particular purposes; scoring models are proprietary and are not available to the public (CFPB 2012).

In addition to the credit reporting agencies, other commercial firms perform background checks for employers. Reports from these firms also come under the FCRA. There are large national firms, such as HireRight and LexisNexis (formerly ChoicePoint), and firms for specialized industries, such as eNannySource. Information provided by these firms may include criminal records, sex offender records, Social Security validation, validation of prior employment, verification of educational records or professional licenses, reference checks, motor vehicle records checks, military records, workers' compensation histories, and former addresses. Employers also use do-it-yourself services online that include much of the same information but are not covered by the FCRA. Reports from these services may state explicitly that they should not be used for pre-employment screening that is legally required. These reports may be less accurate for employers and may subject them to liability risks or risks of employment discrimination (Brooks 2016). Nonetheless, they are inexpensive and quick and they remain in common use.

Should credit information be protected? Why or why not?

Reports by consumer reporting agencies wield a great deal of power. Entities granting credit such as mortgages, automobile loans, credit cards, or bank loans or accounts subject to overdraft may seek to assess whether applicants are good credit risks or are likely to default. Rates for casualty, property, or automobile insurance may be based on information in credit reports; people with poor credit may pay more or may not be offered insurance at all. Landlords may wish to know whether their potential tenants are likely to continue to pay their rent or have a history of moving out with bills unpaid. Employers may be interested in whether their potential employees are financially trustworthy or likely to demonstrate the steadiness associated with regular payment of their bills. Credit reports are also used to grant or price telecommunications services. In short, most of the transactions in the economic life of ordinary people require credit reports: renting an apartment, opening a checking account, buying and insuring a car, getting cell phone or Internet service, and getting a job.

Any of the entities that people must go through to accomplish these basic transactions may seek a wide range of information about whether people are creditworthy. In order to make financial or hiring decisions that are prudent, especially when the risks are significant, it is reasonable to expect them to do this. When unfavorable information is received, the result may be very damaging: individuals not only may not get credit, but also may not be able to function even minimally as an economic agent in contemporary society. Or, they may pay higher prices for the credit they do receive. If the unfavorable information is inaccurate, outdated, or taken out of context, these consequences to individuals are more than unfortunate; they are unjustifiable. Without protections, individuals may not know the source of unfavorable information, its content, or even its existence. They will be unable to correct something that is simply wrong but could hang over them for a lifetime, to respond to something that is being misconstrued, or to explain how they have overcome past misdeeds. All that they will know is that they were turned down for something important that they had sought and perhaps needed badly. An additional problem for individuals is that the algorithms used by credit reporting agencies to determine credit scores remain opaque (Pasquale 2015, pp. 22–23).

How is credit information protected in the United States today?

In the United States, individuals are protected from at least some of the problems in credit reports by the Fair Credit Reporting Act (FCRA). The FCRA, enacted in 1970, was spurred by reports of damaging inaccuracies in consumer credit reports. According to a 2012 Report from the FTC to Congress, this problem has not gone away, and inaccuracies remain; in this report, 21% of consumers had credit reports that contained errors that required at least some modification and 10% that required full rectification of the error. Overall, 13% of consumers had errors serious enough to alter their credit scores, and 5% had errors that would alter the interest rates they paid or that would result in their being denied credit.

Under the FCRA, consumers have important rights to ensure the accuracy of information about them. These include the right to request copies of the information in their credit reports; at least one request a year must be free. Consumers have the right to dispute information and request correction of inaccuracies. When information is disputed, credit reporting agencies must notify the source furnishing the information; furnishers must investigate disputed information and correct or update it if it is inaccurate. The FCRA also gives consumers the right to be informed before unfavorable information in a credit report is used to deny them credit. If employers use unfavorable information to make a negative decision, they must give employees or prospective employees a copy of the report and information about how to request its correction.

There are also limits on the information that may be included in credit reports. Conviction records have no time limit. Otherwise, there is something of a right to be forgotten for credit reports. Bankruptcy reports may be included for the past 10 years. Civil suits, arrest records, accounts in collection, paid tax liens, and other negative information may only go back seven years. Information about medical debts may not provide information that allows the nature of the service provided to the consumer to be inferred (15 U.S.C.§ 1681c(a)). Except for the information about medical debts, these restrictions do not apply for credit transactions involving a principal of $150,000 or more, for underwriting life insurance with a face value of $150,000 or more, or for employment at an annual salary of $75,000 or more.

Other important consumer rights include limitations on the use of credit reports. Credit reports may only be requested for reasons listed in the statute (15 U.S.C. § 1681b). These include court orders, the individual's own written request, credit transactions, employment, insurance underwriting, eligibility for licenses or other government benefits required by law to consider financial status, or certain other legitimate business needs. Reports may also be requested by child support enforcement agencies to establish ability to make payments or paternity. Employers may not request a credit report without the employee's permission. As with the statutes protecting financial information, the FCRA has exceptions for national security investigations (15 U.S.C.§ 1681b(b)(4)).

Critics claim that the enforcement of FCRA rights is very poor—so poor that, in the judgment of the National Consumer Law Center (2016), it is a "travesty." Critics also claim that the protections themselves are inadequate (National Consumer Law Center 2016a). In their critics' eyes, a particularly troubling aspect of the use of credit reports is how they mirror histories of discrimination and inequality. Communities of color that once suffered from redlining—the practice invented by the Federal Housing Administration to refuse to grant loans in neighborhoods judged to be high risk—have accumulated far less wealth than whites and thus have less financial resilience to offset emergencies. (African Americans have an estimated 7 cents of wealth for every $1 whites have, and Hispanic Americans an estimated 8 cents.) The result is poorer credit ratings in these groups, and a cycle of difficulty in obtaining affordable credit or even housing or jobs. Insurers also claim that people with poorer credit ratings are higher actuarial risks and should be charged more; critics point out that people with fewer financial resources may simply be more likely to file legitimate claims because they are less able to absorb smaller losses with their own resources. As of 2016, 11 states had enacted laws that prohibit employers from requesting credit reports. California, for example, prohibits this except for managerial positions, law enforcement positions, positions allowing regular access to the financial information of others, and positions involving regular access to amounts of cash over $10,000 (Cal. Labor Code § 1024.5). Many other solutions also have been proposed to correct these imbalances, including limiting the time unfavorable information may stay in reports and designing analytic tools to adjust for the economic impact of past discrimination (National Consumer Law Center 2016a).

Because unfavorable credit information can have such negative consequences, the Federal Trade Commission suggests that people who are planning to apply for employment or credit should get a free copy of their credit report in advance. That way, they can request any needed corrections beforehand. They can also be prepared about how to respond to any negative information (FTC 2016d). Like so many of the other laws about personal information, this recommendation places the burden on consumers to protect themselves.

What is tax information?

Tax information includes all the information on the returns required to be filed to pay federal, state, and local income taxes. It also may include information on import taxes, sales taxes, and property taxes. This information is possessed by the governmental agency collecting the tax or those entities (such as stores) who collect the tax for the agency. Confidentiality questions arise about whether it should be shared with other governmental agencies or with members of the public.

Should tax returns be confidential? Does it matter whether the taxpayer is an individual or a corporation?

Tax returns reveal a great deal of information about the taxpayer: earned income; income on investments; charitable contributions; and deductions for such matters as child support, alimony, charities, business expenses, or medical expenses. As with financial information, individuals may have both noninstrumental and instrumental reasons for wanting tax returns not to be revealed. The FBI and several presidents have pursued investigations targeting taxpayers for their political views. The government also has an interest in protecting returns because knowing that the returns are confidential may encourage taxpayers to be honest in filling them out. On the other hand, opening individual tax returns to public scrutiny would make it easier to detect fraud. It would also allow the world to see in detail how individuals are benefiting from the many deductions—pejoratively described as loopholes—available to them. Other governmental agencies may need access to tax returns to perform their functions: for example, the Department of Education may need to know eligibility for student loans, or Medicare may need to know income to adjust premiums. Congress has insisted on detailed scrutiny of the tax returns of nominees for positions in the executive branch and the judiciary; revelations of the information in these returns has derailed many nominations, for reasons ranging from the hiring of undocumented domestic workers to the failure to document charitable donations (Tumulty 2009).

Corporate tax returns may reveal business secrets, business relationships, successes, or failures—facts that a corporation might legitimately want to keep from its competitors. On the other hand, publicity in these returns would show whether corporations are paying US taxes or whether they are using a variety of legal strategies to reduce or eliminate their tax liabilities. For publicly traded corporations, public returns would give investors far more information than they now have from the reports that are required by the US Securities and Exchange Commission.

Nonprofit corporations may be—and legally are—a special case. When nonprofits such as religious organizations, charities, or private foundations claim exemption from paying federal taxes, the public arguably has a strong interest in monitoring how such tax-sheltered funds are contributed and used. Such corporations arguably also do not have an interest in the competitive advantages that secrecy might bring. Under the US tax code, they are required to file a form called the 990, which is open for public inspection and copying (IRS 2016). Only private foundations are required to make public the names of their donors, however. This restriction is a very important protection for charities that are unpopular or controversial; it protects donors from becoming targets of criticism, investigation, or threats. But it also allows donors to public foundations to keep their support secret and thus conceal the extent of their influence.

In contrast to income tax returns, property tax assessments and collections are public knowledge. Arguably, they reveal only the value of the property, which is far less sensitive information than the information on income tax returns. Moreover, property values for tax purposes can likely be estimated by observation and by information about comparable sales in the area. Sales taxes and excise taxes are assessed as flat rates, so there would appear to be little reason for disclosure for monitoring purposes, other than the assurance that they are being collected.

How are tax returns protected in the United States today?

Initial (and unsuccessful) efforts to establish a federal income tax in the United States during the Civil War and then again in the 1890s considered the records to be public documents. When the present-day federal income tax system was initiated in 1920, the US government treated tax information as a government asset that could be widely shared within federal agencies (Benedict and Lupert 1979). Rumors abounded that the director of the FBI, J. Edgar Hoover, used access to tax records to maintain power. After suspicions that President Nixon had targeted particular taxpayers for investigations during Watergate, in 1976 Congress enacted the current protections for taxpayer confidentiality.

The Internal Revenue Service (IRS) has a separate set of privacy rules for the tax information it collects. As a general rule, all federal tax return information is confidential, with the exception of nonprofits claiming tax exemptions (26 U.S.C. § 6103(a)). This return information may not be revealed by officers of the US government or of state or local governments who have access to the information, even to other government agencies. Federal returns may, however, be disclosed to state tax officials and to state and local law enforcement agencies. Limited disclosures are permitted for criminal investigations on the order of a judge (26 U.S.C. § 6103(i)). Some disclosures are permitted to people with "material" interests: spouses filing joint returns, spouses of individuals filing separate returns if they have consented to consider gifts as made half by each, individuals designated by corporations, shareholders of record owning more than 1% of corporate stock, estate administrators, and trustees, among others (26 U.S.C. § 6103(e)). Certain congressional committees may inspect reports, and the president of the United States may request them with a specific statement in writing of why they are being requested (26 U.S.C.§§ 6103(f)(4), (g)). Taxpayer information may also be disclosed under certain circumstances for use in terrorist investigations.

People may be required to provide their tax returns when they seek certain benefits. To apply for federal student loans, students must submit their own or their parents' most recent tax returns. People with student loans in default also may want to be aware that the Department of Education has the authority to refer defaults to the Department of the Treasury for collection to be offset against expected tax refunds. Tax returns may also need to be submitted to verify income for courts to determine child support obligations. The Treasury will intercept tax refunds to pay child support obligations that are in default.

What are the major concerns about information used by employers?

In order to decide whether to hire someone, promote someone, or take adverse action against current employees, employers may seek additional information about the employee. On the one hand, employers may have a legitimate need for this information if it is related to job performance. They may be concerned about tort liability for hiring someone negligently without having done the appropriate background check, or about risks of theft or violence within the workplace. On the other hand, employers may seek information that is not job related or that may be used to discriminate against the employee. Especially in states with broad doctrines of employment at will—states in which there are very limited exceptions to employers' authority to fire employees at any time or for any reason except a reason that is illegal, such as prohibited discrimination—protection of information they wish to keep private may be very important for employees. Their very jobs may be on the line.

When the government is an employer, special restrictions and protections may apply. The government may not engage in state action that violates the Constitution. So it may not violate the First or Fourth Amendment rights of its employees, or condition employment on employees' acquiescence to violation of these rights. Employers in the private sector do not have the same obligations to protect their employees' constitutional rights, although they could still be subject to suits for damages under the common law privacy torts (discussed in the Online Appendix).

What can employers request in a background check?

With limited exceptions, employers are permitted to request information about employees in background or credit checks. Under federal law, they can make criminal background checks or credit checks conditions for employment; only 11 states restrict whether employers can use credit checks for employment. The Americans with Disabilities Act (ADA) prohibits requiring medical reports or examinations before job offers are made; job-related exams are permitted after people have been made offers if they are required of everyone. GINA prohibits employers from requesting genetic information. Chapter 3 on medical information describes the ADA and GINA in more detail.

When criminal background checks or credit checks are requested from reporting agencies, employers must comply with the requirements of the FCRA, as described earlier in this chapter. They must have the employee's written consent to make the request. If the employer makes a negative decision based on the report, they must give the employee a copy of the report and a summary of rights, including how to contact the credit reporting agency. It is then up to the employee to tell the employer whether anything in the report is misleading or wrong, or to contact the reporting agency to seek correction. Prospective employees would be wise to check their credit records before applying for jobs, so that they can correct or anticipate any negative information in advance. Unlike with decisions about credit, they will not get notice in advance about an adverse decision; they will only get the information after the employer has made the negative decision. This may be fair to employers who cannot wait to make job offers to others, but it is hard on job seekers who lose out because of damaging information in their credit reports.

Employers may also use the variety of do-it-yourself background checking resources that are available online. These resources do not provide what the law defines as consumer reports, so they are not covered by the FCRA. But they may yield a great deal of information—some of it potentially inaccurate or misleading—to potential employers.

The federal Equal Employment Opportunity Commission (EEOC) is particularly concerned about how the use of criminal background checks might be discriminatory. Because arrest and conviction rates vary by race, blanket use of these records may be expected to have a disparate impact linked to race, which in turn affects employability. The EEOC has issued a guidance document on the use of arrest and conviction information in employment (EEOC 2012). Documents of this type, while not legally binding, indicate how the agency plans to enforce its rules and may have some persuasive force with courts as illustrating agency views. Because arrest information does not demonstrate that an offense has actually occurred— only that the person was arrested—the EEOC considers use of this information to be discriminatory. However, if the conduct underlying the arrest makes the individual unfit for the job, this information may be used by the employer. The EEOC's example is immediate termination of a school employee who has been arrested for inappropriate touching of students, when the case has not yet been tried in court. Also, according to the EEOC, use of conviction information is discriminatory treatment if the employer makes different decisions for applicants of different races based on what is otherwise the same information—for example, if African-American job applicants are disqualified when they have youthful marijuana convictions but white job applicants are not. Some states have laws that do not permit requests for conviction records until after job offers have been made; the EEOC also recommends this policy and suggests that convictions be disqualifying only when they are job related.

Can employers access and use information that employees post on social media?

For the most part, employers may search the Internet, including social media sites, for information about employees or prospective employees. They can also use what employees post on these sites. They can use whatever others pass along to them about what employees have posted. This information can be used in hiring decisions or in decisions to discipline or terminate employees.

The FCRA rules about background checks and credit reports only apply to consumer reports sought from reporting agencies. Only the laws against employment discrimination and some state laws restrict what employers can do on their own. Employers are free to use do-it-yourself look-up sites, to google prospective employees, or to search their public posts on social media, and many do. One recently published study conducted by Microsoft reported that two-thirds of human resource managers browse publicly available social media sites of job candidates, and 75% of companies have policies requiring online research about job candidates (Carter 2016). However, employers may not perform searches for otherwise protected information—such as the genetic information protected by GINA—or use the information they get from searches to discriminate, such as information about race or disability.

Employers may also wish to gain access to private areas of employees' or prospective employees' social media sites. Gaining unauthorized access to these sites may violate federal statutes such as the Stored Communications Act (SCA, described in the Online Appendix) or the anti-hacking Computer Fraud and Abuse Act. These statutes don't prevent prospective employers from just requesting the passwords as a condition of employment, however, because then the access is authorized (Carter 2016). In 2012, six states (California, Delaware, Illinois, Maryland, Michigan, and New Jersey) passed statutes prohibiting employers from requesting or requiring their employees to disclose usernames or passwords for private social media accounts, and a few more states have since enacted similar statutes (NCSL 2016).

Sometimes employees post comments about their jobs on social media sites. Employers have used these posts to discipline or fire employees. Courts arc agreed that even when the comments were posted in areas where the employee had set privacy controls, it is not a privacy violation for the employer to use them for discipline as long as the employer gets the information in a way that is otherwise legal. In two related cases in Texas, for example, employees of an air ambulance company were concerned about their safety in dealing with patients who needed restraints. One employee posted on the wall of a Facebook friend that she had a patient needing restraints and she had wanted to slap the patient (*Roberts v. CareFlite*, 2012 WL 4662962 (Tex. App. 2012)). In later exchanges, her flight partner posted that the company's responses were like a kick in the head (*Sumien v. CareFlite*, 2012 WL 2579525 (Tex. App. 2012)). Both were fired by the company, which took the view that the posts could become public and damage the public's trust in their services. The posts had come to the attention of the company because another employee who was a Facebook friend disagreed with them and passed them on. The Texas court said that the employer's access to the posts was not a violation of the employees' privacy and dismissed their suit. In another case, in Kentucky, a police officer was disciplined for posting on his Facebook page that he'd had a tough night breaking the news of a fatal accident to the victim's family. Even though the post didn't contain any information about the identity of the victim's family, it was against department policy. The police officer claimed that access to his Facebook page was a violation of his privacy, but the court judged that there is no expectation of privacy in Facebook. Even when postings are in an area protected by settings that allow access only to "friends," posting takes the risk that the material will be passed on. According to this and other courts, the Internet is public space, even the privately set spaces within it: "By analogy [to a walk on a public highway], Pearce's Facebook posting was a walk on the Internet, the information super-highway" (*Pearce v. Whitenack*, 440 S.W.3d 392, 401 (Ky. App. 2014)).

Can employers search employees' laptops, email, cell phones, or desk drawers?

Employers may have some legitimate interests in their employees' laptops, email, cell phones, or desk drawers. These interests include monitoring what the employee is doing on work time or with the use of employer resources. They also include assuring that employees are not bringing prohibited materials into the workplace, such as drugs or firearms, or accessing materials such as pornography sites from workplace devices. Employers also may need to monitor the content of employee communications to ensure quality and protect against damaging contents. Even physical searches may be necessary to assure that employees are not stealing company property. To a significant extent, private sector employers can search their employees' laptops, email, cell phones, desk drawers, or even physical persons.

The federal SCA (for details, see Online Appendix) is one limit on employers' access to the contents of their employees' communications. Under the SCA, your employer can't gain access to the contents of your emails or other communications from the provider of your electronic communication services without your consent or the consent of the recipients of the emails (18 U.S.C. § 2701)(a)). This provision includes stored communications on the employer's server, if the employer is a provider of electronic communication services to you. But "stored communications" has a narrow meaning—it's only email before it's been opened, or backup copies of email in transit, not emails that the employer stores long term, so unless your employer is another kind of provider—a remote storage provider, like a provider of cloud storage—the SCA no longer applies to protect you from your employer's access to the content of your emails. Even if your employer gave you remote storage capacity, the employer could access the contents of your communications if the employer is the subscriber to the remote storage. So if your employer subscribes to a cloud storage provider, the employer can gain access to the contents of files you store on it. This provision also does not mean that your employer can't access your cell phones or pagers or other similar devices themselves directly as a way to get what's on them. It only means that your employer can't go to the facilities providing the communication services or remote storage as a way to get the content they have stored (*Garcia v. City of Laredo*, 702 F.2d 788 (5th Cir. 2012)). Some employers have policies that state that employees must authorize them to access company email accounts or company cell phone accounts; these policies are not illegal under the SCA, although they may be limited by state laws. If employers intentionally violate the SCA, employees may obtain remedies, including court orders that the violation should be stopped and recovery of actual damages, profits made by the violation, or punitive damages.

Some state statutes place additional limits on what employers can do. The California Privacy Act, for example, would prohibit employers from installing spyware on their employees' computers so that they can monitor what is up on the screen (*Ribas v. Clark*, 696 P.2d 637 (Cal. 1985); Cal. Penal Code §§ 630-637.22); The New Jersey Wiretapping & Electronic Surveillance Control Act (N.J.S.A. §§ 2A:156A-1 to -37)). Georgia has a statute criminalizing computer invasion of privacy and of computer password disclosure (Ga. Code Ann. § 16-9-93(c)(e)). Many other states have a variety of similar statutes. One of the consequences of federalism is that to know how you're protected, you'll need to know about your state's laws.

State tort law may also restrict the searches that employers may conduct of their employees. The privacy tort of intrusion on seclusion states a cause of action for damages for intrusions that violate expectations of privacy in a manner that would be highly offensive to a reasonable person. (If you are interested, there's more about the privacy torts in the Online Appendix.) Court cases in which employees raise these claims against their employers tend to be very fact-specific and balance the privacy expectations of the employee against the legitimate interests of the employer. Factors counting in favor of the employee may be use of a private email account, unclear company policies, and communications that are otherwise protected, such as communications between the employee and his or her attorney (e.g., *Stengart v. Loving Care Agency, Inc.* 990 A.2d 650 (N.J. 2010)). Counting in the balance for the employer might be use of employer-provided services, need for the employer to monitor the employee's performance or protect its business interests, or the clarity of the employer's policy (*Sitton v. Print Direction, Inc.*, 718 S.E.2d 532 (Ga. App. 2011)). Employees who link their employer-provided email accounts to other social media accounts might therefore find themselves unprotected if the employer seeks to access these other accounts.

Governments, even when they are acting in their role as employers, cannot engage in state action that violates constitutional rights. They thus are limited in what they can do by the Fourth Amendment prohibition on unreasonable searches and seizures, a provision that does not apply to employers in the private sector. Under search and seizure doctrine, the initial question of whether there is a search is whether there is a reasonable expectation of privacy on the part of the employee (see Online Appendix). According to the Supreme Court, the answer to this question in any particular case will be fact-specific. There would not be an expectation in items left out in the open, such as papers on top of a desk. Nor would there be an expectation in furniture or equipment under the employer's control, such as desk drawers. Government policies could make it clear that there is no expectation in laptops or government-issued cell phones or pagers. On the other hand, employees would have an expectation of privacy in personal possessions at work, just as they would outside: purses, briefcases, closed suitcases, and the like. They would have expectations of privacy in their individual email accounts, but not in accounts provided by the government. When there is a reasonable expectation of privacy, the Supreme Court has said, the government does not need a search warrant or a showing of probable cause—that would make it impossible for government workplaces to function efficiently. The standard, instead, is "reasonableness under all the circumstances"; both the intrusion and its scope must be reasonable (*O'Connor v. Ortega*, 480 U.S. 709, 726 (1987)). The intrusion will be reasonable if there are grounds for suspecting that a search will yield evidence that will show the employee has engaged in workplace misconduct, or if the search is necessary for a work-related purpose, such as determining the relevant monthly data allowance for text messaging (*Quon v. City of Ontario*, 560 U.S. 746 (2010)).

Can employers require drug tests?

Employers have justifiable reasons for wanting to make sure that their employees are not impaired on the job. So it seems reasonable to say that they should be able to test employees for drugs or alcohol if there seem to be performance problems. There are also some jobs for which it's too risky even to take the chance that an employee might show up impaired: transportation jobs, for example. For these jobs, it seems reasonable to permit employers to conduct randomized tests of employees in these positions to make sure that they do not pose a risk. But the connection to the employer's legitimate employment-related interests is much less clear when drug tests detect prior use that does not affect on-the-job performance for employees who are not in these risky positions. Examples might be a sales clerk with a Monday to Friday job who smokes recreational marijuana on Friday night after work in a jurisdiction where it is legal, or a university faculty member who teaches during the week and drinks alcohol over the weekend or even on weeknights if consumption amounts do not affect performance the next day. But this isn't quite how the law works in the United States today.

In general, employers in the private sector can require drug tests as long as they do not violate the federal ADA, HIPAA, or provisions of state law. Under the ADA, past use of illegal drugs and present alcoholism are disabilities; present use of illegal drugs is not a disability and hence is not protected by the ADA. Under the ADA, employers may not ask questions or perform tests that are likely to elicit information that the employee has a disability. Tests for actual use of illegal substances (not including alcohol) would elicit information about current drug use, and hence are not protected. Drug tests may also be part of the medical exam employers may require after offers have been made, as long as they are required of everyone and are job related. Employers may have reasonable testing policies if they are job related, such as random testing or testing based on legitimate concerns about performance. But employers may not target employees for testing based on their guesses about likely disabilities such as alcoholism or past drug use; this would be treating employees differently based on regarding them as persons with disabilities.

Some states set statutory standards for employee drug testing; for example, the test for requiring urinalysis under Connecticut law is "reasonable suspicion that the employee is under the influence of drugs or alcohol which adversely affects or could adversely affect such employee's job performance" (Conn. Gen. Stat § 31–51x(a)).

In requiring drug tests, government employers are bound by the constitutional strictures governing searches and seizures. Special needs such as safety may permit suspicionless drug testing; transportation workers are a good example of these interests. The federal Substance Abuse and Mental Health Services Administration (SAMHSA) has mandated guidelines for drug and alcohol testing of federal employees that are aimed to ensure the accuracy of the tests. Other employers are not required to follow the SAMHSA guidelines, although many do (Department of Labor 2016).

*Can employers take adverse action against employees for
what they do in their private lives, outside of work?*

What employees do in their private lives, outside of work,
would seem to be their own business. Employers of course
have an interest in their employees coming to work unim-
paired, ready to work, and in good condition. Some employees need to be on call for their jobs—like health-care workers
who may be called in if patients need them—and so these employees may need to avoid alcohol or other substances even
while they are at home when they are on call. Some employers
may want to assure that their employees are of a particular
religious faith; this is permitted for religious employers, as defined in Title VII of the Civil Rights Act. Employers may also
want to encourage their employees to be healthy to avoid costs
of absenteeism or disability insurance (not to mention costs of
health care itself); this is permitted as long as employers meet
the conditions of the Affordable Care Act and the Americans
with Disabilities Act. Employers also may not want their employees to engage in activities that undercut the employer
economically—such as moonlighting for a competitor.

These aspects of off-work life are at least relevant to reasonable interests of employers. But even these are controversial at the edges, and employers impose other restrictions that
are far more questionable. Should an employer be able to hire
only non-smokers, for example? On the one hand, smokers
might have higher rates of absenteeism due to increased sus-
ceptibility to respiratory infections; on the other hand, hiring
only non-smokers might seem to be an unreasonable imposition of the employer's values on employees. Things get even
stickier when employers assert interests in their reputations,
so they may not want publicity about their employees carousing, being arrested for drunk driving, or indulging in a variety
of sexual practices—even when these will not interfere with
work performance. If the employees' carousing takes place
partially on the employer's dime—say, while the employees

are at a convention paid for by the employer—this may seem different, even when the carousing takes place after all the convention activities have ceased for the day and the employees pay for it themselves. Here, there's a direct connection to the employer; the employees might be regarded as representing the employer at the convention, even during off hours. Employers may also want to try to define very broadly activities that might undercut the employer's interests—such as an automobile worker driving a competitor's car, or an employee of a coal company publicly supporting environmental controls on emissions from coal-fired power plants. But if the employer is just imposing its moral values or political views on the employee, this seems to many to be unfairly overstepping the employer's pursuit of legitimate interests. It seems especially so if the employer is trying to muzzle the employee's freedom of speech or association. Others might respond, however, that employers should be free to hire and fire as they will, as long as they don't violate anti-discrimination laws.

No US federal laws offer general protections for employees in the private sector (nongovernmental employees) for what they do away from work. This includes protection against employers who retaliate against employees for their political views. Specific federal statutes may be applicable to such actions, and of course many people would condemn such actions ethically. Nonetheless, despite what most Americans believe, their rights against their employers, even about what they do when they are off-duty, are very limited in some states. As Justice Holmes once wrote, "There may be a constitutional right to talk politics, but there is no constitutional right to be a policeman" (*McAuliffe v. Mayor of New Bedford*, 155 Mass. 216 (1892)).

Nonetheless, employers cannot violate federal anti-discrimination laws in how they treat their employees for behavior on or off the job. Under federal law, employers with 15 or more employees cannot discriminate on the basis of race, national origin, color, sex, religion, or disability. Employers with under 15 employees are not covered by these anti-discrimination requirements. Also under federal law, employers with under 20 employees cannot discriminate against workers over 40 based on age. Workers who are fired for activities in their private lives, such as expressions of views about race or sex, might be able to claim that their dismissal was discriminatory, but they would need to argue that the employer's adverse action was related to their membership in the protected category. Sexual orientation is not a category protected from employment discrimination under federal law; however, 22 states and some localities protect workers from being fired on the basis of their sexual orientation or related behavior. These 22 states are located in the West (California, Colorado, Hawaii, Nevada, New Mexico, Oregon, Utah, and Washington), upper Midwest (Illinois, Iowa, Minnesota, and Wisconsin), and Northeast (Connecticut, Delaware, Maine, Maryland, Massachusetts, New Hampshire, New Jersey, New York, Rhode Island, and Vermont). Elsewhere, despite federal constitutional protections for same-sex marriage, private employers are free to refuse to hire based on their judgments about sexual orientation.

Also, under the National Labor Relations Act, employees are protected if they engage in concerted activities to improve their working conditions (*Eastex v. National Labor Relations Board*, 437 U.S. 556 (1978)). Employees may not be disciplined if they vote for or join a union—or if they refuse to do so. They also may not be disciplined for more activities about workplace conditions, such as safety, that are not directly related to union activities. Many collective bargaining agreements also contain provisions protecting workers from adverse action-based activities that were not job related (Cox 2015), although union membership has declined significantly in the private sector in recent years.

Federal election laws also prohibit employers from taking adverse action against employees for their participation in federal elections. Employers are also not permitted to require employees to contribute to their political action committees

(PACs) or to political parties. Federal election laws do not apply to employer pressure with respect to political ideas, social policies, or state or local issues or elections, however. Just over half the states do have laws protecting employees from adverse action from their employers because of legal off-work activities. For example, in Colorado employers are liable for damages if they fire employees for engaging in any legal activity off-work, unless the employer's restriction is related to a bona fide occupational requirement or to the employment activities and responsibilities of the employee, or necessary to guard against the appearance of a conflict of interest (Colo. Rev. Stat. § 24-34-402.5). Some states also have laws protecting workers' political activities outside of work in a variety of different ways. For example, in California, employers may not have policies forbidding or controlling employees' engagement in political activities (Cal. Labor Code § 1101). In states without these laws, private sector employers are free to take action against what their employers do either on the job or on their own time, as long as they do not violate the statutes already mentioned.

Government employers are a different matter, however. Governments may not take action in violation of constitutional rights, such as the First Amendment right to freedom of expression, assembly, or religion. This includes actions by the government as employer. In a decision in 1968, the US Supreme Court adopted a balancing test for when government employers violate their employees' free speech rights (*Pickering v. Board of Education*, 391 U.S. 563 (1968)). The case involved a schoolteacher who was fired because he wrote a letter to the editor of a local newspaper criticizing how the School Board had handled bond elections. The School Board contended that the teacher's actions were detrimental to the best interests of the schools. The balancing test adopted by the Court weighed the teacher's interest in speaking out on a matter of public concern and the public's interest in open debate against the government employer's interest in a harmonious workplace and performance of government functions; the Court concluded that the teacher's rights to freedom of speech had been violated. On the other hand, courts have ruled in favor of the government in cases involving a police officer anonymously publishing anti-black and anti-Semitic blog posts (*Pappas v. Giuliani*, 290 F.3d 145 (2d Cir. 2002)) and a lawyer in the state attorney general's office publishing inflammatory blog posts targeting the president of a state university as pursuing a "homosexual agenda." And government employees have much less protection for speech that does not involve matters of public concern, especially when it creates dissension within the workplace (*Connick v. Myers*, 461 U.S. 138 (1983)).

6

LAW ENFORCEMENT INFORMATION

POLICE, VICTIMS, AND SUSPECTS

Introduction

Law enforcement activities involve enforcers, people who are being victimized or protected, and people who are suspected of activities against the law. Because all members of a society have a strong interest in public safety and justice, there is arguably a presumption in favor of openness for law enforcement activities. For example, after a spate of police shootings of unarmed black men, there has been a push toward equipping police officers with body cameras, to ensure that police officers are held accountable for their actions and that there is complete transparency surrounding police actions and whether or not they are warranted. Whether law enforcement activities should ever be private is the subject of this chapter, beginning with police officers and privacy limits on what they may do and what may be done to them.

Are there limits to what police can do when investigating crimes? Can police search your trash or discarded paper cups?

You have a constitutional protection in the United States against unreasonable searches and seizures—but what this means is complex at best (see Online Appendix). Here, we elaborate three points about when you are protected from searches: (1) if you consent, a search is reasonable and does not require a warrant; (2) in deciding whether Fourth Amendment protections apply, courts first examine whether you actually had an expectation of privacy; and (3) courts then determine whether your expectation was objectively reasonable.

At first glance, it seems to make sense that search warrants aren't required if people consent. If people are willing to agree to an intrusion, it seems that protection may not be very important to them and they may not expect privacy (e.g., *Schneckloth v. Bustamonte*, 412 U.S. 218 (1973)). But beyond this simple point, the issues get very complicated, such as who may consent, what constitutes consent, and whether there are circumstances in which consent is coerced and thus invalid.

Suppose that in response to a loud knock, someone within an apartment opens the front door, leads the policemen standing on the threshold inside, and invites them to look around. If the person opening the door is the tenant of the apartment, she has consented to the entry; she has authority over the premises. But if the person opening the door is the landlord, a subletting roommate, or an overnight guest, there may not be consent. The US Supreme Court has suppressed evidence resulting from a warrantless search when the landlord gave consent while the tenant was away from a locked house (*Chapman v. U.S.*, 365 U.S. 610 (1961)). Without an express provision in the lease, the Court said, the landlord didn't have the right to break into the property; the police didn't have the authority to decide on their own that a search was justified, but instead should have gone to a magistrate for a warrant. This case was decided in 1961—over 50 years ago—and quoted ringing language from a case decided in 1948:

> The point of the Fourth Amendment, which often is not grasped by zealous officers, is not that it denies law enforcement the support of the usual inferences which reasonable men draw from evidence. Its protection consists in requiring that those inferences be drawn by a neutral

and detached magistrate instead of being judged by the officer engaged in the often competitive enterprise of ferreting out crime. Any assumption that evidence sufficient to support a magistrate's disinterested determination to issue a search warrant will justify the officers in making a search without a warrant would reduce the Amendment to a nullity and leave the people's homes secure only in the discretion of police officers. * * * The right of officers to thrust themselves into a home is also a grave concern, not only to the individual but to a society which chooses to dwell in reasonable security and freedom from surveillance. When the right of privacy must reasonably yield to the right of search is, as a rule, to be decided by a judicial officer, not by a policeman or Government enforcement agent. (365 U.S. at 614–615, quoting *Johnson v. U.S.*, 333 U.S. 10, 13–15 (1948))

Subsequent cases have determined that for jointly occupied premises, the consent of one who possesses common authority over premises or effects is sufficient (*U.S. v. Matlock*, 415 U.S. 164 (1974)). If both are physically present and one objects, however, a warrant is necessary (*Georgia v. Randolph*, 547 U.S. 103 (2006)). Roommates may consent to searches of their part of the apartment, including common rooms, but not to the search of the other's bedroom. Even overnight houseguests have a legitimate expectation of privacy in the bedrooms they are temporarily occupying; staying overnight is a valuable social custom under which people seek shelter and privacy (*Minnesota v. Olson*, 495 U.S. 91 (1990)). Drop-in social guests are another matter in the view of some courts; just being on the premises in an area where there has been no attempt to exclude others doesn't create a legitimate expectation of privacy (e.g., *U.S. v. Rose*, 613 Fed. Appx. 125 (3d Cir. 2015)). If the apartment is occupied by a guest and the tenant is away, a warrantless search is permissible if the police reasonably believe that the person letting them in has authority over the premises.

Consent to a warrantless search must also be voluntary. This means that the police may not threaten or browbeat people into letting them conduct a search. It does not require that people actually be told that they are free not to allow the search to take place, however. In deciding whether consent is voluntary, courts will weigh all the circumstances; this is a question of fact, and no bright-line rules have been adopted (*Ohio v. Robinette*, 519 U.S 33 (1996)). There are also some circumstances in which consent is presumed; for example, acceptance of a driver's license is presumed consent to a blood alcohol test or mandatory suspension of the license.

Or, suppose that in response to a loud knock, the owner of a house comes to the door and invites policemen in. On the mantel in plain view are elephant tusks, illegal contraband. Because the tusks were in plain view, and the police—invited in—were where they had a right to be, the owner does not have an actual expectation of privacy in the tusks (*Washington v. Chrisman*, 455 U.S. 1 (1982)). It would be a different matter if the tusks were in a locked closet or hidden away in a bedroom. People have actual expectations of privacy in closed spaces: purses, locked suitcases, and rooms closed off from immediate view. On the other hand, people do not have actual expectations of privacy in trash. They have thrown it away, demonstrating that they did not care about it. The same holds true for discarded paper cups (*California v. Greenwood*, 486 U.S. 35 (1988)). There's an aspect of circularity here: expectations of privacy generate constitutional privacy rights, and constitutional privacy rights in turn generate expectations of privacy.

In most cases, these expectations are objectively reasonable. If people take the time and effort to place their belongings within containers, they have an objectively reasonable expectation of privacy about the contents. In the judgment of the Court, it is irrelevant whether the container is a brown paper bag or a brand name leather briefcase: to hold otherwise would be to privilege those who can afford fancy containers over those who cannot in determining the reasonableness of expectations of privacy (*U.S. v. Ross*, 456 U.S. 798 (1982)). It is also irrelevant whether the outward appearance of the container suggests that there is contraband within.

However, if a search of an area is legitimate, so is the search of objects within the area. Police who have a warrant to search a house are permitted to search the luggage within, even if they are locked or in closets. Because there is a long-standing exception to the requirement of a warrant for vehicles—they might move away in the time needed to get a warrant—police may search cars without a warrant if they have the probable cause that would justify them in obtaining a warrant. This means that they may search the entire car, including the trunk and anything within it, as long as they have the probable cause required for a warrant (*U.S. v. Ross*, 456 U.S. 798 (1982)).

Contemporary technologies may allow police to gather evidence without actually entering into premises. Thermal imaging, for example, may detect unusual areas of warmth within a home. In *Kyllo v. U.S.* (533 U.S. 27 (2001)), drug enforcement agents suspected that a homeowner was growing marijuana using high-intensity lamps. The agents used a thermal scanner to detect areas of heat within the home as evidence of probable cause to get a warrant to search the home. The question for the Court was whether by using the thermal imaging the agents had already engaged in a warrantless search. Historically, eyeballing premises was not a search; trespass in the sense of unlawful entry was required (e.g., *Boyd v. U.S.*, 116 U.S. 616 (1886)). Actual physical trespass continues to be sufficient for the Court to find a search today; in *U.S. v. Jones* (132 S.Ct. 945 (2012)), the Court concluded that placing a GPS on a car required a warrant because of the trespass on the car without consent. In addition to the physical invasion, to determine whether there is a "search" today, the Court will also ask whether there is a subjective expectation of privacy that is objectively reasonable. Surveillance of a backyard from an airplane in publicly navigable airspace is objectively reasonable, so police could hover 1,000 feet above a home and photograph marijuana growing in the yard with an ordinary 35-mm camera—even though the owner had manifested his subjective expectation of privacy by building a high fence to obscure the view (*California v. Ciraolo*, 476 U.S. 207 (1986)). In *Kyllo*, the Court said that the thermal imaging technology was a search because to allow sense-enhancing technology to gather information that otherwise could only have been obtained by intruding into the home violated reasonable expectations of the security of the home—"at least where . . . the technology in question is not in general public use" (533 U.S. 27 at 34). What this analysis means for applying search and seizure law to newer technologies such as smartphones equipped with thermal cameras (http://www.catphones.com/en-us/news/press-releases/cat-s60-announced-as-worlds-first-smartphone-with-integrated-thermal-camera) or drones is an unanswered question (Talal 2014; McKnight 2015).

Some states have enacted laws prohibiting what their law enforcement officers may do with these newer technologies. For example, Vermont passed a law in 2016 prohibiting law enforcement use of drones to investigate crimes without a warrant or a judicially recognized exception to a warrant—and then only under stringent limits such as avoiding data collection on anyone other than the target of the drone surveillance (20 V.S.A. § 6421).

Does it violate the privacy of police officers to record them?
The privacy of others who appear in the recording?
Does it matter whether it is the police or members of the public doing the recording?

Video or audio recording is now cheap, simple, and ubiquitous. It can be accomplished with cell phones or other smart devices. Many people now own drones that can be operated remotely and are equipped with cameras. With a flick of a switch, these records can be posted online, and many have gone viral with viewings on sites such as YouTube. In their defense, police departments have also required their officers to be equipped with body cameras and to keep them switched on during their activities.

The Black Lives Matter movement was stimulated by widely circulated video recordings of police killings of people of color (Atkins 2016). The recordings, made by private individuals, revealed what many judged to be unjustified abuse, beatings, shootings, and outright murder. These revelations may be especially important in that police exercise the state's authority for the use of force. Recording may be critical to free expression of ideas and debate in a democracy, powerfully documenting what could formerly only be portrayed by muckraking writers using pen and paper (Marceau and Chen 2016). Recordings may also vindicate police, demonstrating heroism or situations of justified suspicions, threats, and risks to their safety or the safety of others. Surely the public has an interest in knowing whether those charged with law enforcement are performing their duties dispassionately, competently, and fairly. In the words of Justice Rehnquist, "To speak of an arrest as a private occurrence seems to me to stretch even the broadest definitions of the idea of privacy beyond the breaking point" (quoted in Potere 2012, p. 286). Very strong considerations thus weigh on the side of permitting police to be filmed as they perform their jobs.

Many of the arguments deployed against filming police are not arguments directed at the privacy of police. Some argue that video recordings will impede effective law enforcement, getting in the way of officers or distracting them. Or, it may lead officers to be overly cautious and thus put them at risk. Others argue that the idea that recordings depict what actually happened is an illusion: recordings may only capture part of the picture, may be taken out of context, or may be cut or doctored in some way. Recordings may thus foster a climate of mistrust that is not warranted. There are privacy concerns as well, however, both for officers and for others who may be captured in the recording. Officers may argue that recordings can too easily be taken out of context and wrongfully put them in a bad light or compromise their reputations. If recordings are posted online, officers may be identified, located, and subjected to threatened or actual harm; threats to the families of police officers, too, are not uncommon. Bystanders may be recorded, and their identities, locations, conditions, and reactions revealed—even when they had nothing to do with the unfolding law enforcement activity. Privacy concerns of bystanders may be particularly acute when the recording occurs in places such as hospitals or homes.

Some of the concerns about recording may be lessened if police themselves do the recording. Many police departments have instituted recording as a way to monitor the performance of officers, and the Obama administration provided $75 million to departments to support body camera recording (Atkins 2016). Police can be subject to openly discussed public policies about when and how recording should take place. With body cameras appropriately positioned, recording may take place in a manner that does not impede police performance. Police may no longer fear that the recordings will be doctored or published without oversight. Cameras may also aid in prosecuting crimes, if they produce accurate recordings of what actually happened. Policies may preserve the confidentiality of bystanders by requiring cameras to be turned off in some locations such as where patients are being treated or by protecting their contents when they are not. On the other side, keeping recording solely in police control may raise additional problems of public mistrust, especially if videos are not released in timely fashion or are redacted. And if recordings are kept indefinitely, without protection, the privacy of individuals and groups (such as people in a neighborhood) is a significant concern.

Many laws restrict recording of judicial proceedings and law enforcement by individuals. The US Supreme Court and many state courts do not permit court proceedings to be filmed; representations of proceedings only take the form of transcripts and sketches. Outside of courtrooms, the most basic prohibition is the federal prohibition on wiretapping. (Readers who want further information about this federal law may wish to consult the Online Appendix.) Some states have stronger anti-wiretapping laws that forbid recording without the consent of all parties, even when the recording is of the police. Other states, such as Maryland, have statutory exceptions for recording police conduct in public (Potere 2012). Anti-wiretapping statutes have been used by police to justify confiscating devices being used to record, as well as to arrest and prosecute people for recording. Significant constitutional challenges have been raised to these prosecutions, but courts remain divided on their success. One court has found that an Illinois statute forbidding oral recording of police in public without the consent of all parties likely violates the First Amendment (*ACLU v. Alvarez*, 679 F.2d 583 (7th Cir. 2012)). Two decisions have reached different results on whether the right to record is clearly established so that state actors can be sued in tort for violating it (*Glik v. Cunniffe*, 655 F.3d 78 (1st Cir. 2011) (yes); *Kelly v. Borough of Carlisle*, 622 F.3d 262 (3d Cir. 2010) (no)). The primary constitutional arguments used in these cases are either that the recording itself is protected speech, or that it is a low-cost way for citizens to gather and transmit information and thus is protected as freedom of the press.

When recordings are done by police-worn body cameras, however, there may be no privacy protections at all. Jurisdictions vary on how and whether they store and protect the footage. Some store indefinitely, others for lesser periods of time. Some allow the footage to be disclosed in response to Freedom of Information Act (FOIA) requests, but many do not. (See the Online Appendix for more about FOIA.) At present, police are recording massive amounts of data that may reflect individuals in intimate moments of tragedy: weeping or railing at the injury or death of a loved one, seeing a child beaten by a spouse, or exploding in fury at how they are being treated. The irony is that the more privacy is protected by limited storage or disclosure, the less likely it is that police-worn body camera footage will be available to mitigate public distrust of police behavior. Police departments are experimenting with a variety of solutions; clearly this issue will continue to raise difficult questions of balancing privacy with transparency in a free society (Atkins 2016).

Should people be able to make reports of suspected crimes anonymously?

People in the United States do not have a general duty to report actual or suspected criminal activity. (You may yourself be criminally liable if you aid or abet the crime, help to conceal it, tamper with witnesses, or otherwise act as an accomplice to a crime.) A federal statute does require people not to conceal and to report actual knowledge of federal felonies (18 U.S.C. § 4)— but is now interpreted to require both knowledge and conceal- ment (Curenton 2003; Yung 2012). Some state laws also require reporting of crimes, particularly where there may be ongoing victimization of the vulnerable. People in designated positions such as physicians or psychologists—or in some states, anyone with knowledge—may have duties to report suspected child abuse or abuse of an adult with a disability.

There are strong reasons to encourage reports of crimes, particularly when reporting may protect people who cannot protect themselves from ongoing harm. Yet people may be re- luctant to make reports if they fear their identity as a reporter may be revealed. They may face very real risks of retaliation, particularly within families or small social groups. In such cases, protecting the identity of the reporter may be needed for his or her physical security. People in relationships of trust also may be reluctant to make reports out of the concern that these relationships will be disrupted by the knowledge of their involvement. These concerns may only justify assuring the confidentiality of the report, not masking of the identity of the reporter from child or adult protective services or other agencies to which the reports are made. Still, reporters may be reluctant to reveal their identities to anyone, lest they be revealed inadvertently.

Anonymity of reporters, however, raises problems of its own. It may make it difficult to assure the accuracy of reports or investigate them. In acrimonious situations—bitter divorces or custody fights, for example—misleading or false reports may be filed out of spite or in the effort to gain an advantage. Under many state laws, knowingly filing false reports of abuse is criminal; these laws may also give law enforcement the discretion to inform alleged perpetrators about false reports.

Should there be limits to what private individuals may do to investigate?

The constitutional limits on what public officers may do in surveillance do not apply to private individuals. As far as the Constitution is concerned, people may spy on one another with impunity. There is some justification for this difference: public officers act with the blessing and the power of the state. Private investigations may be justified by freedom of speech and the press. Nonetheless, from nosy neighbors to privately contracted security services, private sector surveillance may feel—and may be—as intrusive as surveillance by state actors.

For the most part, private surveillance is regulated by the states. One exception is the federal statute prohibiting wiretapping (see Online Appendix). Beyond the variety of state laws about wiretapping, a number of states have passed statutes limiting the use of private surveillance technologies. Drones have been a popular target of these statutes. States limit using them in tracking game for hunting, filming forest fires, photographing schools or prisons, or committing voyeurism. California now has a tort of constructive invasion of privacy for using a device to capture images or recordings that would invade privacy if they could not otherwise be achieved without trespassing (Cal. Civil Code § 1708.8(b)). (In other words, in California what you can't do unless you sneak into someone's house you can't do by flying a drone instead.) Florida's "Freedom from Unwarranted Surveillance Act" prohibits the use of drones to capture images that violate reasonable expectations of privacy without written consent (Fla. Stat. § 934.50(e)). There is a great deal of legislative activity at the state level in this area, as people have become more concerned about what can be done with drones.

The federal government has also played a role in regulating drones. Under its authority to protect aviation, the Federal Aviation Administration has issued a rule requiring registration of larger drones (over .55 pound) and regulating their flight patterns. The rule includes a restriction on flying drones over unprotected people on the ground who are not participating in their use.

Not all of the laws about private sector surveillance have been designed to stop invasions into personal space. Commercial interests have also used state laws to gain protection from investigative activities. Many agricultural states, for example, have what are called "ag gag" laws that prohibit people from recording agricultural activities even when they are on the premises legally. These statutes have been used to prohibit publicity about the treatment of non-human animals on factory farms; significant questions have been raised about whether they violate freedom of speech (Bambauer and Bambauer 2017), and at least one court has agreed (*Animal Legal Defense Fund v. Otter*, 118 F.Supp.3d 1195 (D. Idaho 2015)).

Should there be actions that are legal "in the privacy of the home" but illegal in public?

Behind the protection of persons and their spaces from searches and seizures lies the idea that people ought to be able to do things "in private" that they may not do "in public." Activities done outside are not self-regarding in the way that activities behind closed doors may be. Public activities may be seen by or impinge on others—unless they take steps to overlook them. Thus many activities may be restricted or even criminalized when they occur in public, even though they are entirely permissible at home: having sex, urinating, watching pornography (for adults), or smoking marijuana (in states where recreational use of marijuana is legal). US constitutional law has recognized this distinction for many years (e.g., *Stanley v. Georgia*, 394 U.S. 557 (1969) (obscenity)). This distinction between the public sphere and the private sphere is not straightforward, however. Some things done within the home may be so harmful or difficult to contain that they should be regulated or prohibited: elder abuse is an obvious example, as is making pornography with children. And the mere fact that something done in public is offensive to others is not enough to subject it to legitimate regulation; interracial marriage and, more recently, same-sex marriage are illustrations. Whether the conduct occurs in public or in private, the question is whether it is properly subject to public constraint. That conduct is exposed to the public may mean that it has impacts on others that are different or broader in scope than when the same conduct occurs behind closed doors, but the considerations that justify regulation are the same in either case.

Should the identities of crime victims or descriptions of crimes be made public?

The public has an interest in knowing the demographics of crimes: where crimes occur, what crimes are most frequent, and what kinds of people are most likely victims. Both social justice and public safety are served by this information. It can tell us whether some kinds of people are more likely to be victimized and whether, in response, patterns of policing should change. It might suggest the need for victim restitution policies. The information can also suggest where communities are less safe for some community members or for everyone—and thus help people decide what risks they are willing to take and impel communities to take action. These concerns have led to the requirement that colleges and universities that receive federally funded student aid publish their crime statistics, although these reports often cover only the campus itself and not adjacent neighborhoods. But these considerations by themselves are insufficient to require publishing the actual names or contact information of individual victims.

Several other justifications support actually naming alleged victims, however. One is the public's interest in being able to discuss and assess the accuracy of the report. The public has an interest in being assured that the criminal justice system is fair; if those who report being victims of crimes remain anonymous, there will be no way for the public to determine whether individuals are making frivolous or spiteful accusations. Relatedly, those accused of crime should have the right to confront and examine the credibility of their accusers. This right is made explicit in the Confrontation Clause of the Sixth Amendment: "In all criminal prosecutions, the accused shall enjoy the right . . . to be informed of the nature and cause of the accusation; to be confronted with the witnesses against him; . . ." Without the right to confront witnesses in the setting of a trial, people may be convicted on unexamined but apparently plausible or sympathetic accusations. They may also quite justifiably believe that they were treated unjustly by the system, because they were not allowed their full day in court.

Nonetheless, it can be very painful for victims to be named. Just having to hear or read about the experience again may be deeply troubling. Victims may be embarrassed or publicly shamed by what happened or their reactions to it. This is particularly likely when the alleged crime involved sex. Monica Lewinsky, in her recent TED talk, "The Price of Shame," (https://www.ted.com/talks/monica_lewinsky_the_price_ of_shame?language=en) recounts how terrible it was for her to hear over and over again how she was a "slut" or a "whore" for having had legal, consensual non-penetrative sexual relations with President Clinton. Victims may be shunned or even disowned, particularly in cultures where virginity is judged necessary for marriage or when people close to them do not believe their claims that they did not consent to the sex they say was forced on them. They or their families may be threatened—with new rapes, stalking, or assault—and may need to change phone numbers, addresses, or known locations such as jobs or schools. The fear of such consequences reportedly deters many from reporting sexual victimization.

Based on concerns about dignity, trauma, and safety, victims and their advocates have increasingly been calling for victim confidentiality, if not in courtrooms, at least in the press and over reports on the Internet. A more limited argument is that victims should be identified by numbers or pseudonyms when they testify in court—or that testimony and cross-examination should be performed only in front of the judge, lawyers, and court personnel, and not in open court (Campbell 2013).

Publicity about what is reported to have happened in crimes or about the identity of victims is magnified by the Internet. Forty years ago, if crime victims testified publicly in court, reports of their names and what they said would only surface elsewhere if the press was covering the crime, and then likely only in a local paper and its archives. Anyone wanting to know about the crime or the victim would need to go to the physical site of the court or the newspaper archives—or to a local public library that might have the newspaper on microfiche. Today, public court records are searchable over the Internet. So are newspaper archives. If names and other identifying information are in these records, they would be likely to turn up in Internet searches.

Many states now have laws that permit victims of domestic abuse or sexual crimes to claim anonymity in disclosures to the defendant and in court records (e.g. Mo. Stat. § 566.226). Advocates for victims, such as counselors in domestic violence shelters, also have confidentiality protections. State laws protect the identity of juvenile crime victims. These statutes may be limited to certain sexual offenses and may not apply if the victims sue convicted offenders or schools or churches that have employed them for damages. Yet in some courts the identity of alleged crime victims may still be made public in court so that those who are accused may confront witnesses against them. In the trial of Jerry Sandusky, for example, the football assistant coach at Penn State who was convicted of child molestation, some of the victims requested anonymity, but the court refused to grant them this during the trial itself (Campbell 2013). In denying the anonymity request, the judge wrote,

> courts are not customarily in the business of withholding information. Secrecy is thought to be inconsistent with the openness required to assure the public that the law is being administered fairly and applied faithfully . . . . A criminal prosecution is not brought to vindicate the rights of only a victim of crime, but to vindicate the rights of the public as a whole to live secure and peaceful lives. (http://co.centre.pa.us/centreco/media/upload/ SANDUSKY%20MEMORANDUM%20AND%20 ORDER%20REGARDING%20THE%20REQUEST%20 FOR%20PSEUDONYM.pdf)

Official court records in the Sandusky case, however, only identify the victims by number, as victims one through eight. As of this writing, an online search for the victims reveals that major news outlets follow the norm of not revealing their names, although they do describe the testimony of each in great detail. A news report on YouTube is followed by comments about the victims, Sandusky, and those alleged to have participated in trying to cover up the abuse; comments range from the ugly to the obscene and include graphic threats of retaliatory sexual assault (https://www.youtube.com/ watch?v=OGFHMbiGqjQ). When Monica Lewinsky's TED talk about how she was treated during the Clinton scandal went online, it apparently triggered similar vitriol. The curator of the comment section for TED talks observed that the comments became more civil after she moved the nastier ones to the bottom of the list (Goodman 2015).

When information about crimes is otherwise public, gathering and publishing it is protected as freedom of speech and freedom of the press under the First Amendment (*The Florida Star v. B.J.F.*, 491 U.S. 524 (1989)). In 1983, before newspapers were routinely archived and searchable on the Internet, the *Florida Star* published a report of a rape victim using her full name. The newspaper had gotten the report from the county sheriff's department, which had placed it in its pressroom where it was publicly available—despite the fact that under Florida law, victims of alleged sexual assaults should not have been made public. The newspaper story was written by a trainee reporter and was published, also in violation of the newspaper's policy of not stating the names of rape victims. Under Florida law that made it unlawful to print, publish, or broadcast in any means of mass communication the name of a sexual assault victim, the victim, listed in the case as B.J.F., sued both the newspaper and the sheriff's department, claiming that she had been damaged emotionally by the publication, that her mother had received threatening phone calls stating that she would be raped again, and that she had been forced to change her address and phone number, seek police protection, and receive mental health counseling. The US Supreme Court stated this principle in determining that the state damages remedy against the newspaper was unconstitutional: "If a newspaper lawfully obtains truthful information about a matter of public significance then state officials may not constitutionally publish publication of the information, absent a need to further a state interest of the highest order" (491 U.S. at 533). Florida could have classified the information, or extended a damages remedy against the state for making the information public— but could not provide a remedy against the newspaper for getting it out into the world once the information was public.

Suppose the story remained in the *Florida Star*'s archives today, now available in digitized form over the Internet. (Actual *Star* archives on the Internet only go back to 2009, but the point remains that earlier archives could be digitized.) Under the Supreme Court's holding, publication of such lawfully obtained information could not be sanctioned "absent a need to further a state interest of the highest order." Nor would there be any obvious US legal means to sanction search engine links to the information. The United States thus stands in sharp contrast to the European Union, where the individual could request delinking of the material from a search of her name. Indeed, in the European Union, Google reports delinking stories about rapes from searches for the victim's name. Neither the US nor the EU approach seems entirely satisfactory, however: the US approach tips the scale broadly in favor of free speech, without specification of public interests sufficiently powerful to support sanctions for publication, while the EU approach leaves it up to search engines to balance interests in privacy against interests in information access in deciding whether to delink. An alternative would be regulations devoted specifically to public records, including which types of these records should be subject to delinking or suppression, on what grounds, and through what procedures.

In short, crime victims may have very strong reasons for not wanting to relive terrible moments in their lives. But the legal protections they have may be limited, in light of constitutional concerns such as the rights of those accused of crime and the freedom of the press. By far the most effective protection in the United States today may be journalistic norms of not identifying victims—norms that are more settled for publication in print than for publication over the Internet.

Are witness protection programs that suppress identities justifiable?

The US federal witness protection program aims to both protect the safety of witnesses and to encourage testimony that can convict people of crimes when witnesses would otherwise not be available to testify. Begun in the 1970s as a way to protect people who would testify against organized crime, the program now protects people who testify against drug traffickers, gang members, and terrorist organizations (Mack 2014). The US program has also been used as a model to protect witnesses in other countries and in trials before international tribunals. Clearly, when people are likely subjects of assassination for testifying, protecting their safety is a paramount concern. One of the most effective ways to do this is to alter their identities altogether. In one way, this secrecy is the ultimate in privacy, although some in the program have reported the devastating effects of the loss of identity.

These programs, moreover, may hide more than intended. Witnesses have used them as a way to avoid paying debts or to hide their own criminal activity (Mack 1992). A 2013 Department of Justice Audit Report indicated that some suspected terrorists have been enrolled in the program and that this may have created national security issues (Mack 2014). At a minimum, if such programs exist, they should be subject to careful oversight and reporting. One way to regard them is as a form of governmental secrets: information suppression that is necessary, but justified because the need for it is explained and monitored.

Should arrest and conviction information be publicly available? Why or why not?

Criminal history records may include arrests, convictions, and convictions that have been overturned for the alleged offender to be released or retried. These records may not only affect alleged offenders themselves; they may also affect the opportunities of people who are close to them, such as parents or siblings who cannot obtain public housing. If these records persist over a lifetime, they may stretch a long pall over people's lives. On the other hand, public safety may require that the information be available so that society can be aware of and avoid dangers from people who may pose very real risks.

One problem with publicly available criminal history records is that they are often mistaken. Background checking agencies that compile these records make mistakes in linking the information to particular individuals. Information that is about John A. Doe may instead turn up in the record of John B. Doe, or in the record of a different John Doe with the same birthday, or the record of a different John Doe who once lived in the same community. Or, information may be miscopied or incomplete. Information that Jane Roe was arrested may not contain the information that the charges were immediately dropped as unsubstantiated. By the time the error is corrected, it may be too late for a job or an apartment.

Posing yet another problem with these records, there are significant differences between arrests, convictions, and convictions that have been overturned. Arrests just signify that you came sufficiently to the attention of law enforcement (or other citizens, in jurisdictions where citizens' arrests are recognized) to be taken into custody. They don't mean that you were officially charged with a crime—that's a decision made by the prosecution based on whether it's likely there's enough evidence to prove a case against you in court. A conviction means that the finder of fact has determined beyond a reasonable doubt that you were guilty of the offense charged. So convictions have been vetted by a court. Convictions can be overturned for many reasons, including procedural ones, such as the admission of evidence that was obtained in violation of the Fourth Amendment. Having a conviction overturned doesn't mean that you were actually innocent—it means that there was some flaw in the original trial that convicted you, sufficient for an appeals court to decide that the conviction could not stand. After a conviction has been overturned, the prosecution might decide to retry you for the same offense (if they can do so without violating the constitutional protection against putting you in double jeopardy for the same conduct).

Or, they might decide that there just isn't enough evidence to make it worth prosecuting you again. So arguably overturned convictions are a little like arrests—maybe smoke or mist, without fire. Or, maybe they do signify fire.

Because of the difference between arrests and convictions, the US Equal Opportunity Commission guidance states that arrest records should not be used for employment unless the underlying circumstances are directly relevant to the fitness to perform the job in question. The US Department of Housing and Urban Development states that arrest records should not be used for denying admission to federally subsidized housing— although it may trigger an inquiry into whether the resident or a household member engaged in disqualifying criminal activity (https://portal.hud.gov/hudportal/documents/huddoc? id=PIH2015-19.pdf). At a minimum, arrest records should be used only when what they reveal is directly relevant to qualifications, whether or not a conviction was eventually to be the result.

Still another problem with arrest and conviction records in the United States is that they are skewed by race. The higher arrest and conviction records among African Americans may reflect differences in policing patterns more than they reflect actual differences in crime rates. If so, they may replicate ongoing patterns of discrimination. Even to the extent that they reflect actual rates of underlying offenses, their use may have a differential impact on the ability to live or to function as a citizen. How these issues affect employment was discussed in Chapter 5; here, we concentrate on other examples of the impact of criminal records: housing, student loans, and voting.

Consider public housing. There are legitimate reasons for public housing and its residents to be protected against crime on the premises. On the other hand, stringent bans, especially if they are applied to members of the household in addition to the tenant him- or herself, can cause severe hardships. Becoming a tenant in federally subsidized housing requires a criminal background check of the tenant and any other adult members of the household: everyone the tenant currently lives with, everyone age 16 or older who might live with the tenant, and biological parents of any children in the household, even if they don't and aren't planning to live with the tenant. So the criminal record of a son can result in a prospective tenant being denied—even when the tenant herself has no criminal history whatsoever and is trying to live as far as possible from the person who does (http://www.reentry .net/ny/help/item.2912-Housing_and_Reentry). Public housing must impose lifetime bans on registered sex offenders, people convicted of manufacturing methamphetamine while in public housing, or people evicted for drug-related offenses within the preceding three years unless they have successfully completed a rehabilitation program. These are the minimums, and public housing may impose stronger restrictions (http:// homeguides.sfgate.com/criminal-history-policy-low-income-housing-8476.html).

Or consider student aid. Anyone convicted of a drug-related felony or misdemeanor that occurred while they were receiving federal student aid is ineligible to receive further aid for at least a year (https://www.whitehouse.gov/sites/default/ files/ondcp/recovery/fafsa.pdf). Some might regard the conviction as demonstrating that the offender was undeserving of the aid—even if the conviction was for possession and the student had maintained a perfect grade point average. On the other hand, the connection between drug-related offenses in particular and academic performance is less than clear; the ban may reflect moral condemnation of these offenses more than a reasonable judgment that people who have been convicted of them are unlikely to be successful students. Moreover, academic success may be the best way for people with convictions to demonstrate rehabilitation; waiting periods for student aid will delay or deny this opportunity.

Finally, consider voting. Current controversies over access to the franchise are intense. Critics argue that insistence on voter identification, lengthy intervals between registration and voting, shortened period for mail ballots, and long lines at polling places are thinly veiled efforts to discourage participation by younger and minority voters. Supporters contend that the restrictions protect the integrity of the ballot against voter fraud. In many states, convicted felons are denied the right to vote; whether this choice is a legitimate judgment that these voters do not deserve to participate in political life or another way to suppress a portion of the electorate is hotly contested. In these states, criminal records can bar political participation. Some states have purged voter rolls based on supposed criminal records; when these records are inaccurate or poorly matched, people who could legitimately vote even in these states are turned away on election day (Brennan Center for Justice 2006). In the Florida purge of voter records in 2000, any voter was purged if his or her name matched 80% of the letters in a name on a national database of convicted felons— a matching standard that was in error over 50% of the time (Brennan Center for Justice 2006). This is one illustration of the interconnections between privacy and democracy, a topic we take up more fully in Chapter 10.

What about offenses committed by juveniles? Should they be confidential?

The movement for a separate system of criminal justice for juveniles was based on the ideas that juveniles may be immature, more easily swayed by others, less responsible, and more open to change and rehabilitation. Juvenile courts were structured to avoid labeling children as criminals and subjecting them to lifelong stigma. As a result, the presumption was established in many states that the records of these courts should be confidential as to the general public, although they could be disclosed to state agencies such as law enforcement (Jacobs 2014).

One of the arguments for a right to be forgotten is that people should be able to outlive their earlier mistakes. This argument is especially strong for juveniles who may be thought to be immature, less responsible, easily swayed by others, and more open to change. If these considerations are persuasive, they suggest that some or all records of juvenile offenses should eventually no longer be available. One possible approach is a bright-line rule, such as one that makes unavailable offenses committed when the offender was under a specified age, or specified offenses, or offenses for which the offender was tried in juvenile court rather than as an adult. Another bright-line approach would be to sunset any juvenile offense after a given period of time or at the time the offender turns 21, an approach that was enacted in many states. These approaches can be administered mechanically but will not take into account any features of particular offenders, such as whether they have changed. A case-by-case approach would allow people to petition to have convictions sealed if after a period of time they have not been in further trouble with the law. It would also allow for consideration of whether the offender has been rehabilitated or is likely to pose ongoing threats to public safety.

The argument on the other side is that juvenile records do have implications for later conduct and the public safety. When the crimes are ones for which recidivism is believed likely, such as certain sexual offenses, the case for openness is strengthened. Juvenile sex offender convictions are required to be reported to sex offender registries if the crimes were sufficiently serious. The case for openness is also very strong when offenders are being tried for subsequent offenses as adults and the issue is whether prior convictions as a juvenile should be taken into account in sentencing decisions. Concerns about violent crime rates among juveniles led many states by the turn of the twentieth century to cut back significantly on sealing juvenile court records. Many police departments now maintain electronic databases of juvenile suspects, for example, gang members (Jacobs 2014).

Even when juvenile records are confidential, what this means has never been entirely clear. One option would be that the situation is supposed to be as though the offense had never occurred: the person can say "no" in response to inquiries about prior convictions, and any record of the conviction should be taken out of background reports, Internet searches for the individual's name, or any other places in which it may have been replicated—at least, to the extent possible. A far more limited option is that the court in which the offense was tried should never include the offense in records it provides—but the record continues to exist elsewhere and the offender must respond to direct questions about its existence, such as when she applies for a professional license. A Supreme Court decision in 1979 concluded that a state law prohibiting newspapers (but not mentioning electronic media) from publishing the otherwise public names of juvenile offenders was an unconstitutional limit on freedom of expression (*Smith v. Daily Mail Publishing Co.*, 443 U.S. 97 (1979)). Likely any limits on publication of already public information about juvenile offenses would not pass constitutional muster in the United States today. So even when the case for confidentiality of juvenile records is strong, privacy may be very difficult to achieve.

What about convictions that have been exonerated, pardoned, expunged, or overturned?

Exoneration means that the individual who was once convicted of an offense has been determined by a court to have been not guilty. Exoneration signifies that the original conviction was a mistake. The exoneration movement has gained steam with the availability of DNA evidence in some cases, evidence that can demonstrate that the person originally accused of the crime was not in fact the person whose DNA was found on the victim. Rape cases are examples of this, if semen are still available to be tested to see if there is a match with the person originally convicted of the offense. So it would seem that a crime that has been exonerated should no longer be linked to the person—that would be double victimization, first in the mistaken conviction and then in the continued linkage of the conviction to the person's name. At a minimum, the link should come with the explanation that the crime has been exonerated—failure to include the exoneration would convey the mistaken impression that the individual's conviction has been allowed to stand. Or, exonerations should be revealed only if the individual wants them to be so, perhaps to explain gaps in the person's history. Some remain suspicious of exonerations, however, especially in cases where DNA evidence is not available.

A pardon means that there has been an official determination that the individual's crime should be forgiven. Individuals may be pardoned because the executive believes that the behavior should never have been criminal, or because the offender has already served more than the appropriate sentence. With pardons for these reasons, the original offense and conviction stand; perhaps this is an argument for continuing to include pardoned offenses in records, but with the notification of the pardon to place the conviction in context.

Expungement means that there has been an official determination that the crime should no longer be on someone's record. Expungement of records sometimes occurs because the conviction was determined to be erroneous. Expungement is available for many offenses committed by juveniles if a certain number of years pass and they have not offended again. It also may be available for offenses that are not serious if, after a period of time, the offender has not been in further trouble with the law. If expungement is genuine erasure of the fact of the offense, the information should no longer be in the offender's record: it should be as though the offense never took place. And the offender ought to be able to reply to direct questions as though the offense never took place. In European terms, there should be the most complete right to be forgotten, to have the offense deleted. But this is frequently not what happens in the United States. Depending on the jurisdiction and the case, expungement orders may require destruction of the record, or may only require its sequestration. Evidence, moreover, suggests that "expungement" is in practice any-thing but—in one study, 42% even of exonerations remained in the individual's record and available for background checks without correction. Even when the information is removed from the original record, copies may be available elsewhere and subject to search (Shlosberg, Mandery, and West 2012; Schlosberg 2014). The result may be irremediable, lifelong damage, if a conviction that has been formally determined to be erroneous or outlived continues to disqualify the individual for employment, housing, public benefits, or even the vote. (Yu and Dietrich 2012; Paul-Emile 2014). Unlike with medi-cal records, there would appear to be no offsetting reason to retain the content of the record. There might be reason to retain the fact of expungement, such as to protect law enforcement officials against a charge of improper conduct, or to use the expungement to correct a lingering copy of the individual's record, but even this might be offset by the potential harm to the individual if notation of the fact of expungement is con-sidered prejudicial, as it might be by some. Surely there is no good reason to permit continued linking of the record to the individual in any search engine results. This is arguably one of the most persuasive examples of the need to consider the European right to be forgotten in the United States.

The United States does not have laws crafted specifically to protect expunged criminal records. The FCRA requires consent to criminal background checks for employment and notice if adverse action is taken on the basis of the report, as we discussed in Chapter 5. However, there is no affirmative duty to ensure the accuracy of the report, only a duty to make "reasonable efforts" to do so.

Should there be public registries of sex offenders? Of offenders who have committed other types of crimes, such as fraud?

Public registries of people who have been convicted of sex of-fenses have become a popular method for alerting the public about people believed to be dangerous who may live in their neighborhoods. They came into widespread use out of the belief that children could be protected from predators if people in their neighborhood were alerted to their presence. Many of these statutes were stimulated by grisly rapes and murders of identified children: Megan Kanka, Jessica Lunsford, and Adam Walsh. The federal Adam Walsh Child Protection and Safety Act requires states to participate in a national program of registering sex offenders or risk losing 10% of federal enforcement funds. Registries must meet minimum national standards and must include convictions for all sexual offenses involving sex acts or sexual contact with another and certain additional offenses against minors, such as possession of child pornography. Offenses committed by juveniles don't necessarily require registration unless they were especially serious offenses committed by older juveniles. State registries can require listing of additional crimes, and many do (SMART 2016).

There are important pros and cons about these registries. One hope was that they would reduce the overall frequency of sex offenses, but the evidence on this is mixed at best. Another hope was that they would put people on notice so that they could protect themselves or their children against known offenders. Surveys indicate that people do believe they are safer because of the registries. However, one problem with some state registries is that they are so overbroad that they do not send accurate signals about who might be a danger, so people don't consult them. Broad registries might include everything from arrests for teenage sexting to public urination—crimes that may just signify youthful indiscretion, rather than any kind of public threat. And another problem with overbreadth, of course, is that these registries really do have serious consequences for people: job loss, housing loss, harassment, assault, and lasting psychological damage (Lobanov-Rostovsky 2016).

Sex offender registries are unique in the United States, but other types of registries might be possible as well. Fraud offenses are a possibility with some of the same supposed characteristics as sex offenses: likelihood that the offender may commit the offense again, likelihood that the offender might prey on those who are vulnerable, and possibility that potential victims who are on notice might take steps to protect themselves or their loved ones from identified offenders. In 2015, Utah became the first state to establish a registry for white-collar crimes (Harvey 2015).

Law enforcement raises very difficult issues of privacy. On the one hand, public safety is undeniably important. On the other hand, arrest or conviction records can have a very long impact on the lives of alleged offenders and their families. These impacts may persist even when the records were wrongly disclosed or were themselves erroneous. Victims may want privacy, too, as may law enforcement officers.

7

PRIVACY WITHIN AND BEYOND FAMILIES AND GROUPS

Introduction

So far in this volume, we have considered privacy as a value for individuals. Yet families or groups might also want to assert privacy as a value. Children, parents, or other family members might want to keep secrets from one another, but may be met with the response that because they are within the family there are special responsibilities to share. Families might also claim privacy against the larger world: that what goes on within the family should be for the family to decide, and not a subject for social or state intervention. Yet feminists criticize the distinction between the private and the public sphere, and the assignment of the family purely to the private, on the basis that this masks the oppression of women at the core institution supporting patriarchy. Claims about intra-group privacy—the ability of group members to assert privacy claims against one another—likewise may be countered with the claim that the group has special claims against its members to share information with each other. The group may assert privacy claims against the rest of the world, too, either on its own behalf or on behalf of its individual members. Group claims also can mask oppression within the group, or secret planning of terrorist acts against the world.

Do families have special claims to privacy?

On a variety of views in political philosophy, families have been thought of as having special claims to privacy against the world. Forms of both liberalism and communitarianism have given special status to the family. So also have views that assign special status to relationships, in this case relationships among family members.

Traditional liberal theory draws a line between the public sphere and the private sphere. Some versions of this view then allocate the family to the private sphere, a realm where people live beyond the interference of society and where what they do is no one else's business. For many of these theorists, the family is a quintessentially private institution, a bulwark against the state. It is where new members of society are created and nurtured, where people are educated into citizenship and supported as they go out into the world to flourish. Family is home—"where the heart is," or "hearth and home." Families have strong privacy rights against the outside world; they can choose which language to speak, who does the cooking and the dishes, whether to homeschool, and whether to go into business together and give special preference in hiring; whether to engage in common activities in a family room, whether to have family meals, and whether to share bedrooms or computers. Only at the very boundaries of severe harm may the state intervene: abuse of elderly parents, child neglect or abuse, or incest, for example.

More recent versions of liberal theory have criticized this assignment of the family to the private sphere as both too strong and too weak. It is too strong because it lets too much injustice fester. Egalitarian liberals argue that the family can be a fundamental site of injustice, if care-work is predominantly assigned to women, caregiving is devalued, and women are undereducated and underpaid. In this view, injustice within the family is as much a social concern as manifestations of injustice in other social institutions (e.g., Kittay 1999). If justice is the first virtue of social institutions, as the philosopher John

Rawls wrote in his widely read *A Theory of Justice* (1971), it is the first virtue of families, too. Critics of these more egalitarian views evoke an image of the "nanny state" telling people what they need to do to provide for the welfare of their members. The picture of the family as squarely within the private sphere is too weak, if the family assigned to the private sphere is conceived in limited terms—as a heterosexual union of one man and one woman, for example. Libertarian liberals, who believe that as long as individuals do not coerce or defraud one another their only obligations are those they voluntarily assume, argue that there must be as much individual liberty about the family as there is about any other institution. Obligations among family members, like other obligations, are a matter of agreement. Even the allocation of child support responsibilities can be a matter of choice within the family. Seen as the result of agreements, families may take a variety of different forms, and members should be at liberty to come and go, constrained only by obligations that they have voluntarily taken on. How far this libertarian position can be extended, given that children cannot be expected to take care of themselves, is a difficult challenge. Think about how people who believe that families should be free to choose whether or not to have health insurance answer the question of whether these families should still be required to get insurance for their children.

More radical feminist theorists argue that the family is the starting point of patriarchy. Patriarchal oppression will continue as long as male-dominated family structures continue. Some of these theorists argue further that patriarchy will continue as long as heterosexual nuclear families continue. The early feminist Charlotte Perkins Gilman, for example, wrote a novel called *Herland* about a society made up only of women who lived idyllic lives (Gilman 1979). For these feminists, the private is the political; assigning the family to the private sphere is a manifestation of the politics of patriarchy. Some radical feminists have suggested abolishing the family altogether;

others have argued for the importance of novel family structures, including same-sex relationships or polyandry. Communitarians also take a variety of positions about the family. For some communitarians, the community, not the family, is paramount. Children should be raised within communal structures such as the kibbutz, lest they acquire the individualist attitudes associated with the nuclear family. The psychologist Urie Bronfenbrenner (1970) studied the differences between children raised in the Soviet Union and in the United States and concluded that children raised in communal settings had lessened expectations for privacy and individual property rights. For other communitarians, traditional family structures are the hearthstone of communities. These communitarians oppose the idea that there are privacy rights to form non-traditional families.

Views about the family as a social or political institution may find support in ethical theories that assign a special status to relationships. Individualist ethical theories start with the separate self—you as a separate person—as the locus of obligations, rights, and responsibilities. Relational views picture you not as a separate self, but as embedded in relationships. You are a son or daughter or possibly both, a mother or father, a branch on a family tree, a Smith or a Rossi or a García or a Wang or a Kumar. Relations are not something you have only if you choose to take them on; they are intrinsic to your identity. There are many complex questions about how relational theorists identify the relationships that have special status, how they justify special moral obligations based on relationships, and whether relationships can ever be undone. (Can you disown your family, for example?) Your views about privacy within and beyond the family may take very different forms, depending on whether you start by thinking of yourself as a separate individual who then chooses whether or not to form relationships, or as someone who is fundamentally a nexus within a web not of your own choosing.

Do children have privacy from their parents? When and why?

From *The Chronicles of Narnia* to the *Harry Potter* series, secret lives of children are the stuff of absorbing fantasy. Children can be very effective in keeping secrets from their parents— but should they be protected in keeping these secrets? Parents might argue that for the most part they should not be, at least before they are old enough to make wise judgments for themselves. Parents might also argue that they are best positioned to make good judgments for their children: they care about their children, know most about them, and have their best interests at heart. Parents might also argue that they have an appropriate role in shaping their children's values, perhaps because of the relationship they hold to their children. They are *parents*, after all. If parents are to judge well on behalf of their children, they might say, they need to have full knowledge about what their children are thinking and doing. From baby monitors to parental control of TV shows to drug testing of hair samples, the parent-surveilled child is the safe, healthy, and well-adjusted child, likely to become the successful adult. He or she is also the child most interconnected with his or her parents.

Each of these claims on behalf of parents has been challenged, however. Sadly, some parents do not have their children's best interests at heart; they are abusers, or may become so if they find out that their children have been doing things that are deeply offensive to their values. This is the reasoning that has led even proponents of parental notification when minors seek abortions to concede that there may be cases in which judges should be able to override the notification requirement. Children may have a pretty good sense of their own interests and the ability to act on them, especially as they become older; thus children can't be included in most research studies in the United States without their assent. And there may be limits to the extent to which parents should be able to impose values on their children; Joel Feinberg (1980) and others have defended the liberal idea that children have rights to an open future in that parents should not be allowed to foreclose options for their children which should be left open to decision when they become adults. Assurances of confidentiality for children may also be necessary to encourage them to open up to others about things that are bothering them, and may thus be a needed form of protection for them. Finally, the surveilled child may be the fearful, conforming child, who grows up afraid to imagine and experiment.

Professionals who deal with children, such as physicians, psychologists, or school counselors, face especially difficult dilemmas about confidentiality. On the one hand, telling parents that their children are suicidal or reporting abuse to child protective services may be critical to protecting children against very serious harm. And parents may argue that because they are in a parental relationship with their child, and have the rights and responsibilities that go with this, they should know. On the other hand, children may not be honest without confidentiality protections. The AMA recommends that physicians should encourage minors to consult their parents, but should also permit competent minors to make their own decisions to the extent permitted by law and should not notify parents without minors' consent (AMA 2013). School counselors may be in an especially difficult position when they act as state employees; their national association advises them to protect the privacy and confidentiality of students and their families, but also to advise them about the limits to confidentiality. Limits to confidentiality are especially important when the student poses a danger to self or others, or when legal requirements may mandate disclosure (American School Counselor Association 2014).

Even when they become adults, it is not always clear that children should have complete privacy from their parents. Parents may care deeply about their children and may have important interests in seeing that their children flourish. If children are secretive about their finances, their marital troubles, or their health, these important concerns of parents will be thwarted. Think of the sadness of parents whose children commit suicide and who wish they had only known. To be sure, the image of parental busybodies perennially checking to make sure that their children's houses are sparkling clean— the image is always the stereotypical mother-in-law—is a reminder that children are adults with their own lives to lead. On the other hand, if relational bonds matter ethically, there is something to be said for children sharing with their parents, too. In the worst case scenario of adult children who cannot look after their own safety, some form of supported decision-making or even guardianship might be appropriate.

Do parents have privacy from their children? When and why?

Parents can be as secretive as their children, hiding everything from when (or whether) they got married, what they did before their children were old enough to know them, to medical histories considered shameful or frightening. The story line of the movie *The Kids Are All Right* was that parents don't always tell children the circumstances of their conception, and that this secrecy may be a mistake. Parents arguably have a right to keep things from their children, just as they do from other people. But there are times when information that parents uniquely possess may be very important for their children to know. Moreover, the parent–child relationship is two-way; if it gives rise to parental rights over children, reciprocally it also ought to give rise to children's rights over parents. Parents nurture, love, and grieve over their children; but children may nurture, love, and grieve over their parents as well.

Family medical history information is probably the best example of information that parents should not keep from their children. Knowledge about inherited cancers or other diseases could be life-saving. Or, it could be information that children would want to take into account when they make important life choices; an example is the possibility that they might have inherited the deleterious form of the HTT gene that causes

Huntington's disease, an adult-onset disease in which people gradually lose control of their emotions and physical movements and ultimately die. When children should know, however, is disputed. There is general agreement that children should be told when they become adults about conditions that might make a difference to their opportunities or their decisions about their health. If the conditions require action before children reach the age of majority, they should also be told so that their health and life are not compromised.

For adult onset diseases such as Huntington's, however, there's nothing medically to be done to prevent them during childhood—or, sadly, in adulthood either, given the current state of medical knowledge. Whether parents should be able to test their children for these conditions before the children can make their own decisions about testing and whether they should tell the children about test results are hotly contested. This issue will only become more complicated as parents contemplate whole genome or whole exome sequencing for their newborns—or even for embryos being considered for transfer during in vitro fertilization. The American Academy of Pediatrics and the American College of Medical Genetics issued a joint statement in 2013 that testing children for adult-onset conditions should be based on the best interests of the child and generally should be deferred until adulthood to protect the child's right to choose whether to be tested, but may occur if deferring testing would place a significant psychosocial burden on the family (AAP 2013). This last qualification reflects a moral framework in which the interests of the family may be considered in decision-making about medical care (Hardart and Chung 2014).

A related topic of controversy has been whether parents may preserve confidentiality about the circumstances of their children's conception. Some parents who adopt may not want their children to know that they were adopted. Historically, adoptions were confidential and often were kept secret even from the adoptees themselves. Even if they wanted to try to find their birth parents, children were unable to gain access to the information. In one well-known decision about medical confidentiality, the Washington state court held that it was a violation of the birth mother's confidentiality for her physician to have disclosed her identity to her daughter and awarded her damages against the physician's estate (*Humphers v. First Interstate Bank of Oregon*, 696 P.2d 527 (en banc) (Wash. 1985)). But children may have strong interests in knowing their birth history. Some of these interests are psychological, involving the child's sense of identity or origins. Other interests may be medical; in some cases, the information may even be life-saving. Recognizing these interests, some states have voluntary adoption registries where birth parents and adoptees may register their interest in being contacted by one another (e.g., Or. Rev. Stat. § 109.430). Especially for medical reasons, courts increasingly will unseal once-confidential adoption records; even when confidentiality was originally promised, it can no longer be guaranteed. Similar questions arise about conception through gamete or embryo donation or surrogacy. Parents may want to keep this information confidential; children may have strong desires to have it or may have medical needs for it. Some jurisdictions now do not permit anonymous donation, although critics claim that this violates the autonomy of both parents and potentially also children (e.g., Cohen 2017). The American Society of Reproductive Medicine strongly encourages disclosing this information to children, but does not require it (ASRM 2013).

Children also may want to know about their parents' circumstances or health. As parents age, children may become their caregivers and may want to know medical information. Parents may want to share this information—many are willing to give their children access to their medical records portals with their physicians—but they may not. Children may also have access to their parents' medical records under HIPAA and state laws if they are their parents' decision-makers and their parents have not denied them access. On the other hand, some parents may not want their children to know details about their health or the fact that they are in increasingly fragile economic circumstances; protecting confidentiality respects this choice, even at the expense of the parents' own interests. And just as some parents abuse children, some children abuse parents or try to exploit them economically. In more individualist views, it's up to parents to decide what information about their circumstances to share with their children. In more relational views, children may have justifications for knowledge about and involvement in their parents' lives, just as parents have justifications for the reverse.

Do spouses have privacy from each other? When and why?

Spouses also may have many reasons for wanting to keep information from each other. Sharing information is part of how people establish intimacy; intimacy may be more precious if not everything is shared. Spouses may enter their relationship based on identities that are at odds with what they were like in the past; there's one famous tort case in which a former prostitute acquitted of the murder of her pimp had reformed, married, and lived an upstanding new life—until a filmmaker told her story without her consent (*Melvin v. Reid*, 297 P. 91 (Cal. App. 1931) (recognizing a cause of action for public disclosure of embarrassing private facts)). Stories of princes or princesses hiding their origins from one another in order to be sure that love is pure are common in fairy tales—and maybe in real life, too, at least in modified form.

But sometimes keeping information from one another is dangerous or potentially harmful in other ways. Before HIV was a treatable disease, physicians debated fiercely about whether they had duties to reveal to the spouses or sexual partners the HIV status of their patients (e.g., Cundiff 2005). Fertility physicians today face questions about whether to treat couples when one member of the pair is withholding information from the other about the infertility or its cause.

Sometimes, withholding the information could put the other person at medical risk, such as a small chance of HIV infection. In other cases, the information might be relevant to whether the use of expensive reproductive technology is needed at all, as when one partner refuses to disclose or discontinue steroid use that is causing infertility. Or, it might be that one partner does not want to inform the other of prior cancer treatment and risks of recurrence that may leave the partner raising a child on his or her own.

Except when there are direct risks of physical harm to another, there is general consensus that people don't have an obligation to reveal their medical information to each other and that their health-care providers should respect their confidentiality (see Chapter 3). Here, the question is whether being spouses makes a difference to this background assumption. Some might argue that it does: that spouses actually make or should be thought of as making a special commitment to protect each other's welfare and look out for each other's interests. Others might note that even the loyalty expressed in traditional wedding vows ("to have and to hold, in sickness and in health, for richer or poorer . . .") stops short of spouses sharing their most intimate secrets with one another.

Libertarians might argue that confidentiality between spouses depends on what they have agreed to share; communitarians might contend that it depends on what is necessary to maintain the family as a traditional institution. Egalitarian liberals might consider when secrets create or reinforce inequalities of wealth or power—as might happen when spouses keep financial information from each other. Feminist theorists would express the further concern that secrets—or the inability to keep them—can be a source of domination. Think about male partners keeping secrets about vasectomies, female partners hiding whether they are using birth control, women keeping secretive abortions from their husbands, or the tragic histories of the many women in sub-Saharan Africa who have been battered or abandoned by their male partners when the knowledge of the HIV infection they caught from them comes to light.

Do family members have obligations to share certain kinds of information with each other, such as family medical history?

Family members may want to keep many kinds of information, including medical history information, confidential from one another. The phrase "skeletons in the family closet" captures it all. Family members may not want to share the information with anyone, or they may be estranged from their families and may be so resentful that they don't want to help other family members, even when they might be willing to help someone completely unrelated. But there are several reasons for thinking that family members may have special obligations to share personal information with one another that require strong reasons to override.

Probably the most persuasive reason is that family members may be in a unique position of knowledge with respect to one another. They may have inherited memorabilia or family papers that no one else has. They may have heard stories from older members of the family before they died. They—or their tissues—may have information about inherited conditions that could be very important for their family members. Even quite weak principles about duties to give aid could support a duty to disclose in such cases of special knowledge: for example, if you could act to prevent serious harm to someone else at little or no inconvenience or harm to yourself, you ought to so act. Potentially life-saving medical information would likely fall under this principle, unless the disclosure would risk serious harm to you, such as physical abuse (e.g., Rhodes 1998). It is less likely that family memories would rise to the level of life-saving importance, as medical information might. But it could be critical to opportunities in life: information about ancestry may be necessary to gain citizenship or some other very important benefit. Of course, this principle about giving aid is not limited to families; however, because of the nature of family structures, obligations under it are more likely to arise within families than among strangers. Other justifications for sharing information with your family members might be that you have benefited from being a member of your family—a reason that is weakened if you have good cause for resentment because of maltreatment. Still another justification is that just being family is enough to generate special obligations. Someone defending this idea would need to explain why family relationships give rise to special obligations, without just assuming that they do. On the other side, family members may have reasons for not wanting to share information with each other. Estrangement is one reason—and a reason that might seem stronger if the estrangement was caused by abuse. Some might contend that any duty to share information is overridden by at least serious abuse—that you don't owe someone aid if she has seriously wronged you, even if you are her closest relative. Others might argue that the balance should still be struck by weighing the benefits of disclosure against whether there is any risk of harm to you from disclosure going forward. The desire not to share information that you are ashamed about, or that you think may cause other family members to think badly of you or someone else you care about, is another reason you might have for not sharing information. People often don't share stories about wayward ancestors for this reason. A further complexity is that you may not want to have the information yourself. Some people do not want to be tested for Huntington's disease, for example. Today, people who want to know whether they are at risk for this disturbing and fatal condition can be tested themselves because the exact location of the HTT gene on the genome is known. Earlier, however, you might have needed genetic information from other family members to assess your own risk. This is still true for genotypes when the phenotypic significance of a variant is unknown; geneticists may need both genetic and medical history information from your family members to figure out whether you might be at risk. Some writers in bioethics argue that you still have a duty to be tested even if you don't want the information yourself—at least if the information could avoid serious disease or death for your relative (e.g., Rhodes 1998; Parker 2015). Others recommend that a physician should explain the importance of disclosure to patients but otherwise keep the confidences (Callier and Simpson 2012).

What if protection of family privacy shields inequality, abuse, or other forms of harm? Should feminists oppose privacy in the family?

Feminist theorists see the family as a social institution subject to interrogation, like any other social institution. From *The Subjection of Women* (Mill and Mill 1869) on, liberal feminist theorists have argued that inequality within the family is inextricably linked to inequality in society more generally. Feminist criticisms of the family as a social institution take many forms, but agree that there is no inevitability about how families are structured. Norms of privacy—how families are structured, what decisions are internal to the family, what information should be kept within the family, or what information should be shared among family members—are subject to critique and change (e.g., Satz 2013). Perhaps the greatest critical concern for feminists is the family as the locus of subordination.

Feminist methodology emphasizes relationships and contexts. Principles that might seem liberating in the abstract can subordinate as they are applied in particular contexts. Consider, for example, the idea of reproductive liberty construed as privacy (see Chapter 1). Defending reproductive liberty on the basis that these decisions are a matter for individuals alone may be viewed as part of a more general view that reproduction, nurturing, and raising children are private matters. But assigning nurturing to a private sphere overlooks the substantive conditions needed for the actualization of reproductive liberty—including funding for abortion, reasonable geographic access to abortion, paid family leave, and available child care.

Decontextualizing the privacy of genetic information is similarly problematic. If women bear the primary responsibility for child care in contexts in which very limited services are available for children with disabilities, their needs or desires for access to genetic information might be different than in more generous settings. Protecting the privacy of sperm donors might have different consequences in contexts in which lesbian couples have limited options for childbearing. If women are blamed for fertility problems—as they are in some patriarchal societies—genetic information that implicates women, or is believed to do so because it is misunderstood, may disempower (Boetzkes 2001).

These examples and many others indicate that privacy within the family is neither subordinating nor liberating by itself. This is true whether the privacy in question is decisional or informational. Rather, in some contexts, protecting choices, family structures, or information-sharing may enhance women's flourishing, whereas in others it will not. For feminists, the question is not public or private in the abstract, but concerns the impact of decisions about privacy in given social circumstances.

Can membership in a group justify restrictions on privacy within the group?

Many different types of groups may wish to insist on norms of privacy or disclosure within the group: clubs, sororities, tribes, religious sects, even virtual groups. Insistence on disclosures may be a ritual of membership, for better or worse. Think about fraternities expecting openness about sexual exploits or grades, private clubs expecting disclosure of financial information to demonstrate worthiness (or the likelihood that club bills will be paid), or religions expecting confessions. Sometimes these norms impose privacy restrictions as well; when sins are confessed to priests, priests must take their knowledge to the grave. Or, group members who are otherwise very close to one another may develop privacy norms as a way to keep at least some personal space among each other. Think about keepsake boxes or lockers in crowded living conditions, personal diaries with tiny keys, curtains on dressing rooms, or enclosed bathrooms. But sometimes the space or the information is shared among all members of the group, like a community bulletin board. Some virtual groups function in these ways, too; for example, the website Patients Like Me designates some data as shared data among members of the site community and other information as "restricted" (https:// www.patientslikeme.com/join).

Intra-group disclosure practices can be liberating, but they can also be severely repressive. They can be a way for group members to shame one another and to impose cultural norms. In some liberal views of groups, it is permissible for groups to impose illiberal values within the group, as long as group members have the freedom to leave. Political scientist Chandran Kukathas, for example, describes a "liberal archipelago" of different group-islands, with many different practices and degrees of freedom within (Kukathas 2003). If there is freedom to move among islands, so that people can choose the mix of privacy norms that best suits them, Kukathas argues that it is permissible for some islands to be illiberal.

Whether and how the conditions of this archipelago can be realized are deeply problematic, however. It may be very difficult for people to leave if they lack resources. They may have family ties or other commitments that would be hard to break. There may be no suitable alternative island that is willing to accept them or where they would fit in—and the open border conditions the archipelago assumes may prove unacceptable to the values of some group-islands. For relational theorists, the individualism assumed by Kukathas's model is misleading from the start: individuals simply are group-related and can't just up and leave by resolving to do so. Religions may be a good example of this: an ex-Catholic is not a non-Catholic, and a non-observant Jew remains Jewish.

Restrictions on privacy within the group thus may be more or less justifiable depending on how individuals enter or leave the group. If individual entry into the group is voluntary, as with fraternities or sororities, the claim to impose privacy restrictions is stronger, at least if individuals are fully informed about the privacy practices before they join. If individual entry is not voluntary—especially if individuals are born into the group, with the ties of identity and relationships this might bring—the case for privacy restrictions is far weaker. If exit is easy, too, the case for restrictions is correspondingly stronger, as individuals are free to avoid them. The worst case would be to lack privacy and to be born into a group with limited prospects for exit.

Further problems arise about group privacy if individuals can choose to leave, however. Suppose that someone is a member of a cult with strong rules about secret rituals. Perhaps the rituals are open only to some group members: males entering adulthood or male members of privileged clans within the groups. These secret rituals are a source of power over other group members for those who are admitted to them. Someone who has been initiated into the most secret of rituals becomes ethically critical of how the power of the rituals is used, and decides to leave the group. On privacy norms within the group, it would have been impermissible for him to share his knowledge of the secret ritual. But is the same thing true once he leaves? This isn't the same question as whether the group can insist on outsiders not learning about their rituals—the topic of the next section—it's about what it means for individuals to be free to leave the group. If it means that individuals are no longer bound by group norms, then departing members should be free to tell the stories of the group. But if departing members remain bound by intra-group norms, they cannot fully leave the group. One motivation for departing might be the freedom to tell people back in the group the secret knowledge that is the source of power over them and thus mitigate their repression. The group might want to forestall this—if privacy norms within the group forbid sharing the knowledge, why should someone be able to share the knowledge just because he has left? On the other hand, if people leaving the group can't share their knowledge to encourage others to leave, the vision of a truly liberal archipelago may fade because people won't have the knowledge they need to decide freely about whether to stay or to go.

This problem about whether people leaving the group remain bound by intra-group privacy norms may seem fanciful, but think for a minute about some actual cases. In one very high-profile example, discussed in Chapter 3, members of the Havasupai tribe objected when DNA samples that had originally been collected from them for research on diabetes were later de-identified and used for research on tribal migration patterns. One source of the objection was that their DNA had been used for a purpose they would not have permitted. But another source of concern was that the research results yielded information they did not want—information about tribal origins that conflicted with group beliefs. This information could also have been obtained by research involving only Havasupai descendants who had moved away from the tribe and agreed to participate—and would have been as disturbing to the tribe's origin beliefs as if the information had been obtained directly from active tribal members (Francis and Francis 2010). Or think about social media groups. If people are free to come and go from them, do they remain bound by the norms of privacy that prevailed among group members? There may be contractual agreements, such as terms and conditions of site use that include continuing obligations of confidentiality, but there may not be. And there may be limits to any contractual obligations, such as disclosures for public safety protection. Or, think about fraternities that share stories of sexual exploits among subsets of group members with the expectation that these stories will go no further. Perhaps those who resign from the fraternity because they object to how women are treated by their brethren should be able to reveal the stories they have been told to fraternity group leaders—or to others outside of the group—to investigate the sexual violence the stories might reveal. If it is permissible to share the information, this suggests that there are limits to the intra-group privacy norms a group might impose. One quite plausible limit might be that groups should not be able to impose strong intra-group privacy norms if the result is serious harm to others outside of the group.

Do groups have privacy? What kind of groups and why?

Like families, groups may wish to protect themselves from the outside world. They may have rituals, oral traditions, sacred objects, or ways of life that they wish to keep separate from the larger society in which they are located. These groups may wish to protect their privacy to build a different social order, or to focus on their chosen way of life without distractions. Historically and still very much with us today are religious communities, from monasteries to small churches, that have moved to isolated rural areas to practice their faith without distraction. These groups may have established rules under which only designated members of the community serve as intermediaries with the world to secure needed services and supplies and to negotiate with the state regulatory agencies and tax collectors. There are even entire countries, or rather their respective leaderships, that have chosen to isolate themselves to the extent possible from the rest of the world. North Korea is a major example today; in the recent past, Myanmar was also a somewhat more limited example. Japan during the Tokugawa Shogunate confined outside contact and trade to a limited space and only reluctantly opened to the outside world. As these examples of states illustrate most clearly, there are interrelationships among intra-group privacy, inter-group privacy, and democracy. Whether leaders can choose privacy on behalf of their populations without democratic deliberation—and whether they can impose information restrictions that make informed deliberation increasingly difficult over time—is one of the issues discussed in Chapter 10.

On liberal theories of groups, the rights that groups have against the outside world may differ from the rights that they have within the group. Liberal theorists such as Will Kymlicka (1989) have argued that groups may require their members to speak a certain language or to be educated in a certain way or to live within stipulated family structures when the larger society could not justifiably impose these rules on the group.

These requirements may be needed so that a group may continue to flourish as its members want— a good that they could not achieve on their own, but that is pursued as a means to the flourishing of individual group members. Or, the group may be thought to be the bearer of rights on its own behalf, as discussed in Chapter 1. These rights may include privacy: Norman and Kymlicka (2000, p. 258) write: "... a liberal society is premised on freedom of conscience, principles of non-discrimination, and a robust zone of privacy, and a liberal nationalism must respect these limits." As we will discuss further in Chapter 10, the presence of many different kinds of groups within a society may be critical for democracy to flourish.

Group secrets may even include the identity of group members. At times, groups have sought to keep their membership lists confidential because they take unpopular positions and are concerned about reprisals. The protection of legitimate dissent may then require protection of these membership lists. Such was the case when the State of Alabama sought to get membership lists for the NAACP during the early days of the civil rights movement. When the case reached the US Supreme Court, Justice Harlan wrote for the Court,

We hold that the immunity from state scrutiny of membership lists which the Association claims on behalf of its members is here so related to the right of the members to pursue their lawful private interests privately and to associate freely with others in so doing as to come within the protection of the Fourteenth Amendment. (*NAACP v. Alabama*, 356 U.S. 449, 466 (1958))

But all is not benign, either within or beyond groups. We've already discussed how intra-group norms of privacy may cause harm to group members. Groups may also be places where harms against others are plotted and fomented. Terrorist groups can wreak grievous harm, even more so than individuals. How protection for legitimate groups such as the NAACP can be juxtaposed with the need to protect others from groups such as ISIS poses enduring tensions between democratic freedom and security. We will see these tensions further illustrated in the discussions of privacy in social media, security, and democracy that follow.

8

PRIVACY ON THE INTERNET AND IN SOCIAL MEDIA

THE WORLDWIDE AND INTERACTIVE INTERNET

Introduction

This chapter addresses three sets of questions concerning privacy, the Internet, and social media. We first consider features of the Internet that are particularly important to whether you can have privacy on it. Then, we explore privacy policies: where they can be found (if at all), how some of them are designed and what they are likely to say, what legal requirements may apply to them, and what you should look for in trying to negotiate privacy. Finally, we consider the difficult issues in negotiating privacy in using social media.

What do people do over the Internet? Is it really like a "superhighway"?

The Internet today is estimated to have over three billion users. According to the International Telecommunication Union, the UN agency for communication technologies, in 2015 57% of the world's population had broadband access. This still leaves 43% unconnected—and the United Nations continues to take bridging this "digital divide" as a critical goal for sustainable development. To this end, the UN's Broadband Commission seeks "to promote the adoption of effective and inclusive broadband policies and practices in countries around the world" (Broadband Commission 2015, p. 8). Although inclusive broadband use is described as allowing individuals to use the Internet in private, rather than in public facilities (Broadband Commission 2015, p. 64), nowhere in the report is the question of Internet privacy itself taken up. Nonetheless, if the Internet is thought of as the location for global interconnection and inclusivity, difficult privacy questions arise.

The Internet is a method for allowing computers to communicate with each other. The development of packet-switching technologies and open architectures in the 1960s enabled computers to be networked, rather than being routed through point to point connections as telephones are (Leiner et al. 2016). The possibilities blossomed quickly. Email arrived in the 1970s, commerce in the late 1980s (with Amazon.com in 1994), the World Wide Web for linking accessible hypertext documents in the 1990s, and user-generated content capabilities such as wikis, blogs, and social networks not long after. The word "blog" (from web log) came into the English language in 1999, Facebook was started at Harvard in 2004, Apple announced podcasting in 2005, and the first Tweets twittered along in 2006 (Thompson 2016). Pandora started streaming audio—like your own customized radio station, they said—in 2000. Netflix started streaming videos in 2007, allowing customers to bypass the annoying step of returning a CD or taking a video back to the rental store. The first Web 2.0 conference was launched in 2004, promoting ideas for crowd-sourcing over the Internet (O'Reilly 2005). Google was incorporated in 1998 and launched its first 10 language versions in 2000. Today, people use the Internet to communicate by email, phone, Twitter, Instagram, and many other ways; to read newspapers and magazines; to buy things and services, stream audio and video and watch TV on demand; to seek content for research; to communicate information, including from biosensors; to collaborate on documents; to post photographs; to form groups; to get crowdsourced recommendations for everything from restaurants and hotels to physicians; to get directions and identify locations; to monitor their homes and their children; to get rides or book stays away from home; and to do just about anything you can think of that doesn't involve actual physical presence together.

The idea of the Internet was, from the beginning, freedom and openness. Thought of in this way, the image of the Internet as an information superhighway is misleading: the Internet would be a very strange superhighway that lacks fixed geographical coordinates, routes, intersections, entrances and exits, borders, or endpoints. The openness of the Internet has been subject to continuing challenges, however. There are the questions of whether areas of the Internet can be owned, fees charged for services, or priorities given to users with more power (see, e.g., Goldsmith and Wu 2006). There are questions of national borders and cultural differences, such as whether China can control access to the Internet, whether France or Germany can prohibit use of the Internet to purchase Nazi memorabilia from abroad, or whether the European Union can insist on worldwide de-listing when it recognizes the right to be forgotten. There are questions of whether materials transmitted among Internet users must follow intellectual property laws—and which jurisdiction's laws apply when this and many other legal questions arise. There are the many questions of cyber-security and how to protect it in a world of open access, questions that we address in Chapter 9. And there is privacy of both individuals and groups as they negotiate their way around the web.

What information about you is likely to be on the Internet?

The answer is that it depends. But it doesn't just depend on what you do. It also depends on what others report about you. Even if you have never accessed the Internet yourself, you could still have a massive and detailed electronic profile. That profile may include all of the kinds of records described in the chapters in this volume on health information, education information, credit and financial information, and law enforcement or employment information. It may also include all the newsfeeds or photographs your friends post about you, the newspaper stories describing your achievements or disasters, your GPS coordinates obtained by sensors you pass as you move through the environment, any public records about you, any records pirated from hacked computers storing information about you—and much, much more. So the prudent course is to assume that there is more information on the Internet about you than you might have imagined. And you don't know where it is, who has it, or what they are doing with it. In the words of a recent US court decision:

> Most of us understand that what we do on the Internet is not completely private. How could it be? We ask large companies to manage our email, we download directions from smartphones that can pinpoint our GPS coordinates, and we look for information online by typing our queries into search engines. We recognize, even if only intuitively, that our data has to be going somewhere. And indeed it does, feeding an entire system of trackers, cookies, and algorithms designed to capture and monetize the information we generate. Most of the time, we never think about this. We browse the Internet, and the data-collecting infrastructure of the digital world hums along quietly in the background. (*In re Nickelodeon Consumer Privacy Litigation.* 2016 WL 3513782 (3d Cir. 2016))

Does this mean you should just get over privacy? No! There's a lot for everyone to learn about what is going on with the Internet, what you can look for and make decisions about, and what policies might better reflect your preferences or the preferences of many people about privacy and the Internet. It's also critical to recognize that issues of Internet privacy and security can't be tackled by individuals on their own; they present serious collective action problems. Whether the best way to solve these collective action problems is to allow industry to innovate and evolve common norms, to adopt regulatory standards requiring minimum protections, to try something in between, or to invent wholly new methods of governance remains up in the air. Descriptions such as the "new frontier" or the "wild West" applied to the Internet suggest accurately that at present there are many different actors, and limited coordination is occurring. This chapter is about privacy on the Internet and in social media. Chapter 9 is about security—making sure that the information protections that you want really stay in place and that you aren't hacked or leaked or unaccountably erased.

What are "cookies"? What are cookie blockers?

Cookies are one of the technical ways to stabilize Internet browsing. They are small bits of code installed on your computer by a website you visit so that the website will recognize you. When you are on a website, for example, you may click between pages of the site and want to be known as the same user when you do. Or, you may store information on the site and expect it to be there for you when you return. Or, cookies may identify you to one website as having browsed on another. The first kind of cookies, operating just as you scroll around on a single visit to a website, are "session cookies." The second kind are cookies for a single website only—first-party cookies installed so that you can use the site's services or "to improve your experience on the site," as many websites say. The third kind are "third-party" cookies, the kind that enable you to be tracked. Here's how third-party cookies may work. You type an address for a website in a web browser like Google; Google sends a "get" signal to the server that is the host of the site. If the site carries advertising, your computer will also be directed to send a get signal to the server of the host of advertising for the site. (Although everything appears to happen simultaneously, this is actually a complex interplay of messages, and you don't see any of what's actually going on.) Either of these servers may post a small text file (a "cookie") on your computer; the cookie placed by the server for the website you sought to visit is a first-party cookie, and the one from the advertiser's server is a third-party cookie. If Google placed the cookies as the ad server, it can then figure out all the websites you visited for which it was requested to serve ads. That way, it decides what ads to serve in a targeted fashion. It can also link this with any of your activities on Google's own sites, such as YouTube or maps.

Cookie blockers allow users to prevent the installation of cookies; Internet browsers may give you different settings to allow you to block them. Internet Explorer does this by allowing you to opt in to block cookies. Safari has an opt out blocker that is a default setting for third-party cookies. Firefox has a variety of privacy settings, including an opt in to block third-party cookies; it also offers a variety of methods to allow you to browse privately, some free and other more advanced options for a fee. You can usually find out how to block cookies or clear your browser by checking the menu options on the top of your browser. Google and other Internet advertisers figured out a way to bypass the default Safari settings on Macs, iPhones, and iPads, however. Although it represented to Safari users that they did not have to separately opt out of Google tracking cookies because their browser settings did the same thing, Google instead exploited an exception to the browser setting for temporary cookies that then let in the Google advertising cookie. When information about this came to light, the FTC investigated and ultimately settled with Google for a $22.5 million fine; the fine was sizable because the FTC concluded that Google was in violation of a prior order requiring them to keep their privacy promises (FTC 2012a). Users also sued Google under a variety of federal and state law theories. Although the court dismissed the claims under the federal Electronic Communications Protection Act (ECPA) (because the user's computer was a party to the communication), the federal Stored Communications Act (SCA) (because the user's computer was not an electronic communication service), and the federal Computer Fraud and Abuse Act (because there was no showing that the users had tried to monetize their own data and then been fraudulently deprived of it), it did let the case go forward under California law, particularly the tort of intrusion on seclusion (*In re Google Inc. Cookie Placement Consumer Privacy Litigation*, 806 F.3d 125 (3d Cir. 2015); for more about the FTC, EPCA, and the SCA, see the Online Appendix). Thus it's a violation of US law for a website to represent that it will respect browser settings about cookies and then try to get around them in a way you are unlikely to detect. It's also possibly a violation of the tort law or privacy statutes of some states for websites to ignore browser settings—even if they don't affirmatively promise to respect them.

What is "do not track"?

In 1994, Congress passed a statute to address fraudulent and abusive telemarketing practices. Of particular concern to Congress was how telemarketers preyed on vulnerable and unsophisticated persons with high pressure sales tactics and outright fraudulent propositions. In 2003, Congress ratified the do-not-call registry provision of the Telemarketing Sales Rule adopted by the FTC under the statute 15 U.S.C. § 6151. The Registry lets you add your phone numbers for free, either by visiting a website run by the federal government (donotcall .gov), or by telephoning a dedicated phone number, 888-382-1222, from the number you want to register. Being listed on the Registry will block cold calls for sales. It won't block political calls, calls from charities soliciting donations, debt collection calls, informational calls, and telephone surveys. It also won't block calls if you have a recent prior relationship with the caller unless you make a specific request not to be called. "Do not call" really resonated with consumers—perhaps because it enabled them to limit all those annoying interruptions that came just at dinner time when telemarketers would expect everyone to be home.

Privacy advocates have sought to get an analogous "do not track" system implemented for the Internet. Except for some browsers that offer you the option, do not track proposals haven't succeeded. Do not track was proposed by FTC staff in a preliminary report (2010a) and was further studied by a group set up by the agency that included many industry representatives. One problem with formulating a do not track proposal is whether there should be an exception like the one in do not call for businesses you have recently had a relationship with. What that relationship might look like for Internet browsing is hard to figure out in the first place—would you establish a relationship by clicking around a website, downloading information from it, or only by making an actual purchase? And smaller companies were concerned that the exception would advantage large established companies such as Facebook or Google with lots of existing relationships and would make it more difficult for new Internet businesses to enter the market. A perhaps more cynical explanation is that industry representatives wanted to block do not track because of the lucrative nature of Internet advertising (Chmielewski 2016). And then there's the possibility that tracking actually benefits consumers by giving them ads that are informative and tailored to their preferences and by getting recommendations from their peers at very little or no cost or inconvenience. Cold-call telemarketing, after all, never had the advantages given by analytics applied to massive amounts of information about the person being called. Ads that pop up in sidebars while you are browsing or even that delay your entry into a website by 20 seconds may be far less annoying than the phone call just as you were taking dinner out of the oven, coming to the climax of the adventure show you were watching, seeing the game-winning touchdown or the elusive soccer goal scored, or curling up with a good book.

Of course, there's a dark side to tracking, too: others may know far more about you than you ever wanted them to know, may figure out how pieces of your life fit together, or may dig up your past. Part of what's difficult in designing a do not track system might be getting a handle on how to separate the kinds of tracking that are benign from the ones that are problematic. In December 2016, the FTC settled a complaint against Turn Inc., a service for targeting online advertising; the settlement requires Turn to represent its online tracking mechanisms accurately and to provide effective opt out mechanisms for consumers (FTC 2016e).

What is the "dark web"? What is going incognito?

The web you see when you use your Internet browser is the publicly indexed web. And your computer is publicly indexed, too—that's what your IP (Internet Protocol) address does. But there is also a largely invisible world of websites that are not publicly indexed. To find one of these, you would need to go directly to its Internet address. It is estimated that the dark web contains over 500 times as much information as the surface web you see. Participants in the dark web may be there because they want to be hidden; dark websites are places where extremists meet to plot terrorism or where sexual predators find victims or where stolen identities are sold. It's where there are websites such as Silk Road for selling illegal drugs. The virtual currency BitCoin can be used to pay for transactions in the dark web—that way, buyers and sellers aren't traceable by the bank accounts or credit cards they use. Since the 9/11 attacks, computer scientists reportedly have been trying to develop algorithms to locate sites on the dark web without already having the Internet address (Ehrenberg 2012).

If you want to browse the web incognito, without anyone knowing your IP address or the URLs (Uniform Resource Locator) you visit, you can do that too. There's a browser called "TOR"—"the onion router," named for how it uses layers of encryption. It's the original brain child of cryptographer David Chaum, who foresaw over 30 years ago the problem of mass surveillance with the use of metadata that we discuss in Chapter 9. Chaum's idea was to encrypt the metadata, too, so no one could figure out the address from which a message came or the address to which it was going. The US Navy financed development of the TOR network, which encrypts in multiple layers and has been used by many who want to communicate anonymously, including WikiLeaks (see Chapter 9). TOR has disadvantages; it's slow and doesn't always encrypt perfectly. Chaum is reportedly working on a new technology called PrivaTegrity. He's concerned about what it can hide, too, so he's building a back door that would allow "something 'generally recognized as evil' " to have anonymity and privacy stripped (Greenberg 2016).

What is the Internet of things?

"Legacy" objects are the objects that made up our world before objects became smart—that is, objects unconnected to the Internet (Rose 2014). Now, objects can communicate in many ways. They may have implanted radio frequency identification (RFID) chips that pick up electromagnetic signals and send back their identification numbers and locations. They may have sensors that can record temperatures, heartbeats, water content, or electrical impulses. And they can connect with each other through the Internet. This last is the "Internet of things"—the IoT. The FTC estimates that in 2015 there were 25 billion connected devices and that this number will have doubled by 2020 (FTC 2016a).

Just think about how the IoT might work on any given day. Your wristband FitBit realizes from changes in your respiration and heart rate that you are waking up. It sends a signal to your thermostat to warm up the house, the lights to turn on, and the electric kettle to start boiling the water for your coffee or oatmeal—or maybe to tell your doctor's office that your arrhythmia has returned. If your wristband realizes that you are very slow to wake up on a given morning, it might send a message to someone you've identified to check on your welfare. If you're out of town, you could use your phone to turn on the lights remotely, or to check to see where the cat is hanging out. Your smart car knows when other objects are too close or when you are going too fast on your way to work or what road hazards lie ahead—and may even drive you someday soon. It lets your office know when you'll be arriving, too. A warm little furry smart robot that looks a little bit like a dog lets you know how your elderly parent is doing in the nursing home where she lives—and gives her cuddles and may even read her the news, too. Smart object designer David Rose, a visiting scientist at MIT, even envisions a smart tooth that would measure how much you've chewed in a given day and lock on to another tooth when you've had enough (Rose 2014).

The IoT is so new that people haven't really caught up with what it might mean. On one level, it seems like a nifty new set of grown-up toys that make life much easier. The control you have over your environment, even from afar, may result in your having more time that you can use for other purposes. It is a very appealing prospect, but using the IoT also poses impressive privacy and even more impressive security risks. The data collected by smart objects provide a remarkable dimension of new knowledge about how you go about your day. The smart objects with which you communicate may be located with spatial coordinates—potentially allowing people to know where you live. They likely will be connected to other objects you use, thus potentially compromising security across a network of objects. To the extent that they record information—and this will depend on their settings—they may be attractive targets for police investigating suspected crimes within the home (Wang 2016). They may help your insurance company determine whether you drive too fast and thus raise your rates (Passikoff 2015). Of course, you could try to opt out of using smart objects, but that may become increasingly difficult, as ordinary appliances come loaded with Internet connectivity in order to function.

Much is subsumed under the "Internet of things" and there is therefore a need for definitional clarity. A "network of things" can be a local area network that is not connected to the Internet. When smart devices are tethered to the Internet, they make up the IoT. Currently, according to the National Institute of Standards and Technology, there is no standard account of the IoT that governs its operation, trustworthiness, or lifecycle (Voss 2016). Objects in the IoT may be sensors measuring physical properties such as temperature or sound and aggregators for the data they collect; methods for weighting the data; channels for communicating the data, products, and decision triggers. A simple example would be motion sensors in restaurants ultimately used in an app that allows individuals to decide how busy their chosen eatery is likely to be at a given time. There are multiple parts to this system and it could go wrong at any one of them, thus vitiating the trust users have in the system. More complex examples include smart cars, smart medical devices, and even smart cities. Commentators contend that definitional clarity about the different aspects of the IoT will help us all to understand what is needed to address privacy concerns. Dieterich (2016) offers three questions that should be asked and answered by consumers and purveyors of IoT products and services: consumers should insist on knowing what data devices are collecting, how the data are being shared, and how they can control data collection and sharing; purveyors should have answers to these questions readily available and communicated to consumers in easily accessed privacy policies.

A 2015 FTC report (FTC 2015a) recommends that IoT creators design objects to minimize data collection and dispose of data as soon as they are no longer necessary. The report also considers how notice and choice might work effectively when devices don't even have a user-facing interface but just have the connectivity built in. It argues that if the data uses aren't clearly what would be expected given the object—a thermostat would be expected to collect information about room temperature but not the number of people in the room, for example—there should be a clear explanation in materials provided with the object. Other methods of informing consumers might also be tried, like online video tutorials or education at the point of sale. The FTC concludes that it will regulate IoT devices consistently with its authority (see Online Appendix)—but that it cannot mandate privacy protections without a specific showing of unfairness or deception. It also recommends that Congress enact minimum privacy standards, for the IoT as well as for websites, social media, and other means for collecting information.

Finally, the Internet of things creates remarkable new forms of cyber vulnerability, too: just think if someone could hack into your thermostat and turn off the heat remotely, turn the water on to boil when you are away, or suddenly instruct your car to drive as fast as it can go down a crowded city street. Particularly frightening are the possibilities with medical devices: cardiac defibrillators going off randomly, insulin pumps shutting down, or blood pressure monitors giving incorrect readings. The FTC report recommends "security by design"—building security into IoT products at the outset, based on risk assessments about the vulnerabilities presented by the object. Risk assessments should consider how consumers will actually use the object and where the greatest points of vulnerability are. Security practices should include encryption of transmitted data, rate limiting to control information traffic and thus reduce the risks of automated attacks, and proper authentication (FTC 2015a).

The Department of Commerce (DOC) is currently engaged in studying the technological and policy landscape of the IoT and the potential role for the federal government in IoT governance. In May 2016 (DOC 2016) it issued a request for public comment on the IoT and in September 2016 it held a workshop devoted to these issues. Among concerns are that a patchwork and even a single-nation approach to IoT governance will prove inadequate to protect privacy and security and will thus hinder commercial development of the smart world.

The Department of Homeland Security (DHS) is also deeply concerned about protection of critical infrastructure from cyberattacks on the IoT. As part of security design, DHS recommends taking operational disruption and its consequences into account. It also recommends developing policies of coordinate disclosure of vulnerabilities and methods for sunsetting outdated IoT devices (DHS 2016a).

What are social media? What privacy concerns are raised by social media?

Social media sites are websites that allow you to make connections with others through the Internet. Depending on how a site is constructed, it may allow you to connect with anyone else with access across the globe, or it might allow far more limited connections with people with common interests. You might establish connections with groups of friends, college classmates, groups with a common medical condition, or groups with common interests, from knitting to politics. Some sites allow you to "follow" others, or others to "follow" you. Social media sites typically let you manage your connections and the information you will share with them. On some sites, you may have layers of sharing with wider and wider groups.

As the editor of one recent book on social media in Europe writes, "Social networking is the new modern zeitgeist" (Lambert 2014). Social media sites are immensely popular among Internet users. Here are just a few recent statistics from the Pew Research Center. Nearly three-quarters of Internet users in the United States are on Facebook—62% of US adults overall—with 70% of them logging on daily. Usage rates are highest among women (77%) and adults under 30 (82%); only the over-65s have less than a majority on Facebook. Twenty-eight percent of US adults use Instagram, 59% of them daily.

Thirty-one percent use Pinterest, and 27% of Pinterest users are on the site at least once a day. About a quarter of Internet users use LinkedIn, 22% of them daily. Among Internet users, 23% use Twitter, 38% of them daily (Duggan 2015). During and after the 2016 election, Twitter has been a favored communication mode of President Donald Trump. Through social media, one critic claims, we create "informationalized versions of ourselves," with every aspect "digitized, tracked, circulated, mined for patterns" (Silverman 2015, p. x).

Closely related to social media sites are sites that allow users to share information. You can rate books or products on Amazon, movies on Netflix, bed and breakfast stays on AirBnB, restaurants on Yelp or Zagat, or attractions on TripAdvisor. You can share medical information on Patients Like Me or get answers from many websites, or maybe even try to buy a term paper safely. And the list goes on. Social media have been hailed as ushering in the perfectionist possibilities of a new information age and have been vilified as creating a state of constant, identity-destroying surveillance. In between these extremes lie many layers of privacy questions for social media users.

For starters, how much information do you need to provide in order to join the site or app in question? Facebook, for example, asks you to represent your true identity as a condition of using the site; you are restricted to one site, may create accounts only for yourself, and may not create a new account without Facebook's permission after Facebook has disabled your account (Facebook 2015). Other sites such as Yik Yak let you sign up without giving any identifying information except your geolocation (Yik Yak 2016). Many sites require you to agree to terms and conditions about yourself: for example, to become a member of Patients Like Me, you must be diagnosed with the disease for the community you are joining (or be a caregiver of someone with the disease); to establish an account with eBay you must be legally able to enter into contracts; to join Facebook you must not be a convicted sex offender; to join

Yik Yak you must not be from a country that the United States has declared as terrorist-supporting; and to join many sites you must be age 13 or older.

A next privacy question is how to manage privacy settings. A first step is to figure out where to find them. Then, you need to know what the default settings are; these are the settings that the site comes with when you sign up. For sites like Instagram where the idea is to share, the assumption will be that you share photos you post with everyone; for Snapchat, where the idea is to communicate with friends, the assumption will be that your posts go only to friends. A fertility tracker, "Glow," reportedly was originally designed to allow male partners to request to link their profiles with female partners by providing her email address; as long as she wasn't already linked, he would be linked and get access to all her information without her having the option to block the link (this feature has since been changed) (Weill 2016). Facebook has probably the most elaborate set of options for most of the information you post on the site, although your profile information is always public unless you hide parts of it, such as your birthday. Many social media sites today now have connections to other apps you might be using, and so it is important to make sure that your settings about what to share through apps reflect your privacy preferences, too.

Some claim that using social media "is anathema to privacy" because you can never be sure that other users will be as trustworthy as you expect (Claypoole 2014). We saw in Chapter 5 how employees have learned to regret sharing information with colleagues that their employers later use against them—and how several states now have statutes that prevent employers from requiring you to share your social media passwords. Keeping your password confidential, of course, won't protect you against what other users of the website do—but it at least keeps you from having to share the information that makes access easy. Pinterest has a secret board function that is visible only to you and to others on the board—but you are warned that anyone on the board may invite others to join it, so you need to trust your fellow board members only to invite others who are trustworthy (https://about.pinterest.com/en/privacy-policy). There are also questions about how much information shared with others may be further transmitted in accord with their settings. Facebook, for example, got into trouble with the FTC for assuring users that their information would only be shared in accord with their privacy settings while allowing information to be shared with third parties through apps used by their friends (FTC 2012b). The problem here was that you might have thought you'd only shared information with a friend—but the friend might have settings that let the information go out more publicly.

Still further questions involve what social media sites will do with the vast amounts of data they may collect about you. One set of issues concerns how they will link this data up into profiles and whether they will share these profiles. Another question is whether they will use these profiles to tailor information back to you, from restaurant selections to job possibilities. Allowing various analytics firms to use information about users is another. Sharing with affiliates such as apps or with third parties is yet another. Allowing researchers to use information—or even to affect what happens on the site—is still another. In a very controversial example, Facebook allowed researchers to adjust users' news feeds in order to see whether social media content affected moods; the research found that users who were given more positive news feeds tended to post happier status reports, and those who were given sadder feeds were more likely to post negatively as well (Meyer 2014).

Social media sites may also change their privacy policies. Some warn you that they will post changes to the policy on the site, but it is up to you to monitor the site to find out about them. Facebook at one point changed its website so that information that was once private became public, but without notifying users. The FTC included this in charges of deception, and part of the settlement was that Facebook must notify users before changing privacy policies (FTC 2012b).

Another concern is whether you can delete your information, once you have shared it. If you have published things that might be embarrassing, or that might cause you to lose your job, or undermine an identity you have carefully nurtured, it seems you ought to be able to erase what you have said. There should, of course, be exceptions to avert harm to others: if others have relied on what you said, or if you have made commitments such as buying something, or if you have done something to harm others such as bullying. But perhaps it should be different if you injudiciously posted a photograph of yourself having a beer when your employer disapproves of alcohol or clicked a "like" button without checking what you were approving (Mayer-Schönberger 2009). Of course, if others have already copied the content, deletion may be futile.

Examples are notorious of tweets or photos or videos that have gone viral before their contributors realized how damaging they might be. But even if you have deleted your account, sites may keep copies of the information for their own use or for legal protection.

European Union privacy law has far stricter standards than US law on information deletion, providing that data may be kept for no longer than is necessary for its declared purpose. The European Court of Justice (ECJ) ruled in 2014 that there is a right to be forgotten, and the new European data protection regulation recognizes this as well (see Online Appendix). After the ECJ decision, Google entertained requests for breaking search links on a country-by-country basis and by late 2015 had deleted nearly 450,000 links. California, however, enacted a statute that became effective in 2015 to allow minors to request removal of content posted on websites; such deletion only applies to public posting of the content on the site, not to copies kept by the site that are not visible or to copies made by others (Cal Bus. & Prof. Code § 22581).

Social media sites also have become a major source through which people get news. As of 2016, data indicate that social media had passed TV as a source of news for people under age 25 (Wakefield 2016). Controversially, social media have also become mechanisms for sharing fake news and hate speech. Efforts by the sites to correct misinformation must contend with difficulties in assessing contested claims and support for freedom of expression (Seetharaman, Nicas, and Olivarez-Giles 2016).

Social media sites are also a source of information for government surveillance. Communication scholar Philip Howard and colleagues have analyzed information from Facebook, Twitter, and YouTube and concluded that social media played a central role in political conversation during the Arab Spring (Howard et al. 2011). Social media accounts have also been extensively used by ISIS; researchers at the Brookings Institution conservatively estimate that at least 46,000 and possibly as many as 70,000 Twitter accounts were used by ISIS supporters in Syria and Iraq between September and December 2014 (Berger and Morgan 2015). (Twitter's terms of service prohibit unlawful use of the site and use of the site for threats of violence or promoting terrorism; https://support.twitter.com/articles/18311.) For good or for ill, governments may wish to gather information in bulk about use of these sites—the US government certainly did after 9/11. The US government's collection of information from Facebook is currently under challenge in the European Union. We discuss these issues further in Chapter 9, on national security and privacy.

What is a privacy policy and how can you find it?

A privacy policy is a statement by a data collector such as a website about the information it collects, how it will protect that information (or not), what it will do with the information, and whether it will ever share the information. When you visit a website today, it is likely that you will find a privacy policy. A few years ago, many websites didn't have privacy policies at all, but the FTC has determined in some cases that it's an unfair trade practice not to have one—particularly when the website is using information it gets from you in a way that might surprise you. In the European Union, anyone collecting identifiable information about you (that isn't just for personal use, or otherwise outside Regulation (EU) 2016/679; see Online Appendix) must tell you what they are going to do with it.

Usually, there are hot button links to privacy policies at the bottom of the web page. Sometimes, you'll also find information about privacy under a button labeled "Terms and Conditions" (T&C). Here, the website tells you what it expects of users of the website. You're expected to abide by the T&C, just as you're expected to abide by the terms of the lease you have with your landlord or the service provider of your cell phone. If you violate the T&C, the website will think you are in breach of contract. So they may say you can't continue to use the website, because the deal is off. Or, they might even sue you for breach of contract if they have damages because of what you have done, like pirating something from the website that you were not supposed to use, or damaging the credibility of the website by what you do with other information on it or what you post on it.

Privacy policies will generally tell you what information the website will collect. Some of the information will be up to you to provide, but some may be passively collected, like your location. Some may also be collected from third parties; Internet sales sites like Amazon or eBay tell you that they will collect credit information or other information to help them to guard against fraud, for example. Privacy policies will likely tell you if the website uses cookies and how it does so. They will tell you how they share information either internally or with third parties; for example, Google makes it clear that it shares information among all the services provided on the site. Policies will also tell you the conditions under which they share information with law enforcement, either in the United States or abroad. It is typical for websites to say that they will share if they have a good faith belief they are legally required to do so. They also will tell you whether you can adjust privacy settings and how to do this.

Terms and conditions are written to be explicitly contractual. Websites such as Pinterest or Instagram, where users share information, are likely to state explicitly that users must be age 13 or older. Websites where content is shared may also state explicitly what kind of content is acceptable for the site; for example, Instagram makes clear that it is not a site for the exchange of explicitly sexual photographs. Many websites state that you waive any liability as a condition of using the site—even the liability of the site for content that might be very damaging to you and that was not even posted by you. Some may also explicitly limit any liability for damages; Pinterest, for example, limits its damages to $100. Whether these liability limitations would stand up in court is another question—but you should also know that many websites also limit your ability to go to court by stating that you agree to individual arbitration. That means that if you have a dispute with the site, it will be resolved via alternative dispute resolution. There will be no possibility for a class action suit in which you could form a group with other site users who claim they have been similarly harmed, and there won't be an opportunity to create legal precedents that might benefit consumers in later disputes. Interestingly, Facebook and Google are exceptions to the arbitration requirement; if you have a dispute with them, you'll be able to sue in California federal or state courts.

What are desirable practices for privacy policies?

Posted privacy policies and privacy settings are the core tools of the notice and choice approach of FIPs. Yet, as we discussed in Chapter 2, the notice and choice approach is often ineffective in enabling consumers to realize their privacy preferences. An important starting point in addressing this problem is developing an understanding of what makes for good privacy policies. These policies might be regarded as best practices, published as guidelines, or used to construct model privacy notices. There have been a number of efforts along these lines;

here, we distill what we think are some of the most important suggestions, based largely on our own experience, research regarding Internet privacy policies in use today, and legal models from the European Union and California.

1. Privacy policies should be *very* easy to find. We mean *very*—not hidden in obscure corners of the website or difficult to find after a long scroll down past products or posts.
2. Privacy information should be in one place, not scattered among different documents. Website "terms" or "terms and conditions" or buttons like "about us" should not be places where important privacy information is scattered.
3. Each section of the policy should begin with an easily understood summary or abstract of the section that follows. Although we understand that lawyers will want to review privacy policies—one of us is, after all, a lawyer—privacy policies should be drafted for consumers. Estimates place the average US reading level at 7th or 8th grade; given the high percentages using social media, this should be the maximum reading level for privacy notices.
4. There should be an explicit commitment to notify subscribers when a privacy policy has been changed. It should not be up to the subscriber to check every so often to see if the privacy policy has been amended. If notice is provided only through the website, people who don't check the website often—or who have forgotten they've even signed up—won't find out about it. It is typical for websites to collect email addresses when people sign up—this is what could be used. (Of course, websites can't control when people change their emails, so there will be some loss in communicative effectiveness in any event.)
5. If a site de-identifies personal data for third-party users to analyze, its privacy notice should include a description of likely types of users and uses, as well as an assessment of the risks of re-identification and how they

will be addressed. Today, most websites assume that de-identification solves privacy problems, but as we saw in Chapter 1, this is not always the case.

6. The privacy policy should contain a list of third-party partners with whom subscribers' data are shared. There should also be links to the privacy policies of these third-party partners. Many policies simply state that data will be shared with partners, but without indicating what these partners might be. This is particularly concerning when websites partner with many of the wide variety of apps in use today because subscribers' information may go out through apps in ways they do not anticipate.

7. If the firm shares subscriber data with its parent company or the family of companies it owns, that updated list should also be included in the privacy statement, with links to privacy policies.

8. There should be a clear statement, with illustrations, of how tracking from the website may take place.

9. If the subscriber terminates his or her membership in the social media site, personal data concerning the former member should be deleted within a specified period of time. Any exceptions should be clearly stated and based on the original purpose for collecting the information.

10. If the firm cooperates with security agencies or the police in the release of subscribers' names or other information, the conditions of that commitment to cooperation should be stated. Statements such as "we share information if we have a good faith belief that sharing is legally required" are too vague. Sites should say whether they will permit any bulk sharing of information, or whether they will respond only to individualized requests and the terms on which they will respond. Sites might also consider giving users very understandable illustrations of what they have actually done about sharing.

11. Privacy policies should state explicitly what they will do to notify you if there has been a breach of identifiable individual information.

What is "privacy by design"?

Website design is as important as privacy notices in helping to make sure that users understand the site and are able to implement their privacy preferences. Privacy by design has been suggested for Internet firms that have large subscriber bases. It means that the site is designed, from the beginning, to be privacy protective. Privacy by design features build protections into the site, rather than expecting users to construct them for themselves. The idea of privacy by design comes from Ann Cavoukian of Ryerson University in Toronto, when she served as privacy commissioner for the Province of Ontario. Cavoukian describes privacy by design in seven foundational principles:

1. Being proactive rather than reactive
2. Making privacy the default setting
3. Embedding privacy into design
4. Avoiding the pretense of false dichotomies, such as privacy versus security
5. Providing full life-cycle management of data
6. Ensuring visibility and transparency of data
7. Being user-centric (Islam and Iannella 2011; Leonard 2015).

The EU data protection directive and regulation incorporate the first two principles. Supporters of the adoption of privacy by design standards argue that privacy must become integral to how we use the web for the services it provides. If for some reason privacy is not articulated, it nonetheless must be the default mechanism for firms that rely on the use of personal data in the services that they provide.

What can you do to protect yourself on social media?

As we've said before, you can't eliminate risks. But you can reduce them. Here are some suggestions.

First, read privacy policies. If the website lets you adjust privacy settings, figure out how to do this before you put any information that you wouldn't want to have shared up on the website. A good rule of thumb is to assume that the default settings will be in favor of sharing—that will remind you to go in and adjust if you have concerns.

Second, assume the worst about information being shared. Before you click that "post" button, think about how you would feel if your worst enemy had the information and could use it against you. This isn't likely to happen, but it could—especially with the length of time social media sites have information, the extent of the interconnection among sites, and the vast numbers of people using them. So be cautious about what you post. The European Union requires websites to limit data collection to what is needed for a stated purpose—in the same way, you might want to limit the data you provide to what is needed in order to get what you want out of the website. Here's an illustration from Laurie Davis, the founder of eFlirt, a coaching site for people about online dating. She suggests four rules of thumb to reduce the chances of a potential online suitor learning too much about you: don't use the name of your employer (but list the field instead), don't list the college or high school you attended, don't use an unusual first name, and do use a temporary phone number that will transfer calls to your cell phone without revealing the number. Otherwise, be prepared for someone to figure out a great deal about you, just by Googling. And remember that a lot of that information might be used to figure out answers to your "secret questions." For example, if somebody knows you were married during college and has the name of the college you attended, they might easily guess where you met your spouse.

Finally, if you think it's hard to figure out how information might be shared, just be aware that hacking and data breaches happen all the time. You may not even know the breach has occurred. If a website has inadequate security policies, it may not have detected the breach. Outside of health and financial information, the United States doesn't have any general federal breach notification laws. There are such laws in the European Union, in California, and in a few other jurisdictions.

The Ashley Madison Internet dating site is an excellent cautionary tale about what a breach could mean. Ashley Madison was a website aimed at married people thinking of dating people outside of the marital dyad; it claimed to have 30 million site users. Because more men than women signed up for the site, it charged men for use but admitted women for free. Although users could delete their visible presence on the website for a fee, Ashley Madison retained copies of the files. In July 2015, hackers breached the site, claiming that they were engaged in a justified attack on an immoral service. The hackers then published the data from the site on the dark web on a site only accessible through the TOR browser. The result was widespread embarrassment, divorces, and in several cases, sadly, suicide (Lamont 2016). There were apparently a number of Saudi Arabians with accounts who could have been at risk as citizens of a state that imposes the death penalty for adultery.

The FTC investigated the Ashley Madison site for alleged deception and lax security practices that left the site vulnerable. The site's parent company, Ruby, reached a $1.6 million settlement with the FTC in December, 2016 (FTC 2016f). The implication of the modest settlement is that the embarrassed users are unlikely to receive compensation for the loss of their privacy. The FTC apparently recognized that the penalty was modest and but at the same time did not want to bankrupt the firm. Site users are pursuing a class action suit but one reasonable inference from the settlement is that web users should take into consideration how willing they are to run the risk of having some personal data made public without the expectation of compensation for their loss (Sharp and Bartz 2016).

What is cyberbullying?

Bullying is unwanted aggressive behavior that is used to intimidate. It's often thought of as a problem among schoolchildren, although adults can bully each other, too. Think of how leaders such as Vladimir Putin of Russia or Slobodan Milošević of Serbia have been described as bullies—or even how countries have also been given this description by their critics. Bullying is, of course, long-standing and not uncommon, but it has been given new and more powerful tools by the Internet.

Playground bullies may, by superior strength or social position, embarrass or physically attack other children. Bullies may justify such ill treatment on some difference that the bullied child has that set the child apart from others—a difference that may even be thought of as making the target a deserving victim. Tools of cyberbullying include emails, text messages, posting photographs or videos, or some other sort of electronic communication. Cyberbullying reaches its victims not only at school, but at home when they open up their email or their smartphones and thus can become a far more pervasive intrusion on their lives. The communicative reach of cyberbullying is exponentially greater than playground bullying as well; messages can be copied and recopied, insults or embarrassing photographs can be shared through social media sites, and YouTube videos may be seen around the world. Although cyberbullying is less common than traditional physical bullying, for victims the increased dimensions of violation result in despairing loss of privacy. An Urban Institute study of bullying and dating abuse finds that 17% of students report cyberbullying, 41% report physical bullying, and 45% report psychological bullying (Zweig et al. 2013). The Internet did not bring bullying into existence, but it has raised its privacy dimensions by conveying the sense for some students that there is no place to hide from the forms it takes in cyber space.

But more privacy for those who are victimized by bullying should not be the only response. It should be pointed out that the Internet not only has ways of communicating disconcerting and embarrassing revelations, but also can be a source of effective help. Public health experts point out that the Internet can be a source of education on mental health issues (Luxton, June, and Fairall 2012). It has also been a place for people with rare diseases to find support for one another. Some websites offer support groups for people with mental illness or hotlines for people contemplating suicide. The ones we have found state explicitly that they do not share personal information, so they are not an effective means for direct intervention. As with so many other kinds of shared information, there are trade-offs here between benefits and risks. In the next chapter, we turn directly to these risks in the context of security.

9

PRIVACY AND SECURITY

Introduction

Security appears in many forms in discussions about privacy. There is physical security of persons and their possessions. Attacks on your physical security may be a privacy violation, or they may occur because your privacy is violated in other ways. There is information security—that is, whether information about you is kept without corruption or destruction and accessible only as the privacy requirements you have stipulated permit. Encryption that protects your data is an example of security in this sense. And there is national security: protection of a country from internal or foreign threats. This chapter discusses these three interwoven aspects of security and their implications for privacy.

What is meant by personal security and what are its implications for privacy?

First a note about the word "security." The opposite of "security" is not "non-security"; it's "insecurity," a word created in medieval Latin by adding the prefix for "not" to the word for security. Insecurity conveys not only the absence of security or separation from security—that would be "asecurity" or "dissecurity." Insecurity conveys an active state of being not secure—of distress, fear, or threat—the dark world portrayed in Donald Trump's 2016 speech accepting the Republican Party's nomination for president. Insecurity is not neutral; it is fearful. The desire for security is the desire to live without immobilizing fear. Perceptions of risks and fear, even if unrealistic, may be as much or more of an impetus to seek protection as actual risks—fear is the driver. This connection between security, insecurity, and fear has been central to the role played by security in the privacy debates. This is true whether the security in question concerns your physical person, your information, or the country where you live.

Personal security is the protection of individuals from physical or psychological violence. What such personal safety requires may be very different across cultures, geographies, societies, and states. It may also be very different for men, women, boys, and girls. Some face day-to-day violence, others food insecurity, others job insecurity—and others lead relatively insulated lives but still worry that remote risks may strike them. Some have argued that personal security should be integrated into the UN Millennium Development Goals (e.g., Muggah 2012). However, other United Nations member states are concerned about just how far the "security" agenda should go. While part of this challenge is semantic, it is also political and is linked to judgments about tolerable levels of intrusions on privacy in order to improve security. Recurring terrorist attacks in seemingly innocuous and happy locations from workplace holiday parties to Christmas markets present continuing challenges to support for privacy.

Actual or perceived risks may lead individuals to take actions to protect their own security. Faced with perceived risks of physical attack, theft, natural disasters, or epidemics, you may think about whether to move to areas where there have been fewer assaults or less property crime. Or, recurrent flooding may drive you to relocate on higher ground, and risks of disease may cause you to change travel plans. You may also call on government to reduce or mitigate risks through measures as different as mosquito abatement or flood insurance. Personal security also becomes a political concern in calls for expanding the police force, better training for security officers, or mandatory sentencing. We saw in Chapter 5 the privacy costs of background checks for employment, and in Chapter 6 how fear of predatory sex offenders impelled public registries for offenders.

Privacy in areas beset by daily violence, with bullets passing near and through your home, is likely to be tenuous. Security isn't exactly a necessary condition for privacy, but the two are deeply intertwined: as fears of insecurity rise, support for privacy may wane. Consider living in one of the three countries that account for a quarter of the world's non-war-related homicides: El Salvador, Honduras, or Venezuela. The omnipresent risk of violence in these nations may make security elusive for decades. Privacy and security clearly intersect in this context, as those who have the resources to do so live in highly fortified homes. To the extent these homes can be successfully defended, their residents achieve a measure of privacy, but it may be a distracted form of privacy, confined to a limited space. And they may give up other forms of privacy, if they are subject to ongoing surveillance or are limited in the choices they can make by the constraints of protection.

Advocates for privacy often understand privacy as providing protection against the intrusive gaze of the state or others. With surveillance, privacy and personal security intersect directly. Supporters of personal security often argue for increased surveillance to curtail the risk of violent threats: the ubiquitous CCTV cameras. Today, there is one surveillance camera for every eleven residents in the United Kingdom; and in November, 2016, the United Kingdom enacted a sweeping surveillance law, the Investigatory Powers Act. A December 2016 decision of the European Court of Justice throws this act into question as a violation of EU restrictions on surveillance— although the UK's anticipated withdrawal from the European Union may alter the significance of the decision (Bowcott

2016). Increased surveillance may reduce privacy by subjecting individuals to an apparently continuous watchful gaze, and therefore privacy advocates may oppose it. Still others argue that, rather than an inherent tension between privacy and security, there is reason to regard the relationship as mutually reinforcing. The argument is that a substantive measure of security is needed for privacy to be sustained: that without the CCTV cameras, we'd suffer even more intrusion in the form of threats—or perceived risks of threats—to our very person. With the cameras, we are freer to go about in the world.

One way of calibrating the interrelationship between privacy and personal security is to view each as a matter of degree. Justice Thurgood Marshall observed in his dissent in *Smith v. Maryland* (442 U.S. 735, 749 (1979)) that "privacy is not a discrete commodity, possessed absolutely or not at all." Yes, we sacrifice some privacy for security, but we also sacrifice some security for privacy. The challenge is to sacrifice each in the way that is most sustaining for the other. As we have seen, privacy is also not univocal: it may include protection from physical access, protection of information, and protection of choices, among other ideas. At times, limits on one form of privacy may be an aspect of achieving more privacy in another dimension. Consider information and physical privacy: the information gleaned from surveillance may be critical to the detection and control of disease spread and far less intrusive than mandatory inspections or quarantine. Airport screening—which many consider to be a grievous imposition on physical privacy—may be needed to assure greater freedom to travel. On the other hand, some limits on access to information also may be necessary to protect those with unpopular ideas against coercion, as the problematic use of "do not fly" lists suggests.

Security is similarly both a matter of degree and multifaceted. Lessened information security may increase or decrease physical security, depending on who possesses the information and what is done with it. National security and information security may work together when there are national security implications of attacks on individuals' information—but to some extent, protecting national security may also require upsetting individuals' information security. Even individual security and national security may not always go in tandem, if physical risks to some or even invasive personal searches are needed for national security protection. This is not to say that all or even most invasions are justifiable, but that depending on the context, the balance may justifiably be struck in different ways. In this way we may argue that privacy and security are similar: we can think of security as occasionally lapsing and privacy as fragile—or both as intermittent. But it still is better for each of them to recur than to happen only infrequently or not at all.

What is information security and how is it related to privacy?

When information is stored, electronically or otherwise, its caretakers may be expected to keep it secure. This means that they must keep it from being destroyed, corrupted, copied without permission, or stolen in some other way. Security assures that privacy expectations are honored in that data are not taken for unpermitted uses or accessed by those who are not permitted entry. When these expectations are not honored, there's a security breach. But information security means more than just making sure that the wrong people don't access the information or put it to the wrong uses—it also assures that the information stays safe and uncorrupted. There are thus three aspects of information security: physical security, administrative security, and technical security.

For paper records—like medical records or court records in manila folders—security matters just as much as it does for electronic records. It just may not be as technically complicated. Physical security means that the information is not physically destroyed or defaced. When Vietnam War protesters poured blood on draft files, or when the flooding in New Orleans destroyed files stored in the basement of the courthouse, the physical security of these records was compromised. The physical security of records is also violated if they are allowed to deteriorate so that they are no longer useful—as, for example, has been alleged about the many rape kits thrown out or corrupted over the years in police stations.

Administrative security means that staff and others having access to information are properly trained. For paper records, this means that they aren't misfiled, that proper procedures are followed for people to get access, and that they aren't taken out of private offices and left in briefcases on public transit by employees on their way home.

Technical security means that appropriate technical standards are in place—for paper records, this might be installing locks with sufficiently complicated combinations. Although paper records may be harder to copy or to get to when they are stored at their place of origin, security is still an issue for them.

For electronic records, security also requires physical, administrative, and technical safeguards. For the medical records it covers, for example, HIPAA has a security rule in addition to the privacy rule discussed in Chapter 3. Physical security means that the location where the data are stored is adequately protected against unauthorized access, tampering, or destruction. If your Facebook page is unaccountably de-activated and the data in it are not saved, if your cloud-stored files vanish, or if your hard drive is stolen or burned with the only copy of your novel on it, the physical security of your information has been compromised—just as it would have been if the typescript of your novel had been burned. The novelist Dennis Cooper lost 14 years of content when Google took his blog down—they claim because of a violation of their terms of use, a claim he disputes (Gay 2016). (Quite likely Google has retained a copy of the file; the problem for Cooper is that he no longer has access to it.)

Administrative security means that staff are properly organized and trained, so that they don't share passwords, copy sensitive documents onto unsecured computers, or peek at documents they shouldn't see, like the health-care records of their neighbors. It also means that appropriate risk assessments are conducted to identify possible vulnerabilities. Staff must be disciplined, too, if they violate good security practices, especially if they do so intentionally.

Finally, security means technical safeguards such as strong passwords or encryption of data in transit and possibly also at rest. It means that there are controls in place to assure that data aren't improperly accessed or modified. Methods for detecting and blocking cyber-attacks are a critical aspect of technical security today.

Information security is not an easy matter, to say the least. Hacking is on the increase, both domestic and foreign, with many causes: recreation, carelessness, criminal intent, terrorism, and political mischief, among others. It is probably best to assume that security will be breached and to think about how to limit the damage if this does happen. In the United States in 2016, the Democratic National Committee learned to their sorrow of the dangers of hacking.

Some writers have suggested distributed storage as a counter-measure—so that with large data sets, not all of it is compromised at once. "Mini-sentinel," a method for detecting unusual side effects of marketed drugs, was constructed in this way, with the information remaining at the health-care provider source but analyzed with standard algorithms. Backups in different locations may help with this, too (see, e.g., Sales 2013; Bambauer 2014). If you don't like storing your data in the cloud as a backup, back up anything that's important very regularly on a different device—and don't keep the device where it will be stolen with your computer. And make sure that you don't confuse versions of a document, either—remember the frustration of losing all your changes when you saved an earlier version of a document in a way that overwrote the later version.

Information security involves hard choices about more or less, as does physical security. Just think about why many people don't use strong passwords—they are hard to remember, and guessing them may mean you get locked out of a website you need access to, like your bank account. What's called two-factor authentication is more cumbersome than single-factor authentication—and three-factor authentication is almost never used. Authentication factors are different types of credentials to verify you are who you say you are, usually something you have, something you know, and something you are. ATMs use two-factor identification: the card you have and the PIN you know. Online banking in the United States uses one-factor authentication—your knowledge of your username and password. If the only way for you to get into an ATM was to screen your fingerprint in addition to your card and your PIN, you'd be using three-factor authentication, adding something you are, to something you have and something you know. Today, signing up for a patient portal with your doctor often requires you to be present in person—so that they can see that it is you. But for people who live far away or who are not very mobile, this can be difficult—even though they may be the people who most need the portals to communicate with their doctors and transmit information obtained by biosensors. Large data systems may encrypt data when it is being transferred remotely, but may not have encrypted the data at rest within its own system because to do so would be expensive or inconvenient—but any unencrypted data are more vulnerable to hacking and other cyber-threats.

As an individual, there are a number of things you can do to protect the security of your electronic information (see Bromwich 2016). You can encrypt the emails and the text messages you send with apps like Signal or WhatsApp. You can encrypt the files on your computer by turning on this functionality—it's offered by both Apple and Windows. You can take a page from the administrative safeguards recommendations: use strong passwords. You can use two factor authentication. When you search the Internet, you can try to use browsers that mask your identity, particularly if you are doing sensitive searches that you don't want others to know about. You can try to keep up to date by reading technology columns in newspapers such as *The New York Times* or magazines such as *Wired*. But the most important thing to recognize is that, whatever you do, your ability to protect the security of your networked information is imperfect at best.

The goal of information security is assurance that choices about information privacy will be respected. This respect is related to other forms of privacy and security in complex ways. When information security is violated, people may be less physically secure if information leads other people to threaten them. An example might be a hack of a court record about someone's sex offender status that was supposed to have been sealed or expunged, with the result that neighbors throw rocks through the supposed offender's windows. People may also be either more or less nationally secure when the security of records is compromised: it depends on what records, by whom, and the purposes for which the records are to be used. The United States is reportedly engaging in "cyber bombing" against ISIS. Although the details have not been disclosed, this presumably involves some form of cyber-attack and likely compromises the information security of at least some involved in ISIS (Sanger 2016). Yet it may at the same time enhance the physical, informational, and national security of people in the United States as well as in the Islamic State, depending on the form of the cyber-attack. Cyber-attacks against targets in the United States may undermine informational or national security here, but guarding against these attacks may require at least some limits on domestic information privacy as well.

What is cyber security?

Cyber security is protection in cyber space, the domain of networked computers. It's the protection of computers and their infrastructure against physical attacks, hacking, malware, viruses and worms, and other hazards. Many crimes can be committed through computers, from stealing intellectual property to selling child pornography to diverting money from bank accounts. Valuable information can also be destroyed: court records, bank records, income tax records, voting records, and many more are vulnerable to cyber-attacks. Passwords can be changed, enabling intruders to inhabit an account while the initial occupants can no longer access it; reportedly, the fertility tracker "Glow" was subject to hacks of this sort (Weill 2016).

One of the most significant concerns about cyber security is the ability to manipulate or destroy information that gives needed direction to infrastructure elements. With the Internet of things, vulnerabilities have increased astronomically. Attacks could reset everything from household appliances to cars, medical equipment, traffic signals, and even voting machines. If voting machines are inadequately protected, elections could be hacked, not rigged, with grievous implications for democracy (Harris 2016). Despite rumors and fears, there is no indication that this happened during the 2016 elections in the United States.

Networked computers are vulnerable in many ways. Unfortunately, networked computers are only as secure as their weakest link. That's why experts are concerned about the Internet of things—that hacking one connected object may bring down everything else that is connected to it. Some critical infrastructure is run by the government, but much is in the private sector: hospitals, power companies, transportation companies, and financial markets, to list just a few. Improving cyber security thus may have implications for privacy, if companies and their workers, or government employees, must themselves be monitored to reduce the risks that they will unwittingly or deliberately compromise network security. Currently, the US Department of Homeland Security (DHS) relies primarily on voluntary and supportive efforts to further cyber security in the United States, but critics worry that this leaves critical infrastructure at risk. Evidence of hacking by foreign governments may stimulate increased cyber security efforts.

What is national security?

National security is generally understood as state-developed policy to protect the nation and its population from attacks. This includes both attacks from outside, such as the strike on Pearl Harbor, and attacks from within, such as the bombing of the Federal Building in Oklahoma City by Timothy McVeigh or the killings at the nightclub in Orlando, Florida. Some attacks come from both outside and within, such as the massacre at the Bataclan Theatre in Paris or the 9/11 attacks on the World Trade Center in New York.

Traditionally, threats to national security were military ones posed by another state. In recent decades, the rise of non-state actors engaged in terrorism has widened the ambit of defense against lethal threats and has blurred distinctions between internal and external threats. The result has been a broadened range of surveillance, from international intelligence to domestic monitoring, with concomitant implications for privacy. Lines between intelligence operations against threats to national security and criminal law enforcement have also been blurred, for example when drug smuggling is thought to be linked to support for terrorist organizations.

As this is security at the national level, it concentrates on threats to the integrity of the country; compromises of national security attack the country as a political entity. Immediate threats may be directed against individuals, as when people supported by terrorist organizations open fire in a nightclub or slit the throat of a beloved village priest, but the ultimate aim is to destabilize the society through instilling fear broadly among the citizenry. Counteracting threats to national security may require commitments from community and state institutions to provide public support for the exercise of police powers to protect personal security. But ultimately, protection of national security is at a different level than the protection of personal security.

Threats of violence within a society, even when quite widespread, don't always threaten national security, although they may increase personal fear. The difference is whether the threats of violence are aimed to risk—or do risk, or even are feared to risk—undermining the country politically. When national security is threatened, more is on the line than individuals' lives—and so the stakes seem higher and compromises to privacy more justifiable in the eyes of defenders of the nation. The US Supreme Court has expressed this idea consistently: "It is 'obvious and unarguable' that no governmental interest is more compelling than the security of the Nation" (*Haig v. Agee*, 453 U.S. 280, 307 (1981)).

Terrorism and the fear it introduces are perhaps the greatest contemporary threats to privacy as protection against state intrusion in our lives—a very result that acts of terrorism, both domestic and foreign, aim to produce. Bruce Hoffman, director of the Center for Security Studies at Georgetown University, recognizes that terrorism lacks a concise definition but argues nonetheless that fear is essential to our understanding of what is meant by terrorism: "... terrorism is the deliberate creation and exploitation of fear through violence or the threat of violence in the attainment of political objectives" (Hoffman 1986). The next few sections concern how this has played out with respect to privacy in the United States after 9/11.

What is the US National Security Strategy?

National security strategies are not new in the United States. In 1947, just after World War II, Congress created the National Security Agency (NSA). In 1949, in the wake of the Soviet Union's first detonation of an atomic bomb, President Truman requested a comprehensive security strategy (Goldgeier and Suri 2016). Since that time, there have been many different security documents, shaped by the events of the time, from the Cold War to perceived economic instability during the Clinton presidency. But security strategies were given new impetus by 9/11; the Bush administration, for example, issued a strategy premised on the need for preventive war. Successive strategies were issued thereafter by both the Bush and Obama administrations, each emphasizing the perceived security threats of the year.

The last security strategy published by the Obama administration in 2015 emphasized a wide range of initiatives, from security, to prosperity, to values such as equality and support for emerging democracies, to a strengthened international order (White House 2015). "Privacy" is mentioned in the 35-page document only twice, and then only as a vague commitment. It appears first in President Obama's introductory letter:

> I have worked to ensure that America has the capabilities we need to respond to threats abroad, while acting in line with our values—prohibiting the use of torture; embracing constraints on our use of new technologies like drones; and upholding our commitment to privacy and civil liberties.

The second mention is in the section of the document that discusses the importance of the United States living by its values:

> Our vital intelligence activities are also being reformed to preserve the capabilities needed to secure our interests while continuing to respect privacy and curb the potential for abuse. We are increasing transparency so the public can be confident our surveillance activities are consistent with the rule of law and governed by effective oversight. We have not and will not collect signals intelligence to suppress criticism or dissent or to afford a competitive advantage to U.S. companies. (p. 19)

The document has been criticized for its generality (e.g., Goldgeier and Suri 2016), and it is fair to say that controversies over the extent of surveillance, government transparency, and public oversight have not abated.

An important outcome of 9/11 was the perceived need to address failures of coordination, including the failure to share surveillance information that could have led to the recognition of threats before they turned deadly. The US Department of Homeland Security was founded in 2002 to fill this role. Among other responsibilities, DHS has responsibilities for border security, citizenship and immigration, anti-trafficking enforcement, disaster relief, and cyber security. It has a privacy office, mandated by statute, which has developed policies and creates privacy impact assessments for activities such as cyber security initiatives.

DHS has established a National Terrorism Advisory System that issues alerts to the American population if there is an imminent or elevated risk of a terrorist attack. DHS defines threat levels as follows:

- An imminent threat warns of a credible, specific, and impending terrorist threat against the United States.
- An elevated threat warns of a credible terrorist threat against the United States.

This threat alert system publicizes warnings in many venues, including social media. The current system replaced color coding of threat risk.

The previous color coding system created a sense of hypervigilance, parallel to the warnings associated with forest fires in the American West. Throughout the summer, in most parts of the West, the highest risk of fire remains the unchanged message on Forest Service billboards. Orange, warning us of a "high risk of terrorist attacks," just under the red of "severe" danger, also seemed never to change. DHS now issues advisory system bulletins that continue to identify a high threat level and reiterate that "our concerns that violent extremists could be inspired to conduct attacks inside the U.S. have not diminished" (DHS 2016). Results of these signals may be mixed. If the threat of risk is assessed as chronically very high, but if terrorist attacks or wildfires occur only infrequently, people may no longer correlate risk with the posted assessment. It may be difficult to maintain high alert status and concomitant willingness to compromise values such as privacy for security. If periodic disasters seem to recur at reasonably predictable intervals, this may engender prudential but not overwhelming fear. Expected crises could result in less panic and reduced willingness to see the maintenance of security as overwhelmingly important. On the other hand, a state of chronic threat could generate a kind of social chronic fever, in which people become weary and acceptant of threats to both their security and their privacy. We'll return to the question of fear as the prioritization of national security over privacy in a later section of this chapter, after fuller descriptions of what has actually happened in the United States after 9/11.

What is FISA and what are FISA courts?

Spying on enemies has always been regarded as a fair way of preserving national security. As law professor Laura Donohue recounts, advance intelligence about British plans was critical to colonial efforts against the British at the Battle of Bunker Hill (2016, p. 1). Under the US Constitution, different rules have been applied to spying on foreign enemies and to spying on domestic enemies. This separation was reflected institutionally, as well: the Central Intelligence Agency (CIA) didn't investigate US citizens at home, and the Federal Bureau of Investigation (FBI) didn't pursue spies abroad. With periodic and growing fears of domestic terrorism, especially after 9/11, pressures for the two to merge have intensified. The original idea of separating foreign intelligence from criminal law enforcement is that it is permissible to have lower standards for protecting individuals who are under investigation for national security reasons than for protecting individuals who are suspected of ordinary crimes. At one point, this distinction seemed largely to track the difference between foreign intelligence and domestic mischief. As the lines have blurred between international and domestic terrorism, however, the lines have also seemed to blur between intelligence activities and the criminal law, with resulting serious issues for privacy. The attacks on 9/11 didn't start this process, but took it to a very different level.

In 1978, Congress passed the Foreign Intelligence Surveillance Act (FISA) to govern domestic surveillance (50 U.S.C. §§ 1801–1885c). FISA was passed after reports that the FBI had engaged in domestic counterintelligence against anti-war and civil rights protesters, a CIA special unit had created intelligence files on many US citizens, and the NSA had engaged in widespread domestic surveillance. Such spying on US citizens was heavily criticized, and the original aim of FISA was to rein them in and subject them to oversight. FISA established a special court, the FISA court (FISC), made up of 11 federal district court judges from around the country serving staggered terms. There is also a court to review decisions of the FISC, the FISCR, made up of three federal judges appointed by the Chief Justice of the US Supreme Court. Decisions of the FISC and the FISCR were to be secret—because of the supposed need to protect the integrity of investigations.

Under FISA, the role of the FISC was to review the government's case for electronic surveillance before it could occur against US citizens or lawful permanent residents.

To be authorized in conducting domestic counterintelligence under the 1978 law, the government had to show probable cause that the purpose of the search was to obtain foreign intelligence information, the target of surveillance was acting for a foreign power, and the target was going to use the facilities being surveilled. Probable cause is the relatively high standard for getting a search warrant under the Fourth Amendment (see Online Appendix). Surveillance of electronic communications conducted abroad, surveillance that does not involve electronic communication, and incidental collection of communication were not covered by these FISA protections—these remained under the rules governing foreign intelligence. Congress subsequently expanded FISA to allow the FISC to authorize physical searches, searches of some business records such as car rentals or transportation, and pen register and trap and trace devices (these are described in the Online Appendix)—all before 9/11 (Donohue 2016, p. 13). Immediately after 9/11, the USA PATRIOT Act expanded FISA much further, as did legal interpretations and other government actions after the terrorist attacks. It is ironic that FISA, originally intended to protect people lawfully in the United States against sweeping surveillance in the name of foreign intelligence, became the structure for the most widespread information gathering by the government that the United States has ever known.

What is the USA PATRIOT Act?

The Uniting and Strengthening America by Providing Appropriate Tools Required to Intercept and Obstruct Terrorism Act of 2001 is the USA PATRIOT Act. Enacted quickly and overwhelmingly after 9/11, USA PATRIOT vastly expanded government powers for domestic surveillance. The expansions have since been somewhat modulated, but many of the powers created in 2001 remain.

A first important expansion of USA PATRIOT, § 215, applied to pen register and trap and trace devices. These are electronic devices that record all outgoing and incoming contacts of a communication device such as a telephone (see Online Appendix for further information). Although these formerly could only be used to identify caller and recipient telephone numbers, now they could be used to capture any information, identifying the destination or source of electronic communications—this means destinations and senders of email, text messages, twitter feeds, and many other types of electronic communication. In 2006, this authority was expanded still further to allow capture of past records of these communications. The showing required to gain this authority was lessened, too; instead of probable cause that the target of surveillance is acting for a foreign power and that the target was going to use the device being surveilled, all that was now required was evidence that the information sought did not directly concern a US citizen and was relevant to protect against terrorism. This provision was interpreted to allow collection of all Internet metadata by the Bush administration. It also meant that tracking could be applied to devices used by anyone—not just targets of investigation (Donohue 2016, pp. 24–25).

Another significant expansion of USA PATRIOT concerned the scope of physical searches that could be authorized by the FISC. Instead of just a limited set of business records, such as car rental records, searches could now apply to any business or personal records and to any data within a company's possession, whether inside or outside the United States. The showing required to get authorization for a search or tracking authority from the FISC was also lowered. Instead of showing that the purpose of the search was foreign intelligence information, the government would only need to show that a significant purpose of the search was foreign intelligence. This brought many more searches with possibly mixed goals under the jurisdiction of the FISC. If, for example, the government thought you were a drug dealer and might be using your earnings to support jihad, that would suffice under USA PATRIOT for the FISC to authorize a clandestine search of your apartment. This is one of the provisions that blurred the lines between foreign intelligence operations and the criminal law.

Delayed notice search warrants were another important expansion of USA PATRIOT. The purpose of a warrant is to require a showing before a neutral magistrate of the need for the search and to define the parameters of the search. When police officers go to your house with a warrant to search, they are supposed to show you the warrant; you may object to it if there are mistakes or the police are overstepping their limits. If you are not at home, they may search but must give you notice that the search has occurred. When pen register or trap and trace devices are used, you are not aware of them unless you are clever enough to detect them on your own. That's part of the point—if you knew that someone was watching the numbers dialed from your phone, you wouldn't use it. Under Federal Rule of Criminal Procedure 41(f)(2)(C), you must be given notice within 10 days after use of a tracking device. USA PATRIOT § 213 allowed officers to request judges for delayed notice warrants in circumstances on this list: endangering physical safety, flight, evidence tampering, witness intimidation, jeopardizing the investigation, or delaying a trial. Jeopardy to the investigation is a broad standard, and the use of delayed warrant searches has expanded greatly, especially for investigations of illegal drug trafficking (DOJ 2004). Since 2007, the US courts have been required to report to Congress on the numbers of delayed warrant search requests; there were 690 in 2007, and the number had risen to 12,870 in 2014, the most recent year for which a report is available (US Courts 2007, 2014). Over 80% of these delayed notice warrants were in drug enforcement cases, illustrating once again a blurring of how USA PATRIOT authority has been used for what might be viewed as domestic criminal law enforcement.

National Security Letters (NSLs) allow the FBI director (or the special agent in charge of one of the 56 FBI offices) to issue an administrative subpoena for the production of records in connection with national security investigations. The NSL provision of USA PATRIOT, § 505, allowed NSLs to be issued to telephone companies, financial companies, Internet service providers, and consumer credit agencies. (Far more limited NSL authority had originally been created for financial records in 1978 and required an affirmation that the information must pertain to a foreign power or an agent of a foreign power.) NSLs can be written for financial information, including account and safe deposit box records. They can be written for information about subscribers to electronic communications services, and can include subscriber information, email records, and records of telephone calls made and received from a phone. They can include credit reports and all the other information in the files of consumer reporting agencies. (See Chapter 5 for a discussion of what information these agencies have.) NSLs present unsupervised powers of administrative authority, as they may be issued without judicial scrutiny—even the secret scrutiny of the FISC. All that is needed is a certification in writing by the head of one of the local FBI offices that the information is relevant to an authorized investigation to protect against international terrorism or clandestine intelligence activities. And there is a proviso: the investigation of a US person cannot be "conducted solely upon the basis of activities protected by the first amendment to the Constitution of the United States." This means that you could be the subject of an NSL even if you were being investigated for activities protected by the First Amendment, such as freedom of speech or the free exercise of religion, as long as you were also being investigated for national security reasons. The implications of this provision for the privacy of religious organizations and their members that are believed to have connections to terrorism are significant.

As it was originally enacted in 2001, the NSL provision had two additional aspects that were antithetical to the protection of privacy. First, any recipient of an NSL was subject to a "gag" order and could not disclose receipt of the letter, the target of the letter, or the letter's contents under any circumstances. This was the situation of the Connecticut librarians who received an NSL for patrons' records (see Chapter 4). Second, there was no right of judicial review for an NSL—indeed, under the gag rule you couldn't even consult an attorney to consider whether to go to court to oppose the NSL. Not surprisingly, civil liberties and privacy advocates were deeply disturbed by NSLs. The Connecticut librarians—under pseudonyms—went to court to challenge the gag order procedure as a violation of the First Amendment. In 2005, amendments to USA PATRIOT required the FBI to certify that disclosure of the NSL could result in a specific harm: danger to national security; interference with criminal, counterintelligence, or counterterrorism investigations;

interference with diplomatic relations; or danger to life or physical safety (18 U.S.C. § 2709(c)(1)). The 2005 amendments also permitted judicial review of NSL requests or gag orders. A report issued by the Department of Justice Office of the Inspector General in 2007 (and reissued with fewer redactions in 2016 (US Department of Justice 2016)) indicated that in the year before 9/11, there were about 8,500 requests for NSLs; in 2005, the number had increased by nearly a factor of 6 to over 47,000. The report also found many inaccuracies in the FBI's records of NSLs, significant confusion over the requirements for issuing NSLs, and a pattern of circumventing even the NSL requirement by claiming exigent circumstances (DOJ 2016). Controversies over NSLs continue with ongoing challenges to them in court and efforts in Congress to either strengthen or weaken the FBI's authority to issue them.

What is bulk surveillance of metadata?

Metadata is information about data, such as their originating source or location, their duration, or their destination. Because metadata is not information about the actual content of data, defenders of its collection argue that collecting metadata is less serious as an invasion of privacy. However, metadata can reveal a great deal of information. From metadata, the government can construct chains of communication—they can see who has communicated with whom, who might be the center of a communication structure, and where was their primary location. Metadata can also allow you to be traced as you go about your activities. It's metadata that might let someone know that you had made a phone call from a Planned Parenthood office, had visited a cancer treatment facility, or had been in a city's red light district late at night. Metadata about users of social media allows collectors to understand networks: who your friends are, how you are linked into groups, who might be the group's central organizer, who lurks on the outskirts of the group, and who is no longer in communication with the group.

Bulk collection of metadata is collection of metadata about large groups of communicators. Targeted collection of metadata, by contrast, would be collection of metadata pertaining to a particular communicator—the kind of information that might be sought via a subpoena or an NSL listing a specific target. Beginning in 2001, without proceeding under the provisions of USA PATRIOT, President Bush authorized the NSA to collect all telephone and Internet metadata from communication service providers in the United States. John Yoo, then at the Office of Legal Counsel in the Department of Justice, wrote memos supporting the program's legality. The program continued until 2004, when officials at the DOJ balked at reapproving it. The collection of Internet metadata was then shifted to approval by the FISC under the FISA trap and track provisions; it was reapproved until 2011, when the government no longer sought reapproval. FISC approval, secret as always, was based on acceptance of the government's argument that the entire database was relevant to threat detection. According to legal scholar Laura Donohue's comprehensive account of the program, which we have found very helpful in constructing this summary, this was an interpretation that took away all the protections Congress had intended from the statute governing domestic surveillance: "The prevention of widespread collection absent particularized suspicion was one of the most important safeguards introduced by Congress to protect citizens' privacy" (Donohue 2016, p. 46).

Telephone metadata also was shifted over to FISC approval in 2006. Under this program as approved by FISC, the government received metadata from all of the US major carriers in bulk. It would then query the bulk data using an identifier that had been linked to a terrorist organization for calls to and from the identifier, calls to and from callers to the identifier, and so on. Beginning in 2009, the NSA understood its authorization to go three "hops" away (in Facebook lingo, friends of friends of friends of the identifier). In 2014, President Obama limited the queries to two hops (Donohue 2016, pp. 48–49).

What was PRISM?

Collecting and analyzing the content of communications was also thought to be critical for national security after 9/11. The same program that initiated collection of metadata in 2001 also initiated collection of the contents of international telephone and Internet communications that passed through the United States. Because Internet communications move around the world in a non-geographically bounded way, communications among people entirely outside the United States, communications between people in the United States and people outside, and communications between people entirely within the United States aren't confined to the geographical spaces where they occur. Links between Facebook friends in the United Kingdom and in France may pass through the United States; links between Facebook friends in Kansas and California may be routed through Ireland. Proponents of surveillance within the government wanted broad authority to gather international information as it passed through routers in the United States, but it wasn't clear how this could fit comfortably within the FISC approval process, which covered domestic surveillance rather than international intelligence. Nonetheless, the collection occurred, even with FISC approval, for several years. Amendments to FISA in 2007 and 2008 provided a statutory solution: a new § 702 of FISA allowed the acquisition of foreign intelligence information from communications within the United States sent by non-US persons reasonably believed to be outside of the United States, subject to approval of the FISC (Oversight Board 2014, p. 5). NSA received annual approval from the FISC for this program, without specifying who would be targeted but with a statement about how the government would determine that people were believed to be non-US persons outside of the United States and that the information would be relevant to foreign intelligence.

PRISM was one of the ways the government got intelligence information about non-US persons outside of the United States. The government would identify a selector—for example, an email address—to an Internet service provider. The provider would then send all the communications to or from that address to the NSA. Providers sending information under PRISM were Microsoft, Google, Yahoo!, Facebook, PalTalk, YouTube, Skype, AOL, and Apple. Under § 702, data were also collected "upstream," through the telecommunications backbone, and included information "about" the target in the sense that the target was mentioned in the content of the communication. For a number of reasons, it was difficult to limit § 702 collection to non-US persons outside of the United States: for example, if a non-US target were mentioned in the email of a US sender, that email would be collected (Oversight Board 2014, p. 7).

Who is Edward Snowden?

Edward Snowden was a contract employee for the NSA who became deeply concerned about its surveillance activities. In 2012, he copied a large number of records from NSA files that revealed the scope of the collection of metadata and content information. Through contacts with the civil liberties lawyer Glenn Greenwald and the documentary filmmaker Laura Poitras, Snowden released a number of his findings from the copied data files to *The Guardian*, *The Washington Post*, *The New York Times*, and *Der Spiegel* (Greenwald 2014).

Snowden's revelations became globally important immediately and led to sharp criticism of US data-gathering policies as spying on its own citizens as well as leaders of friendly foreign powers. Criticism within the United States, Europe, and South America was particularly vehement. It was not that critics were dismayed to learn that the NSA engaged in surveillance, but that they were shocked by the ease and scale with which data were and are gathered on the daily lives of millions of people both inside and outside the United States, with limited resistance from high tech and phone companies, among others. There was also shock at the limited, and secret, oversight provided by the FISC. The ease with which Snowden copied the files raised another concern among advocates of privacy protection: that someone who was not a regular employee of NSA was able to gather vast amounts of data by stealth from the NSA and transfer it out of the agency with seemingly little difficulty. Privacy was compromised twice over.

Snowden now lives in exile in Russia. He has not returned to the United States, as he faces possible prosecution because his acts are regarded as threats to national security. Snowden believes that under the Espionage Act he will be unable to argue publicly that the leaks were justified. He remains a controversial figure, with some regarding him as a civil libertarian hero and others as hiding cowardly behind an authoritarian regime. President Obama's national security advisor Lisa Monaco stated, in response to a WeThePeople petition signed by over 167,000 people, that there were no plans to pardon Snowden (Froomkin 2015). Reactions to Snowden's revelations have brought a number of changes to US surveillance practices, however. These include a five-year limit on the time the NSA can keep even the data of non-US citizens and a three-year limit on the mandatory silence required for NSLs (Childress 2015).

What is WikiLeaks?

Wikis are websites with community-edited content. Anyone with an Internet connection can participate in generating a wiki. WikiLeaks is a site founded by Julian Assange in 2006 to "give asylum" to "the world's most persecuted documents" (WikiLeaks 2015). WikiLeaks collects, analyzes, and publishes data sets of censored or restricted documents involving war, spying, or corruption. It is a nonprofit, funded by Assange, publication sales, and private donations. WikiLeaks lists many partners on its website, from major newspapers such as *The New York Times*, *The Telegraph*, *The Wall Street Journal*, *Le Monde*, *Der Spiegel*, and *The Washington Post*, to organizations for press freedom such as Reporters without Borders, the

Bureau of Investigative Journalism, and the Freedom of the Press Foundation.

WikiLeaks has been controversial for its decisions about what and when to publish. Its publication of leaked documents from the Democratic National Committee on the eve of the July 2016 Democratic Convention brought criticism from many, including Edward Snowden (Chokshi 2016). Further publication by WikiLeaks of hacked documents from Democrats during the 2016 US presidential campaign unleashed a torrent of criticism that Assange had been allied with Russia in the effort to defeat Hillary Clinton, a claim that Assange denies. In the spring of 2016, publisher Julian Assange was under asylum in the Ecuadorian embassy in London; he was wanted in Sweden for questioning over rape allegations. Although a UN working group on arbitrary detention judged that he was arbitrarily detained in February 2016, the Swedish court upheld the arrest warrant for him in May 2016.

What is the USA FREEDOM Act?

Suspicions about the bulk collection of metadata surfaced from time to time in the press but reached a crescendo with Edward Snowden's revelations in 2011. Critical reports also indicated that the mass surveillance had failed to actually identify any serious terrorist threats (McLaughlin 2015). Authorization for the bulk collection programs and for USA PATRIOT both expired in 2015. USA FREEDOM—Uniting and Strengthening America by Fulfilling Rights and Ensuring Effective Discipline Over Monitoring Act of 2015—is the act that reauthorized USA PATRIOT. Its stated purpose is "to reform the authorities of the Federal Government to require the production of certain business records, conduct electronic surveillance, use pen registers and trap and trace devices, and use other forms of information gathering for foreign intelligence, counterterrorism, and criminal purposes, and for other purposes" (Pub.L. No. 114-23, 129 Stat. 268 (2015)).

USA FREEDOM does introduce new privacy protections. It prohibits bulk or indiscriminate collection of all records under USA PATRIOT § 215, the FISA pen register authority, or NSLs. Instead of bulk collection of telephone records and metadata, like all records from a given zip code, it limits data collection to the "greatest extent reasonably practical" for the search in question. If there is reasonable suspicion that an individual is connected to a terrorist organization, data can be collected about others up to two hops away—in Facebook lingo, friends of the individual's friends. NSL gag orders can be challenged in court; to defend them, the government must show a danger to national security or the need to prevent interference with an investigation. A panel of experts was established to provide guidance for the FISC on privacy and civil liberties, among other matters. All significant legal constructions or interpretations by the FISC must now be public, although approvals of actual searches remain secret.

USA FREEDOM's critics contend that much remains unclear about the extent to which bulk surveillance has actually ended. Questions have been raised about the status of ongoing investigations, which may create a loophole (Hackett 2015). There are also concerns about bulk collection of foreign intelligence information, which isn't covered by FISA—FISA is only about domestic surveillance—but which may sweep up information about people in the United States. Ongoing litigation in the European Union is challenging Facebook practices with respect to the information it collects. Facebook has its overseas headquarters in Ireland, which in practice means that over 80% of active users are under Irish law and EU regulation. Privacy activist Max Schrems is organizing the suit, which argues that Facebook uses personal data without informed consent by tracking people who gave a "thumbs up" in response to a posting. It argues that Facebook's default settings favoring open sharing violate the EU requirement of specific consent for data use. It also raises the concern that Facebook is subject to US surveillance protocols, which are inconsistent with EU data protection rules. If successful, the result would be that Facebook could no longer transfer information from the European Union to the United States under the new Privacy Shield arrangement (see Online Appendix). Similar claims might be raised about other Internet companies. The Irish court has referred the case to the Court of Justice of the European Union, and the US government has asked to intervene in the case (Europe versus Facebook 2016).

Clearly, these conflicts between national security and privacy are not going to go away soon. Perhaps the most important and least resolved areas of controversy include whether and how there should be different standards for domestic and foreign intelligence surveillance, how closely targeted and well supported suspicions must be in order for information to be collected about individuals, and the extent to which surveillance may be secret or must be transparent and subject to oversight.

Why is privacy often judged to be a trade-off with national security? Is this too simple?

Since 9/11, but even before, advocates of surveillance have argued that when national security is at stake, trade-offs with privacy are necessary. The actions of the US government after 9/11 demonstrate the significant detriments to privacy that this may mean in action. When the scale of surveillance was revealed by Snowden and others, debates recurred over the limits of privacy in the face of national security threats, and the limits to security in the face of the importance of maintaining privacy as a desired political value.

To some extent, these debates pictured a relatively simple trade-off between security and privacy: the more security, the less privacy, and the more privacy, the less security. Presumably the greater a threat is perceived to be, the greater the measures that should be devised to respond to the threat. Threat response, if it is to be reasonable and effective, requires information that is accurate and presented in real time: in short, intelligence. But this means, some argue, a loss of privacy. If the threat is the rapid emergence of a new communicable disease that requires public health intervention, we need to know who is infected and where they are. But people who fear they are ill know that if they are identified with a lethal variant of the disease, they will be isolated and their family and friends may be quarantined. If they do not consent to testing, they will be compelled by authorities to be tested. When it is urgent to identify epidemics—or even when it is thought to be urgent to identify an epidemic—the expectation is long established that public health officials will exercise police powers to identify those who may spread the communicable disease to the uninfected. Privacy cannot be used as grounds to refuse to cooperate with public health agents; physical and informational privacy will be overridden by others' need for security.

Similar reasoning has been used for national security, in the United States and elsewhere, perhaps at an even greater level of intensity. The images that the concept of national security conjures up are not images of blissful, undisturbed private life in rural settings. Rather, they are images of frightening insecurity of individuals and communities being threatened by a person or groups or the destructive presence of foreign forces deploying lethal weaponry. Threats to the political order are invoked to justify the need for ever greater amounts of information about people within and beyond the policy and thus for weakening privacy protections. The presence of privacy protections, in the view of policymakers, may shield from observation individuals and groups planning to commit violent acts. The premise is that information is needed—indeed, a great deal of information that is gathered from many sources and collected continuously—to detect and to unmask those who intend harm to the nation's population and resources. Privacy is seen as an obstruction to the effort to locate and identify individuals and groups who may seek to perpetrate harm on others and sometimes themselves. This is the picture that was invoked to justify US surveillance after 9/11—that of a stand-off between security and privacy.

But we think this picture is too simple, for either individual or national security. Consider two other nations that judged surveillance highly important to their national security: Nazi Germany and Communist East Germany. If you had lived in the Germany of the Nazis or the East Germany of the Stasi secret police, you might have had both time and space to be yourself, but you likely also would have been entirely unable to anticipate when your space and the time you had to enjoy it would be lost, perhaps forever. The East German state, as the Nazis before them, regarded domestic dissatisfaction as a threat to its well-being. What made private life so hard to sustain in East Germany was the frequent willingness of not just the state but of neighbors and coworkers to report activities and conversations that they considered as violations of state expectations as to how people should lead their lives. This custom of neighborly denunciation revealed the willingness of so many people to report comments perceived as unpatriotic or actions seen as questionable. This random and frequent intervention in your life didn't create security at all, though: it had as a consequence the welling of insecurity, of fear, which meant that many people opted for risk-averse behavior. People tended to avoid going out in public so they would not attract the attention of security personnel or, more important, informants. In the end, the security police could get by without cameras, listening devices, or secret agents; most of the time, they needed only to wait for reports from members of the general population to tell on the perceived misdoings of their fellow citizens. We see some of this today in calls for members of disfavored communities to report on the supposed misdeeds of others among them. The East German state's central commitment to omnipresent surveillance made the idea of effective privacy problematic—but it ultimately made the idea of individual security problematic, too.

In the US surveillance programs after 9/11, distinctions between ordinary citizens and criminals, criminals and terrorists, and domestic and international actors quickly eroded. Rules that had been constructed to protect privacy and to provide oversight to ensure that these protections were being honored, even when information gathering needed to be hidden from its targets, were bent, worked around, or simply ignored. Perhaps the connection between security and privacy, especially security beyond the individual, just is zero-sum, with more of one meaning less of another. This picture is misleading, however, if decisions that are made to undermine privacy undermine basic commitments of the nation, a point to which we will return in the next chapter on privacy and democracy.

What is the role of fear in how the relationship between privacy and security is understood?

If privacy and security are viewed as two vertices of a triangle, fear is the third. President Franklin Roosevelt famously described one type of fear as an immobilizing reaction to economic crisis: "So, first of all, let me assert my firm belief that the only thing we have to fear is fear itself—nameless, unreasoning, unjustified terror which paralyzes needed efforts to convert retreat into advance" (Roosevelt 1938). FDR identified fear as a dysfunctional response to the Great Depression, characterized by high unemployment and very little money. But fear may arise in many areas of our lives: random attacks, hunger, disease, death.

The Cold War (1947–1991) was a high point for clarity in understanding national security. There was a single enemy—the Soviet Union—and a common threat: nuclear war. The focus of the US national security debate in that era was how best to respond to what was judged to be the formidable and enduring external threat of the Soviet Union. The Cold War was global in scope, with a world divided into rival blocks with a large number of aligned states. It was both an ideological competition and a series of proxy wars in various parts of the planet, but was defined by the dominant theme of the fear of global nuclear war. The decline of the Cold War and the rise of terrorist threats posed by non-state actors, both domestic and international, made fear both more diffuse and not only distant but locally omnipresent.

Today, national security embraces a number of diverse fears that are not even necessarily interconnected. The overriding fear of nuclear war has been supplanted to a large extent by an expanding set of threats to our well-being. Fears today embrace such diverse possibilities as the traditional fear of war among major powers, the rise of terrorism sponsored by non-state actors, economic decline, climate change, and the spread of diseases that achieve epidemic scale, among others. By the time of the Obama administration, the list of catastrophic threats for the federal government to address was long:

- Catastrophic attack on the US homeland or critical infrastructure;
- Threats or attacks against US citizens abroad and our allies;
- Global economic crisis or widespread economic slowdown;
- Proliferation and/or use of weapons of mass destruction;
- Severe global infectious disease outbreaks;
- Climate change;
- Major energy market disruptions (White House 2015).

Many of these have been elevated to the level of national security threats.

Fear is omnipresent. The British historian Joanna Bourke argues that fear is very much a part of the human condition (Bourke 2005). Highly salient events such as 9/11 have wide and variable impacts on people, from increased attendance at religious services to demonization of those who bear some similarities to the group who performed the terrorist act. We use fear to persuade people to change harmful behaviors such as driving while drinking, smoking, failing to take appropriate shelter in a tornado, or engaging in unsafe sex. But we also celebrate people who endure during terrorist attacks and carry on (Bourke 2005). Public opinion survey data indicate that fear is not confined to threats of terror, whether they originate domestically or from abroad. People who are fearful of crime may be just as willing to give up liberties as they are to sacrifice to reduce the threat of terrorism (Mondak and Hurwitz 2012). Public opinion data also suggest that the more threats are perceived as pressing, the greater the likelihood that popular preferences become more supportive of increased security, informed by increased surveillance and realized at the expense of reduced privacy protections. Fear, especially when its sources are diffuse and unpredictable threats, contributes to the conventional understanding that there is a trade-off between privacy and security.

Although omnipresent, fear takes different forms and waxes and wanes. In the immediate aftermath of the terrorist attacks in Paris, US public opinion surveys reported a significant increase in the number of Americans who expected a major terrorist attack in the United States. There was a 12 percentage point increase among those who expressed a great deal of concern, from 39% to 51% (Newport 2015). When fear is the driver, there are spikes in the numbers of Americans concerned about security threats, whether the threat be Ebola or a terrorist attack in Europe. The finding does suggest that Americans see terrorist threats as interconnected, at least between Europe and the United States. But a longer review of fears of terrorist attacks in the United States suggests that they are strongly event-driven. As we have suggested earlier, chronic high alerts may lead to weariness and resignation, rather than heightened fear.

To what extent can we integrate privacy and security?

As we have suggested earlier, the conventional understanding of privacy and security as antithetical is too simplistic. The way forward is to recognize that both privacy and security are multifaceted and that the facets that matter may vary with the context. The assumption that more privacy means less security treats privacy as one-dimensional. An argument that national security always trumps privacy—or for that matter that privacy always trumps national security—assumes that the balance will be struck similarly at different times and places. But suppose privacy is understood as a set of interrelated but different goods that we value for different reasons and that are not interchangeable. In Chapter 1, we saw some of the different goods that have been associated with privacy: physical security, private space, liberty, confidentiality, anonymity, the ability to outlive the past, and even secrecy. In this chapter, we've seen some of the different values that have been associated with security: protection of the physical person, assurance of informational privacy, and national security. These have different dimensions, too: we saw in Chapter 3 the importance of health information, in Chapter 4 of educational information, in Chapter 5 of financial information, and the list goes on. The data we cited in Chapter 2 indicate that most people today do value privacy in some forms of information more than in other forms. In some contexts, you might care more about your physical security, in others more about the security of one type of information over another, and in still others national security might be paramount. Depending on the likely types of threat, different types of information may be relevant, too: large, real-time data sets of health information might be needed for the syndromic surveillance used to detect suspected bioterrorism, but would be utterly useless for figuring out who is trying to steal uranium supplies from a nuclear power plant. The point is that these are complex choices, about which individuals and societies may need to think hard about what information is needed and what compromises of privacy are best at given points in time. That's why the lack of oversight of what happened in the United States was so disturbing: there was no opportunity for democratic deliberation about what surveillance really mattered, how it could be limited, and whether it was really worth the privacy costs.

Moreover, these are not decisions that can readily be made at the individual level. You don't get to decide whether your social media accounts are available to national security scrutiny in the same way that you get to decide whether they are shared with friends. There are good reasons for this. National security is a good for everyone. It's what economists call a public good: a good that everyone gets, to the extent it is provided, whether or not they contribute to it. We can't assure desired levels of national security without coordination of individual decisions, either. But if decisions about how much security to provide, and how, are social decisions, it's critical to have appropriate social oversight over them. So government needs to be transparent, and citizens need to stay informed about and to participate in democratic oversight of what government is doing. These are not issues that will go away; pressures to augment security arise as levels of perceived threat heighten.

Attention to dimensions of security matters, too. National security, personal security, and informational security cannot be entirely separated from one another. Some have argued that we should rethink the idea that privacy and national security must be traded off against each other by giving sustained attention to how individual security and privacy are related. The importance of such a focus is apparent in the rapidly expanding Internet of things. The millions and soon possibly billions of devices that secure your home, order food, locate your clothing, pay your bills, access your personal records, arrange your entertainment, and drive your car (to some extent) are vulnerable. If they are hacked, not only would your privacy be compromised, in some areas seriously so, but your life could be disrupted and your safety seriously jeopardized. Strengthening encryption strengthens privacy, but it also strengthens both individual and national security.

The Digital Equilibrium Project (2016), a group of experts concerned about privacy and security, has argued that governments need to address how civil liberties are maintained, as well as the security of their citizens and the infrastructure that serves them. They write that the interconnected world of the Internet is so new that we have not yet developed the structures to figure out how best to negotiate it:

> It is a new dimension where individuals, organizations and governments must interact in ways that are productive, safe and socially acceptable. But the laws, policies and social norms we have developed over centuries in our physical world are not capable of providing the structure we need to inhabit this new dimension peaceably, happily, and prosperously. (2016, n.p.)

There are links between personal security, information security, and national security. There are also clear connections between these and the many forms of privacy, as well as other civil liberties. Making these links explicit is one approach to what we need to know about the future of privacy. Both privacy losses and security losses may also be distributed unequally—if certain groups who are thought to be associated with threats bear the burdens of privacy loss more heavily, or if some groups are less well protected than others. One important dimension of working out the new norms called for by the Digital Equilibrium Project is the relation between privacy and democracy, to which we now turn as the final topic in this volume.

10

PRIVACY AND DEMOCRACY

Introduction

How privacy is understood and valued varies among democracies and non-democratic states. Some of the sharper variations may be attributed to whether privacy is viewed from the perspective of the individual participating in politics or from the perspective of a state's policymakers about how transparent their decision-making should be to the people they govern. Political theorists also differ on whether, when, and why privacy is necessary for democratic institutions to function or to remain secure. Finally, a very distinctive understanding of privacy and the political order is to understand privacy as an attribute of the society as a whole that is insulated, creating a sort of *cordon sanitaire* for social privacy that protects the populace from foreign observation and social/cultural influences. This chapter considers the role of privacy for democracies and for other types of states as well.

What is democracy and how is privacy related to it?

Political participation is a core expectation for people living in a democratic political order. But this expectation is not uniformly practiced in most democracies. Nor is participation understood in the same way. Expectations for participation are sometimes embraced, sometimes treated skeptically, and sometimes rejected entirely. Privacy may play many roles in the forms taken by democratic participation (e.g. Lever 2006). Many argue that some or a great deal of privacy is needed for participation to occur without fear or to be genuinely meaningful. Some argue, to the contrary, that privacy means that they should be free to decide not to participate and that it is an imposition on their privacy to expect them to become publicly engaged.

Participation at its most minimal is just casting a ballot. Many democratic theorists defend more robust ideas of participation, lest democracy in their judgment disintegrate into mere populism. Privacy is often judged as needed to sustain thoughtful political engagement in many ways. For some, privacy protects the ability to gather the information and exercise the intellectual freedom for thoughtful participation. Surveillance states, their critics argue, curtail freedom of exploration, thought, and expression, without which participation will become empty. Others argue for the privacy of the ballot on the basis that public knowledge of how you have voted risks subjecting you to unwarranted pressures. Still others contend that you should have further privacy about whom you support and how you give money to causes or candidates, lest you be discouraged from making political commitments and taking actions.

On the other hand, if democracy requires an informed citizenry, it also seems to require transparency that is at odds with privacy. If people don't have adequate information about political candidates or other leaders, they may not be able to select intelligently. The public may want to know not only candidates' political positions, but also information about their private lives that may be relevant to their honesty, the sincerity of their views, or their capabilities for office. If political contributions can be concealed, corruption and influence may thrive—or you may not know whether people whose views you dislike are supporting a given candidate. Transparency is often suggested as a corrective for conflicts of interest in politics.

Another way in which democracy and privacy may be related pertains to the extent to which the state itself must be transparent about what it is doing. Transparency about government affairs may reveal information about individuals that is possessed by the government but that they regard as private—that's why Freedom of Information Acts have exceptions for information about individuals (see Online Appendix). Advocates for increased security may argue that the state must keep surveillance secret, at least some of the time, if it is to protect its citizenry adequately. If security fails, these security advocates claim, democracy itself may fail. On the other hand, privacy advocates claim that the surveillance state gives up some of the most basic protections that are needed for democracy. The more government is transparent, the more the citizenry will be able to scrutinize whether security measures are appropriate to threat levels and as limited as possible to meet actual threats. Such oversight of decisions about how to mesh security and privacy, these advocates claim, is at the very heart of democratic engagement.

Can you be a thoughtful democratic citizen without privacy?

Liberals have long defended the importance of freedoms of speech, association, and conscience for a democratic society. Without these freedoms, individuals may be unable to acquire the information necessary to evaluate the claims of competing candidates, assess the merits of alternative public policies, and enter freely into community life. John Stuart Mill's *On Liberty* is a stirring defense of how freedom of expression is necessary to ensure that ideas don't become stale dogma and are continually tested against new challenges. Freedom of expression is a form of liberty privacy—the freedom to choose what to say. But it may also require information privacy, if surveillance makes people less willing to entertain unpopular thoughts, think for themselves, or speak up.

Many defenses of the importance of privacy to democracy see it as primarily instrumental. Citizens in a democracy may need the free flow of ideas to understand issues and to vote intelligently. They may also need the private space to obtain and thoughtfully consider the information on which to base decisions about candidates and policy positions. This is why librarians are so fiercely protective of the privacy of their patrons, as we saw in Chapter 4: they see libraries as protected space where people can encounter unfamiliar and unpopular ideas. Libraries are also places where groups come together to discuss issues of public concern. Citizens in democracies also may need to associate in groups to discuss ideas, reassured by the protection that privacy provides against interference and coercion. In these multiple ways, privacy becomes a necessary condition for sustaining meaningful democracy, for it enables individuals and groups to choose aspects of their lives that will remain private or that will be disclosed as they engage in political participation and glean information about candidates and issues.

In this view of privacy as instrumental in sustaining democracy, it is of course possible that under certain conditions, privacy protections might undermine democratic values. This claim is made by those who worry that surveillance prevents subversive and terrorist groups from growing in privacy's protective shadow. Yet privacy, in the view of some theorists, is not merely instrumental for the functioning of democracy; it is a value intrinsic to "the importance that a democratic society will attach to people's abilities to develop and exercise their capacities for personal reflection, judgement and action" (Lever 2015, p. 2; see also Brettschneider 2007). For these theorists, privacy is implicit in the creation of truly democratic citizens. Democratic citizens are people who can think and choose for themselves. Privacy—in the form of freedom of thought, expression, and even action—is part of what it is to be citizens who are autonomous in this way.

Does privacy provide the protection needed to participate without fear in the electoral cycle? What is the role of the secret ballot?

Over the course of the nineteenth century, voting became the preeminent political struggle in maturing and emerging democracies. Who should be given the suffrage and how public or private the voting act should be were the dominant questions in political debates. In elections in Britain and elsewhere, the standard practice up through the early decades of the nineteenth century was for voters to announce their votes to the clerks keeping the tallies. Such open voting was associated with fights and intimidation if employers or others of local importance disapproved of voters' choices. A growing reform movement favored the introduction of the secret ballot. In opposition to the secret ballot, the liberal theorist John Stuart Mill argued that voting was a trust, not a right: just as we require members of legislatures to declare their votes openly, so should we require voters to announce their choices publicly. Mill contended that if votes were cast in the open, voters would be more likely to vote in the public interest rather than their narrow selfish interests (Lever 2007).

The triumph of the secret ballot has placed privacy at the center of democratic elections. As Lever (2015, p. 14) writes, the standard justification for ballot secrecy is that it is necessary "to prevent corruption, coercion and intimidation from undermining the fairness of elections." Not all problems were solved by the secret ballot, however. There was the dilemma of someone who could not read or write or speak the name of a favored candidate that raised possibilities of corruption if others assisted them in casting ballots. In the United States, the recent Help America Vote Act seeks to address the problems of assuring ballot independence and secrecy for people with disabilities. There are the current battles over the documentation required to confirm eligibility to vote and the privacy issues this raises that we discussed in Chapter 6. Moreover, in a very real sense, Mill's concern about selfish voting has come to pass. It is widely expected in contemporary electoral behavior that people will vote what they suppose to be their interests within the confines of the voting booth or mailed-in ballot. Critics of contemporary ballot secrecy argue that openness is a corrective for mistaken, ignorant, or prejudiced voting, for ballot openness can encourage people to vote responsibly (Brennan and Pettit 1990). Supporters of the secret ballot justify their position by invoking the democratic ideal that everyone should participate politically and that the right to vote does not depend on the approval of others (Lever 2015). With secrecy, you don't need to explain to anyone why you voted as you did. You can even lie about whom you voted for. And so you have a kind of immunity from the criticism that might stimulate you to vote more responsibly.

What's more, the rise of mailed-in or electronic ballots makes voting even more a private act, far removed from the expectation that by traveling to the polling station you signal the public importance of your political participation. Concerns have been raised that removing voting so far from the public gaze as a very private act may also decrease the expectation that voters become informed. When you go to the polling place, you may get some information, even if it is at the last minute— or you may talk to your neighbors or the person standing in line next to you about your planned votes. Another problem with the mailed-in or electronic ballot is that there is little check on whether it is really you filling it out—or someone else filling it out for you. The farther voting is removed from the public sphere and the more it takes place in private, critics say, the less likely it is to reflect robust democratic participation.

Should you have privacy about whom you support politically?

The secret ballot is now standard practice around the globe. But perhaps secrecy should not stop with the ballot. Perhaps others areas of political participation would benefit from privacy as well. If protection from a public declaration of how you are going to cast your ballot is to be valued as avoiding strife and embarrassment, perhaps you should also be able to avoid disclosure of the contributions you make to political candidates, just as you can avoid disclosure of your ideas about candidates and your ultimate decision about how to cast your vote. This, too, is a question about privacy in the public sphere: How private or public should other political participatory actions be?

There's the question of speech and how much it should be protected in public spaces. Privacy protects your ability to think and talk to yourself in the shower or your home. But robust democracy, theorists such as Mill argue, also requires the public expression of diverse political views. In the United States, robust expression is protected at least in the public square—although there have been times, particularly when threats of subversion are perceived as high, as during the McCarthy era, when freedom of expression has been curtailed. As we saw in Chapter 5, however, protections for the expression of your political views may not always extend to the workplace of a private employer. There, we also saw how critics of this damper on robust expression have succeeded in achieving statutory protection of the right to speak out, at least when you are away from the workplace.

The openness—or lack thereof—of political contributions is perhaps the most significant flash point for conflict about privacy in political action in the United States today. As we saw in Chapter 7, the privacy of group membership and contributor lists may be critical to allowing unpopular groups to engage in dialogue and seek democratic change. But unless this commitment to group privacy makes distinctions among groups based on what they support, others think it may sweep too broadly. It was proponents of democratic transparency who tried unsuccessfully to require the Americans for Prosperity Foundation to release their donor lists (see Chapter 5). And security advocates worry that there is a darker side to protecting group privacy in this way—that it allows illiberal groups to flourish.

One way to try to draw the line at disclosure is at contributions that directly relate to elections: contributions made to support candidates or issues that are on the ballot. US politics has a complex history of efforts to try to keep money, especially hidden money, from influencing elections. At present, federal election campaign contributions are regulated only incompletely in the United States. In 2002, Congress passed the Bipartisan Campaign Reform Act (also known as the McCain-Feingold Act), which prohibited corporations and unions not only from using their general treasury funds to make direct contributions to candidates in connection with certain federal elections, but also from making contributions to support "electioneering" communications. Electioneering communications were defined as communications referring to an identified political candidate and occurring within 30 days of a primary or 60 days of a general election. Citizens United, a nonprofit corporation, wanted to support a movie that was highly critical of Hillary Clinton, then a candidate in the 2008 presidential primaries. They went to court, claiming that the prohibition violated the free speech rights of the corporation—and the US Supreme Court agreed (*Citizens United v. Federal Election Commission* 558 U.S. 310 (2010)).

Current federal law—which applies to elections for federal offices—limits the amount that individuals may give to $2,700/ year for federal candidates, $5,000/year to a political action committee (PAC) supporting federal candidates, $10,000/year to a state or local party committee, and $33,400/year to a national party committee. There's also a stringent limit on cash contributions, because these are so difficult to track: $100 to any political committee (and only $50 if the contribution is anonymous). Spouses each have their own limits. Groups that band together to solicit or spend contributions in elections count as a PAC if they raise over $1,000. Corporations and labor unions are not allowed to use their general funds to contribute to electoral campaigns. *Citizens United* has had a major impact in the face of these limits. It allows virtually unlimited contributions for communications that are not directly coordinated with political campaigns but that might be very impactful in influencing how people vote. These independent organizations are described as super PACs. Corporations, trade unions, and anyone else are allowed to donate without limitation to super PACs, and the super PACs may in turn donate to political campaigns. Since the *Citizens United* decision, there has been a major shift in the patterns of political donations in the United States, with super PACs emerging as major donors to electoral politics. Major shifts also have occurred at the state and local levels, depending on how the respective state regulates campaign finance. Impressive amounts of new money have moved into school board, local government, and state campaigns.

This indirect path of contribution allows donors to remain in the penumbra, if not in complete privacy, in funding various political campaigns. Critics have argued that the only solution is increased transparency about contributions, and especially about contributions to super PACs, given the current sweep of Supreme Court free speech doctrine. From a privacy perspective, campaign contributions are done in the glare of full disclosure. Given that only about .28% of the American electorate who qualify by age to vote donate in excess of $200, it is relatively easy to identify and to publish the names and amounts and addresses of donors to campaigns, making this expression of political engagement a very public action. But the contributors to super PACs may remain hidden, if they are themselves contributors to a corporate entity that contributes to the super PAC. Thus the Americans for Prosperity Foundation, a non-profit corporation, would not need to disclose its independent donors if it contributed to a super PAC, and the super PAC could then simply disclose that the Americans for Prosperity Foundation was one of its contributors.

In response, you as a contributor may fiercely defend your privacy. You may wish to be politically active but to engage privately. The explanation for your discretion may be that you are intensely shy. Or, you may think of yourself as a member of a vulnerable group that is treated disagreeably for taking an interest in political participation. Or, closer to home, you may be concerned that your political activities may be scorned by family, friends, your employer, or others in your community.

Today in the United States, many critics think that privacy has been given greater weight than is wise, given the current level of influence of the super PACs. However, one might easily imagine situations in which protecting the privacy of political participants is critical for their engagement in democratic politics, as it was for the NAACP in Alabama in the United States only a little more than 50 years ago.

Should candidates for office have privacy? How much?

If we shift the focus from voters to candidates seeking office, questions about the extent of privacy also arise. The stakes are surely higher for democratic citizens in knowing more about their candidates than they are for knowing about their fellow voters. Chapters 3 and 5 have already considered questions about candidates' disclosure of health and tax information, respectively. Here, we consider questions of disclosure more globally.

US candidates for federal office (president, vice president, senators, and representatives) are required to file certain financial disclosures. These disclosures include assets and sources of income. Although disclosures give a general sense of a candidate's wealth and where it might be located, critics are concerned that they are less informative than they might be (Rubin 2015). Other personal information is at the discretion of the candidates. It is not clear how much information about candidates is expected by the voters and the various private groups that monitor election campaigns.

But how much personal information should a candidate really be prepared to release? Consider the possibilities: income tax submission at both the state and federal level, dating history, marital status, members of both nuclear and extended families and anything about them, religious attachment and frequency of attendance at religious services, hobbies, preferences for film, reading habits if any, commitment to exercise, travel to other countries and its frequency, charitable endeavors, political activities, health records, or even family health history that extends back generations. There could also be requests to ask for a candidate's encounters with law enforcement and the judicial system, even going back well into childhood. In many respects, what has just been written goes beyond present-day expectations for personal data. It seems unlikely that candidates will be asked to undergo an intensive review of their personal data that is to be vetted by a publicly constituted panel to see if the candidate's background check finds them fit to be considered for a party to select for a major office—although ironically this is what some people may have to do for more ordinary jobs today. Presumably, voters should have the choice of casting their ballots for people about whom they know little—this could be an aspect of democratic choice as well. On the other hand, it seems reasonable to expect candidates to reveal information that is relevant to their political positions, the likelihood that they will be subject to influence or conflicts of interest, and their capacities to serve out their expected terms of office.

Timing matters, too. If people are going to have the knowledge to deliberate about candidates, they'll need to have it before they actually vote. US federal election law states that financial disclosures must be filed as soon as a candidate for the House or the Senate receives $5,000 in contributions, including the candidate's own contributions (many extensions are granted, which has drawn significant criticism) (Rubin 2015). Yet disclosures may place candidates at significant risk before they have even a reasonable idea about their chances of success. Employers, family members, or others close to the candidate may react negatively to the disclosures that accompany the decision to run, or to the decision to run itself. People are not obligated to seek office, although there may be pressures on them to run. But the surrender of significant privacy may discourage potential candidates who want to serve but who wish to seclude a good deal of their personal lives. They may wish to avoid some disclosure about their financial lives and indiscretions that do not violate laws but that do violate confidences shared by others. They may also be concerned to protect family members. One option would be to enforce transparency at a later stage, perhaps on assuming or even on leaving office—although this risks shielding some information from public scrutiny until it is too late to make a difference.

The challenging question for people living in a democracy that is focused so massively on electoral choice is to sort out what the limits to expectations about a candidate's heretofore personal life are, if there are any limits at all. In the American political past, up at least until the Watergate scandal of the Nixon administration, the private lives of candidates and office holders were presented selectively in the press. After Watergate, the chances improved that private indiscretions would become public and might place a person's electoral prospects at risk. But now, in the age of the 24-hour news cycle, people may have become so familiar with the public knowledge of private lives of politicians that the negative shock impact is fading fast. Prospective candidates may be able to pursue unconventional activities knowing that even if they become known to the electorate, they will be discounted when secret ballots are actually cast. If fake news masquerades as real news, or partial truths pass as the whole story, candidates may also have to determine whether they want to respond to apparent errors about themselves, thus risking further spread of the mistaken claims.

What about privacy as political disengagement?

Some may believe that political participation places at risk their understanding of privacy as the right to be undisturbed. There is a strain of individualist isolationism among some supporters of privacy. For people of this persuasion, privacy may serve a very different political goal of disengagement from the political world. They seek a privacy of voluntary isolation and insulation from society, perhaps even living off the grid, disconnected from the service of the state and private sectors. Often such choices may be driven by an abiding sense of dissatisfaction with the existing order and a deep commitment to privacy, understood as the capability to live successfully with minimal dependence on others and without tracking by state agencies or businesses.

If your goal is to escape the gaze and intrusions of others in the conduct of your life and to sustain a deeply private life, a state that makes voting mandatory may meet with some resistance. Being compelled to vote may seem a violation of the private life you seek. This desire to live apart from the state is not confined to individuals but is associated with groups that define themselves by their separation from society and use their privacy to build a different social order, focusing on their chosen way of life without distractions. Historically—and of course very much with us today—there are religious communities, from monasteries to small churches, that have moved to isolated rural areas to practice their faith without distraction. These groups may establish rules for certain members of the community to serve as intermediaries with the world to secure needed services and supplies and to negotiate with the state regulatory agencies and tax collectors.

There are also families that choose to live off the grid or seek to achieve relative isolation from others. In the case of families seeking privacy in the form of detachment from an intrusive world, there is the problem of the household, as we saw in Chapter 7. There may be issues about who within the family gets to enjoy privacy and who does not. A family decision-making structure that confines all decisions to one individual for people living in a defined space with little or no opportunity to possess alternative sources of information or to travel may not have the privacy exercised by the head of the household. Instead, such privacy may be the privacy of oppression, not liberation, as it may also be with groups when decisions to leave are very difficult to accomplish.

Would a privacy state be desirable?

In the European Union, the free movement of ideas, goods, services, and people is celebrated. When nations within the European Union respond to threats by adopting border controls, this can create a difficult challenge. Borders within the European Union are certainly far more porous than borders in the rest of the globe. The idea of walling off a specific society within the European Union as private and not to be disturbed defies the imagination. The concept of societal privacy is not a promising objective to be sought, in contrast to the preservation of individual and often group privacy.

But in some other parts of world, the idea of maintaining a "privacy wall" against external influences is judged to be a realistic and sustained possibility for a state to achieve. Obviously a number of states seek to restrict importation of ideas judged to be socially harmful to the nation and the stability of the regime. In a closed society, all outside influences that are judged distracting are reduced to a minimum. Preservation of the country's cultural identity may be offered as a justification for establishing barriers—be they policies against trade with foreign firms and states, denying visas to foreign visitors, or refusing entry to missionaries of faiths not associated with the country's predominant religion. Barriers, from the physical to the electronic, may be designed in part to keep residents undisturbed by global temptations—just as families or groups may move to remote locations to avoid the distractions, threats, and allures of the outside world.

The textbook example of state-enforced insulation today is North Korea. Few residents can leave, and foreigners who visit have restricted itineraries. Strict censorship is maintained; no competitors, either religious or secular, can challenge the official state ideology and its prescriptions for the society it rules. There is no obvious way for North Koreans to judge comparatively the strengths, limits, or failures of the regime. They have no other sources of information. North Korea has its own distinctive ideology, and apparently it is pervasive.

Saudi Arabia presents a somewhat different illustration of a state deeply committed to sustaining its understanding of what society should be. What matters most in the Saudi Kingdom's Basic Law is sustaining an Islamic identity. The king and his advisors are given the charge to govern in the Islamic tradition as that is understood. Privacy is not recognized as deserving of protection in the way that private property or the family is recognized. Life within the family does afford some removal from state observation and its prescriptive implications, but family life is expected to conform to the expectations of religious life in Saudi society. Two Articles from the Kingdom's Basic Law convey the commitment to a society defined by its faith. Article 9 provides:

> The family is the nucleus of Saudi society. Its members shall be brought up imbued with the Islamic Creed which calls for obedience to God, His Messenger and those of the nation who are charged with authority; for the respect and enforcement of law and order; and for love of the motherland and taking pride in its glorious history.

And Article 10 reads:

> The State shall take great pains to strengthen the bonds which hold the family together and to preserve its Arab and Islamic values. Likewise it is keen on taking good care of all family members and creating proper conditions to help them cultivate their skill and capabilities. (Kingdom of Saudi Arabia Basic Law, www.constituteproject.org/constitution/Saudi_Arabia_2005)

In Saudi Arabia, the state's obligation is not only to maintain but to facilitate the flourishing of a tightly defined Islamic society. But in sharp contrast to other closed states, Saudi Arabia is a well off country (although not as well off as it was when the price of oil was much higher). For a private society, it has the distinctive feature that travel to and from the Kingdom is easy and for students is encouraged in many cases. Estimates suggest that 12 million residents of Saudi Arabia travel annually. A number have houses in the Gulf States. Saudis do not emigrate, at least not in significant numbers, however. In a sense, travel abroad offers the privacy of not being observed by authorities at home, yet returning to the closed society where you are once again subject to observation. This may suggest that material incentives, pull of family, or commitment to the society all work to sustain this private society with the knowledge that exit is possible for private holidays.

Is privacy ever antithetical to democracy?

National security, as we saw in Chapter 9, is about the security of the polity. Some security advocates raise the heartfelt concern that illiberal groups have the potential to undermine democracy itself. This concern reaches beyond the need to detect intermittent risks of terrorist attacks. These security advocates worry that networks might be able to organize so successfully that they can bring down the democratic state from within. We need surveillance to detect the episodic attacks—if they are frequent enough, they may place citizens in a sufficient state of fear to seek an authoritarian leader. But we need surveillance even more to make sure that there are not concerted attacks on democracy itself, either by accumulating power from within, as did Hitler, or by feeding sufficient information about vulnerabilities for external enemies to exploit toward an eventual takeover. At its most extreme, this is the stuff of conspiracy theories—during the Cold War, of seeing communists everywhere, and today of seeing immigrants or other strangers as constant threats. But it has a more rational side, too: that if threats are sufficiently ever-present, and citizens sufficiently on edge, democracy will cease to function well. So, we need surveillance to protect our very democracy, it seems.

These defenses of surveillance are met with the response that a surveillance state cannot be democratic. If people are always aware of being watched, or know that they are being watched, or even think that they might be watched, some argue, they cannot have the independence of thought required for being a democratic citizen. There are several different versions of this view. The strongest seems to make it true by definition: being watched just means that you cannot act autonomously; not being watched is part of what is meant by the exercise of agency. A somewhat weaker view is that choices are almost never in fact authentic if they are subject to, or even believed to be subject to, a watchful gaze. This is a psychological position that holds that it is nearly impossible for people to think independently if they are aware that others might observe them.

Far more plausible views, we think, attend to how in different circumstances watchfulness is likely to affect independence of judgment. There are contexts in which even what might otherwise seem very small leakages of information—an innocuous "like" on your Facebook page leaked to your parents, or your spouse, or your employer, or really anyone you didn't expect—loom very large because of their effect on you. On the other hand, the knowledge that your entire Facebook page might under extraordinary circumstances be queried by the government might seem far less intrusive on your choices—at least, if you can be reassured that queries will only take place under extraordinary circumstances and your information will otherwise be protected.

Is transparency required in a democratic state?

And so we reach the culminating question of this volume, both structurally and theoretically: Should democratic states and those who govern them commit themselves and the state to making decisions in an open and public way? Our answer is "yes," in the full recognition that this will have consequences for privacy that are not always favorable. But we think this answer is ever more imperative in these times of ever-present information availability both in the public and the private sectors.

Over the past 50 years in the United States, the Freedom of Information Act (FOIA) has opened up to some extent the processes of government. Lyndon Johnson at the time of FOIA enactment said, "No one should be able to pull curtains of secrecy around decisions which can be revealed without injury to the public interest." But as we have seen, there are exceptions to FOIA, and other statutes are regularly amended, sometimes to increase transparency and sometimes to diminish it significantly, sometimes in ways that are damaging to individual privacy and sometimes in ways that expand the privacy protections surrounding decision-making and its administration. It is hard even to convey how, over much of the twentieth century, the US federal government has gathered more and more data on both citizens and non-citizens, throughout the country and the world, and at various stages in their lives. J. Edgar Hoover, the longest-serving director of the FBI, built that agency into a major collection of personal data through investigations of crime and groups judged to be threats to the nation. It has been said that the reason Hoover stayed in office for so many decades was the set of files he held on many prominent Americans, who preferred to keep Hoover in office rather than run the risk of having the files released to congressional committees or to the public.

Advocates for transparency in the conduct of government argue that citizens should know what decisions are made, who made the decisions, how they might or might have been influenced, and what information they were able to consider. FOIA-type laws are a start; by latest count, all US jurisdictions and 93 countries have FOIA-type laws (freedominfo.org 2012). But FOIA in the United States has limits. It does not apply to the legislative and judicial branches of government—hence, not to the FISC or the FISCR. Challenges also have been the costs of requests and delays in granting them. FOIA is a very popular federal service, with over 714,000 requests for information annually. DHS, Justice, and Defense are three of the federal government departments that have received the most requests—indicating the interest people have in the issues about surveillance, security, and privacy. Perhaps the most serious concern about FOIA today is that it has exceptions for national security and for privacy. If either is successfully invoked, the request for information will not be granted. Applied in all-or-nothing fashion, these exceptions forestall information and discussion about how to work out the balance between facets of security and privacy in difficult circumstances.

The revelations of Edward Snowden and the continuing disclosures from WikiLeaks have stimulated discussions about integrating and balancing privacy and security. But it is unfortunate that the revelations that got the discussions started had to come through back doors and even the secretive channels of TOR browsing on the dark web. It would be far better to have agencies of government explain fully to the public what information they are collecting, how they are using and protecting it, and how long they plan to keep it. It would be even better if the private sector were to do this as well. We are recommending that data collectors, be they governments or private actors, adhere to the EU standards on specifying the scope and purpose of information collection to allow for public oversight and deliberation. Such deliberation can bring light and thought to forms of privacy as a value, even if individual knowledge and consent might not be either desirable or possible. We hope that reading this book has left you better prepared to participate in these dialogues.

CONCLUSION

Our approach in this book has been to offer responses to the ever-expanding range of questions about what privacy means in our lives. We have explored the value, or the absence of value, of privacy in the conduct of our daily lives, as well as over the course of our lifetimes. We have argued that privacy is often contested as to its meaning and its importance, depending on other concerns and preferences in peoples' lives. Many of the definitions of privacy have in common the importance they assign to autonomy in exercising choices about what to share with others: other people, private firms, or government agencies. Personal information, preferences, relationships, and personal space (to the extent that it exists) may all be shared. These choices raise many questions as to how to secure and maintain autonomy to experience the privacy we desire. Over time, new opportunities and new threats—often generated by technological innovation—may enlarge or contract our expectations for privacy and what is needed to maintain it.

Throughout this book, we have offered generalizations about the state of privacy in this changing era. We have looked at privacy questions in the lives of individuals and families, health and its care, education, finance, employment, and security at home and abroad. We have explored privacy's importance for the political order in which we live. We have encountered the explosive force of big data and the Internet, most notably the social media that define many privacy problems today. We have drawn selective comparisons between the United States' and the European Union's approaches to privacy. Throughout all of these themes, we have emphasized how privacy or its absence may vary greatly in different spheres of our lives.

It is not that Americans and Europeans are utterly divided over what they mean by privacy and how to protect it. Rather, they strike the balance differently between knowledge and forgetting: the right to know and speak freely about others is valued more highly in the United States, whereas the balance in Europe is tilted toward the right to be forgotten. This debate is complicated by recognition that the great Internet and social media firms are based in the United States, where greater latitude is found, but have taken up residence in the more restrictive European Union in countries such as Ireland, where corporate tax treatment may be more favorable. The robust sense of the right to know in the United States disconcerts a number of Europeans for a wide variety of reasons—just as many Americans may be more suspicious of the robust social safety nets in the European Union. This is but one example of how societies vary in how they understand the meaning and importance of privacy.

The Internet is liberating in very powerful ways. With the Internet, you are no longer constrained by the locality where you live and work. Before the Internet, active participation in other areas of the world meant moving. There is a directness and an active engagement that comes with being an Internet user. Your network may become global; at the same time, you no longer are subject to the sometimes unwelcome gaze of people in your neighborhood. But as we have seen, there is a downside to the ubiquity of the Internet. People increasingly have little choice but to use the net. They submit a great deal of personal information with only a limited sense of how well protected their data are from being shared with third parties, or being hacked, or being used for state surveillance. The protection of personal data stored and transmitted on the Internet has significant implications for privacy, as it is so very hard to avoid the net in many areas of life today.

The scale of the Internet has implications for employment, too. In many areas, net-related solutions may reduce the numbers or change the types of workers needed. This observation seems particularly apt in looking at security agencies. Dictatorships of the past often employed thousands of people and tens of thousands of informers. Pattern recognition research strategies for big data allow the veil of privacy to be removed in detecting patterns of communication and interaction judged to be important by security researchers. It is not our intention to express dismay for unemployed security officers in old-fashioned dictatorships, but rather to argue that technological change is often a two-way street in what it offers. It gives more knowledge of the wider world, with the opportunity to participate actively in it, but it also opens everyone to observation from the world in ways that may intrude on privacy. The debate over the US government's efforts to compel Apple to help break into a terrorist suspect's iPhone suggests lively divisions of opinion about the extent to which contents regarded as private should be available even when reasons of security seem strong.

Privacy varies throughout the day and the course of your life, too. Consider expressing your views on political issues or entering into unconventional relationships. Expressing controversial views may result in dismissal from your job if your personal life is not private and your employer judges that what you have said does not meet your employer's expectations. There may be degrees of anonymity in the public square that are not found in the workplace. Or there may not be: in some jurisdictions, it is forbidden for people to take pictures of you in the street without asking your permission first, but in others it is not. You may have different sets of expectations for your health-care records being shared by a number of health-care professionals and assistants. You may have access to your records, and that is the good news, but so do many, many others as well, and that may be less good news. Your educational records at a university are not to be shared with others without your permission, but perhaps they should be if necessary for your own well-being or the well-being of others. It is likely that if you live in a nursing home in advanced old age, your privacy may be greatly reduced, to your great distress—or that new technologies may allow you more privacy in terms of liberty to move about, but less privacy in terms of being free of surveillance.

In the political sphere in the United States, we see privacy at its most paradoxical. On the one hand, a variety of statutes and courts over the past half-century has brought significant aspects of privacy into being. On the other hand, national security pressures have more than once brought privacy up short. Transparency may help to correct these pressures, but at some price to privacy, too, particularly that of participants and candidates in the democratic process. Transparency that is the absence of privacy in managing the affairs of state may coexist uneasily with privacy in casting our ballots and in many aspects of our lives. Privacy and security seem separated and conflictual, especially when modulated by fear. One of the tasks of effective democracy in today's world—which itself requires balancing privacy and other values—is figuring out how to bring these multifaceted aspects of privacy and security together.

It is not surprising that people have very different understandings of what privacy means and how much privacy they have. What forms of privacy matter and how much they matter vary as people move through their days and their lives, develop different interests, and engage in different activities. There is nonetheless value in drawing connected expectations about how robust privacy protections in one sphere of life may relate to other spheres where privacy protection is weak. Perhaps the English novelist E. M. Forster was wise to advise, in the epigraph to the novel *Howard's End*, "only connect" to better understand your own life in context with the lives of others. But Emerson may better serve Americans' more disjointed approach to privacy when he observed that "consistency is the hobgoblin of little minds."

REFERENCES

Adjerid, Idris, Eyal Peer, and Alessandro Acquisti. 2016. Beyond the Privacy Paradox: Objective Versus Relative Risk in Privacy Decision Making. http://papers.ssrn.com/sol3/papers.cfm?abstract_id=2765097.

Alba, Davey. 2014. The Future of Anonymity on the Internet is Facebook Rooms. *Wired* (Oct. 27) [online], http://www.wired.com/2014/10/facebook-rooms-future-anonymity-internet/.

Allen, Anita. 2011. *Unpopular Privacy.* New York: Oxford University Press.

Altman, Irwin. 1981. *The Environment and Social Behavior: Privacy, Person Space, Territory, Crowding,* 1st ed. New York: Irving Publishers.

American Academy of Pediatrics (AAP). 2013. Ethical and Policy Issues in Genetic Testing and Screening of Children. *Pediatrics* 131, no. 3: 620–622.

American Library Association. 2016. Privacy and Confidentiality. http://www.ala.org/Template.cfm?Section=ifissues&Template=/ContentManagement/ContentDisplay.cfm&ContentID=25304.

American Library Association (ALA). 2002. Privacy: An Interpretation of the Library Bill of Rights. http://www.ala.org/Template.cfm?Section=interpretations&Template=/ContentManagement/ContentDisplay.cfm&ContentID=132904.

American Medical Association (AMA). 2013. Report of the Council on Ethical and Judicial Affairs, Amendment to E-5.055, "Confidential Care for Minors." file:///Users/u0035587/Downloads/ceja-3a13.pdf.

American Psychiatric Association (APA). 2013. The Principles of Medical Ethics With Annotations Especially Applicable to

Psychiatry. file:///Users/u0035587/Downloads/principles-medical-ethics.pdf.

American School Counselor Association (ASCA). 2014. The School Counselor and Confidentiality. https://www.schoolcounselor.org/asca/media/asca/PositionStatements/PS_Confidentiality.pdf.

American Society of Reproductive Medicine (ASRM). 2013. Informing Offspring of Their Conception by Gamete or Embryo Donation: A Committee Opinion. *Fertility & Sterility* 100: 45–49.

Atkins, Elizabeth. 2016. #BlackLivesRecorded: Will the Darling Savior of Police Brutality Be the Downfall Of Modern Privacy? http://poseidon01.ssrn.com/delivery.php?ID=319121006065080082000102 0701051081040560740070110890600730950040250960050140730001 25 1230360600240380140020250150991160891100251030540020350310 25 11810612412111800703000808003006701810008102801809610509200 2 083071093112083102007123085065023118011002008100 &EXT=pdf.

Audette, D. Elizabeth. 1998. Confidentiality in the Church: What the Pastor Knows and Tells. *Christian Century* (Jan. 28) [online], http://www.religion-online.org/showarticle.asp?title=317.

Bailey, Melissa. 2015. Should Patients Be Able to Record Their Surgeries? *STAT* (Dec. 15) [online], https://www.statnews.com/2015/12/15/patients-record-hospital-visits/.

Bailey, Melissa W. 2016. Seduction by Technology: Why Consumers Opt Out of Privacy by Buying into the Internet of Things. *Texas Law Review* 94: 1023–1054.

Bambauer, Derek E. 2014. Ghost in the Network. *University of Pennsylvania Law Review* 162: 1011–1090.

Bambauer, Jane R., and Derek E. Bambauer. 2017. Information Libertarianism. *California Law Review* 105: forthcoming, http://poseidon01.ssrn.com/delivery.php?ID=071026118068011015016127 1 1509109200700202502101104303906807506502810009408602708511 70 9911806110110509811212101011908210206512301007801706100008 90 8210207809200412405206504911402906502800106712100609403106 70 86075029127025104090117019096099088106126031 &EXT=pdf.

Beasley, Mike. 2015. Facebook Removes Slingshot, Rooms, and Riff Apps from App Store, Closes Creative Labs [Dec. 7], http://9to5mac.com/2015/12/07/facebook-creative-labs-shutdown/.

Benedict, James N., and Leslie A. Lupert. 1979. Federal Income Tax Returns—The Tension between Government Access and Confidentiality. *Cornell Law Review* 64, no. 6: 940–987.

Benitez, Kathleen, and Bradley Malin. 2010. Evaluating Re-Identification Risks with Respect to the HIPAA Privacy Rule. *Journal of the American Medical Informatics Association* 17: 169–177.

Berger, J. M., and Jonathon Morgan. 2015. The ISIS Twitter Census. The Brookings Project on U.S. Relations with the Islamic World, Analysis Paper No. 20 (March). https://www.brookings.edu/wp-content/uploads/2016/06/isis_twitter_census_berger_morgan.pdf.

Berisha, Visar, Shuai Wang, Amy LaCross, and Julie Liss. 2015. Tracking Discourse Complexity Preceding Alzheimer's Disease Diagnosis: A Case Study Comparing the Press Conferences of Presidents Ronald Reagan and George Herbert Walker Bush. *Journal of Alzheimer's Disease* 45, no. 3: 959–963.

Berland, Leland, et al. 2010. Managing Incidental Findings on Abdominal CT: White Paper of the ACR Incidental Findings Committee. *Journal of the American College of Radiology* 7: 754–773.

Bingham, John. 2015. "Surveillance" Concerns over Private School with 500 CCTV Cameras. *The Telegraph* (Nov. 18) [online], http://www.telegraph.co.uk/education/educationnews/12004297/Surveillance-concerns-over-private-school-with-500-CCTV-cameras.html.

Blakinger, Keri. 2016. A Look at Some of the Ways George Orwell's "1984" Has Come True Today. *New York Daily News* (June 6) [online], http://www.nydailynews.com/news/national/ways-george-orwell-1984-true-article-1.2662813.

Body Project, Bradley University. 2016. Illness & Body Image. http://www.bradley.edu/sites/bodyproject/disability/illness/.

Boetzkes, Elisabeth. 2001. Privacy, Property, and the Family in the Age of Genetic Testing: Observations from Transformative Feminism. *Journal of Social Philosophy* 32, no. 3: 301–316.

Bok, Sissela. 1983. *Secrets: On the Ethics of Concealment and Revelation.* New York: Pantheon Books.

Bourke, Joanna. 2005. *Fear: A Cultural History.* London: Virago Press.

Bowcott, Owen. 2016. EU's Highest Court Delivers Blow to UK Snooper's Charter. *The Guardian* (Dec. 21) [online], https://www.theguardian.com/law/2016/dec/21/eus-highest-court-delivers-blow-to-uk-snoopers-charter.

Bowcott, Owen, and Kim Willsher. 2014. Google's French Arm Faces Daily Fines over Links to Defamatory Article. *The Guardi306 an* (Nov. 13) [online], http://www.theguardian.com/media/2014/nov/13/google-french-arm-fines-right-to-be-forgotten.

boyd, danah. 2014. *It's Complicated: The Social Lives of Networked Teens.* New Haven, CT: Yale University Press.

Brandimarte, Laura, Alessandro Acquisti, and George Loewenstein. 2013. Misplaced Confidences: Privacy and the Control Paradox. *Social Psychological & Personality Science* 4, no. 3: 340–347.

Brennan, Geoffrey, and Philip Pettit. 1990. Unveiling the Vote. *British Journal of Political Science* 20, no. 3: 311–333.

Brennan, Troyen. 1989. AIDS and the Limits of Confidentiality: The Physician's Duty to Warn Contacts of Seropositive Individuals. *Journal of General Internal Medicine* 4 (May/June): 241–246.

Brennan Center for Justice. 2006. Policy Brief on Inaccurate Purges of the Voter Rolls. http://www.brennancenter.org/analysis/policy-brief-inaccurate-purges-voter-rolls.

Brettschneider, Corey. 2007. *Democratic Rights: The Substance of Self-Government.* Princeton, NJ: Princeton University Press.

Broadband Commission for Digital Development, International Telecommunication Union and United National Educational, Scientific and Cultural Organization. 2015 (Broadband Commission). *The State of Broadband 2015: Broadband as a Foundation for Sustainable Development* (September). http://www.broadbandcommission.org/Documents/reports/bb-annualreport2015.pdf.

Brody, Howard. 2011. How Much about a President's Health Does the Public Have a Right to Know? *New Republic* (July 21) [online], https://newrepublic.com/article/92452/michele-bachmann-migraines-health-ethics.

Bromwich, Jonah Engel. 2016. Protecting Your Digital Life in 7 Easy Steps. *The New York Times* (Nov. 16) [online], http://www.nytimes.com/2016/11/17/technology/personaltech/encryption-privacy.html.

Bronfenbrenner, Urie. 1970. *Two Worlds of Childhood: USA and USSR.* New York: Russell Sage Foundation.

Brooks, Chad. Choosing a Background Check Service: Guide for Businesses. *Business News Daily* (Feb. 18) [online], http://www.businessnewsdaily.com/7636-choosing-a-background-check-service.html.

Buchanan, Alec, Renee Binder, Michael Norko, and Marvin Swartz. 2012. Resource Document on Psychiatric Violence Risk Assessment. *American Journal of Psychiatry* 169, no. 3 (data suppl.): 1–10.

Callaway, Ewen. 2013. Deal Done over HeLa Cell Line. *Nature* 300 (Aug. 8): 132–133.

Callier, Shawneequa, and Rachel Simpson. 2012. Genetic Disease and the Duty to Disclose. *AMA Journal of Ethics* 14, no. 8: 640–644.

Campbell, Kellie Wingate. 2013. Victim Confidentiality Laws Promote Safety and Dignity. *Missouri Bar Journal* (March 4) [online], http://www.mobar.org/uploadedFiles/Home/Publications/Journal/2013/03-04/victim-confidentiality.pdf.

Carter, Ralph. 2016. Too Much Information!: The Need for Stronger Privacy Protection for the Online Activities of Employees and Applicants. *Journal of Civil Rights & Economic Development* 28: 291–321.

Cate, Fred H. 2010. Protecting Privacy in Health Research: The Limits of Individual Choice. *California Law Review* 98, no. 6: 1765–1804.

Childress, Sarah. 2015. How the NSA Spying Programs Have Changed since Snowden. *PBS Frontline* (Feb. 9) [online], http://www.pbs.org/wgbh/frontline/article/how-the-nsa-spying-programs-have-changed-since-snowden/.

Chmielewski, Dawn. 2016. How "Do Not Track" Ended Up Going Nowhere. *recode* (Jan.4) [online], http://www.recode.net/2016/1/4/11588418/how-do-not-track-ended-up-going-nowhere.

Chmielewski, Dawn. 2015. When Personalized Learning Gets Too Personal: Google Complaint Exposes Student Privacy Concerns. *recode* (Dec. 9) [online], http://www.recode.net/2015/12/9/11621282/when-personalized-learning-gets-too-personal-google-complaint-exposes.

Chokshi, Nirah. 2016. Snowden and WikiLeaks Clash over How to Disclose Secrets. *New York Times* (July 29) [online]. http://www.nytimes.com/2016/07/30/us/snowden-wikileaks.html.

Chouchane, Lotfi. 2015. Precision Medicine: Paving the Way to Better Healthcare in Qatar. *International Innovation* (Nov. 17) [online], http://www.internationalinnovation.com/precision-medicine-paving-the-way-to-better-healthcare-in-qatar/.

Citron, Danielle Keats, and Frank Pasquale. 2014. The Scored Society: Due Process for Automated Predictions. *Washington Law Review* 89: 1–33.

Claeys, Eric R. 2008. The Private Society and the Liberal Public Good in John Locke's Thought. *Social Philosophy and Policy* 25, no. 2: 201–234.

Claypoole, Theodore F. 2014. Privacy and Social Media. *ABA Business Law Today* [online], http://www.americanbar.org/publications/blt/2014/01/03a_claypoole.html.

Cohen, I. Glenn. 2017. Sperm and Egg Donor Anonymity: Legal and Ethical Issues. Chapter 22 in *Oxford Handbook of Reproductive Ethics*, ed. Leslie Francis. New York: Oxford University Press.

Cohen, Julie E. 2012. *Configuring the Networked Self: Law, Code, and the Play of Everyday Practice.* New Haven, CT: Yale University Press.

Consumer Financial Protection Bureau (CFPB). 2012. *Key Dimensions and Processes in the U.S. Credit Reporting System: A Review of How the Nation's Largest Credit Bureaus Manage Consumer Data* (February). http://files.consumerfinance.gov/f/201212_cfpb_credit-reporting-white-paper.pdf.

Contreras, Jorge. 2016. The President Says Patients Should Own Their Genetic Data. He's Wrong. *Nature Biotechnology* 34, no. 6: 585–586.

Contreras, Jorge. 2016a. Genetic Property. *Georgetown Law Journal* 105. http://papers.ssrn.com/sol3/papers.cfm?abstract_id=2787553.

Cook-Deegan, Robert, John M. Conley, James P. Evans, and Daniel Vorhaus. 2013. The Next Controversy in Genetic Testing: Clinical Data as Trade Secrets? *American Journal of Human Genetics* 21, no. 6: 585588.

Cowan, Alison Leigh. 2006. Four Librarians Finally Break Silence in Records Case. *New York Times* (May 31) [online], http://www.nytimes.com/2006/05/31/nyregion/31library.html?_r=0.

Cox, Jeannette. 2015. A Chill Around the Water Cooler: First Amendment in the Workplace. American Bar Association, *Insights on Law & Society* (Winter) [online], http://www.americanbar.org/publications/insights_on_law_andsociety/15/winter-2015/chill-around-the-water-cooler.html.

Cundiff, Dave. 2005. The Wayward Husband. *AMA Journal of Ethics* 7, no. 10 [online], http://journalofethics.ama-assn.org.ezproxy.lib.utah.edu/2005/10/ccas1-0510.html.

Curenton, Christopher Mark. 2003. The Past, Present, and Future of 18 U.S.C. § 4: An Exploration of the Federal Misprision of Felony Statute. *Alabama Law Review* 55: 183–192.

de Waal, Frans. 2016. *Are We Smart Enough to Know How Smart Animals Are?* New York: W.W. Norton.

DeCew, Judith. 2015. Privacy, *The Stanford Encyclopedia of Philosophy* (Spring 2015 Edition), Edward N. Zalta (ed.), http://plato.stanford.edu/archives/spr2015/entries/privacy/.

Department of Commerce (DOC). 2016. The Benefits, Challenges, and Potential Roles for the Government in Fostering the Advancement of the Internet of Things, RIN 0660-XC024 (April 16), *Federal Register* 81, no. 66, https://www.ntia.doc.gov/files/ntia/publications/fr_rfc_iot_04062016.pdf.

Department of Education (DOE). 2016. FERPA General Guidance for Students. https://www2.ed.gov/policy/gen/guid/fpco/ferpa/students.html.

Department of Homeland Security (DHS). 2016. National Terrorism Advisory System Bulletin (June 15). https://www.dhs.gov/ntas/advisory/ntas_16_0615_0001.

Department of Homeland Security (DHS). 2016a. Strategic Principles for Securing the Internet of Things (IoT) (Nov. 15), file:///Users/u0035587/Downloads/Strategic_Principles_for_Securing_the_Internet_of_Things-2016-1115-FINAL....pdf.

DeWitt, Karen. 1997. Paul Tsongas, Who Made Presidential Bid, Dies at 55. *New York Times* (Jan. 20) [online], http://www.nytimes.com/1997/01/20/us/paul-tsongas-who-made-presidential-bid-dies-at-55.html.

Dieterich, L. Elise. 2016. Benefits and Risks of the Internet of Things. *Law Journal Newsletters* (June) [online], http://www .lawjournalnewsletters.com/sites/lawjournalnewsletters/2016/06/01/benefits-and-risks-of-the-internet-of-things/?slreturn=20161130110145.

Digital Equilibrium Project. 2016. Advancing the Dialogue on Privacy and Security in the Connected World. https://nebula.wsimg.com/3e4ae1cf8da3d560ac319cfa8dcfa298?AccessKeyId=B2921D5064AE5D77DC67&disposition=0&alloworigin=1.

Dignan, Larry. 2016. Big Data, Analytics Expected to be $187 Billion Market in 2019. *ZDNet* (May 23) [online], http://www.zdnet.com/article/big-data-analytics-expected-to-be-187-billion-market-in-2019/.

Donohue, Laura K. 2016. *The Future of Foreign Intelligence: Privacy and Surveillance in a Digital Age.* New York: Oxford University Press.

Duggan, Maeve. 2015. The Demographics of Social Media Users. Pew Research Center, http://www.pewinternet.org/2015/08/19/the-demographics-of-social-media-users/.

Dunbar, John. 2016. Koch Brothers Hide Donations Behind Civil Rights Precedent. *Newsweek* (July 5) [online], http://www.newsweek.com/koch-bros-hide-donations-behind-civil-rights-precedent-477786.

Ehrenberg, Rachel. 2012. Scientists Surf Web's Dark Side. *Science News* (March 10) [online], http://www.jstor.org/stable/pdf/41480481.pdf.

Electronic Frontier Foundation. 2016. *Internet Archive et al. v. Mukasey et al.*, https://www.eff.org/cases/archive-v-mukasey.

Elliott, Justin. 2013. Remember When the Patriot Act Debate Was All about Library Records? *Pro Publica* (June 17) [online], https://www.propublica.org/article/remember-when-the-patriot-act-debate-was-about-library-records.

n, Ralph. 1952. *Invisible Man.* New York: Random House.

ıl Employment Opportunity Commission (EEOC). 2012. EEOC Enforcement Guidance: Consideration of Arrest and Conviction Records in Employment Decisions under Title VII of the Civil Rights Act of 1964. (April 25). https://www.eeoc.gov/laws/guidance/arrest_conviction.cfm.

Europe versus Facebook. 2016. Class Action against Facebook Ireland. http://europe-v-facebook.org/EN/Complaints/Class_Action/class_action.html.

European Commission. 2015. Data protection Eurobarometer (June). http://ec.europa.eu/justice/data-protection/files/factsheets/factsheet_data_protection_eurobarometer_240615_en.pdf.

European Commission. 2011. Special Eurobarometer 359: Attitudes on Data Protection and Electronic Identity in the European Union (June). http://ec.europa.eu/public_opinion/archives/ebs/ebs_359_en.pdf.

Evans, Donald. 1995. The Investigation of Life-Threatening Child Abuse and Munchausen Syndrome by Proxy. *Journal of Medical Ethics* 21: 9–13.

Executive Office of the President. 2016. *Big Data: A Report on Algorithmic Systems, Opportunity, and Civil Rights.* (May), https://www.whitehouse.gov/sites/default/files/microsites/ostp/2016_0504_data_discrimination.pdf.

Facebook. 2016. Statement of Rights and Responsibilities. https://www.facebook.com/legal/terms.

Facebook. 2015. Statement of Rights and Responsibilities. https://www.facebook.com/legal/terms.

Farrell, Kenneth Neil. 2008. Global Privacy in Flux: Illuminating Privacy across Cultures in China and the US. *International Journal of Communication* 2: 993–1030.

Federal Trade Commission (FTC). 2016. *Big Data: A Tool for Inclusion or Exclusion?* https://www.ftc.gov/system/files/documents/reports/big-data-tool-inclusion-or-exclusion-understanding-issues/160106big-data-rpt.pdf.

Federal Trade Commission. 2016a. Electronic Health Records Company Settles FTC Charges It Deceived Consumers about Privacy of Doctor Reviews (June 8). https://www.ftc.gov/news-events/press-releases/2016/06/electronic-health-records-company-settles-ftc-charges-it-deceived.

Federal Trade Commission. 2016b. FTC Approves Final Order in Craig Brittain "Revenge Porn" Case (Jan. 8). https://

www.ftc.gov/news-events/press-releases/2016/01/
ftc-approves-final-order-craig-brittain-revenge-porn-case.

Federal Trade Commission. 2016c. FTC Approves Final Order in
Vulcun Deceptive App Installation Case (May 10). https://
www.ftc.gov/news-events/press-releases/2016/05/
ftc-approves-final-order-vulcun-deceptive-app-installation-case.

Federal Trade Commission. 2016d. Employment Background
Checks. https://www.consumer.ftc.gov/articles/
0157-employment-background-checks#questions.

Federal Trade Commission. 2016e. In the Matter of Turn, Inc., https://
www.ftc.gov/system/files/documents/cases/161214_turn_
agreement.pdf.

Federal Trade Commission. 2016f. Operators of AshleyMadison
.com Settle FTC, State Charges Resulting From 2015 Data Breach
that Exposed 36 Million Users' Profile Information (Dec. 14).
https://www.ftc.gov/news-events/press-releases/2016/12/
operators-ashleymadisoncom-settle-ftc-state-charges-resulting.

Federal Trade Commission. 2015. Wyndham Settles FTC Charges It
Unfairly Placed Consumers Payment Card Information at Risk
(Dec. 9). https://www.ftc.gov/news-events/press-releases/2015/
12/wyndham-settles-ftc-charges-it-unfairly-placed-consumers-
payment.

Federal Trade Commission. 2015a. Careful Connections: Building
Security in the Internet of Things (January). https://www
.ftc.gov/system/files/documents/plain-language/pdf0199-
carefulconnections-buildingsecurityinternetofthings.pdf.

Federal Trade Commission. 2015b. Internet of Things: Privacy & Security in
a Connected World. https://www.ftc.gov/system/files/documents/
reports/federal-trade-commission-staff-report-november-2013-
workshop-entitled-internet-things-privacy/150127iotrpt.pdf.

Federal Trade Commission. 2012. Report to Congress Under Section 319
of the Fair and Accurate Credit Transactions Act of 2003 (December).
https://www.ftc.gov/sites/default/files/documents/reports/
section-319-fair-and-accurate-credit-transactions-act-2003-fifth-
interim-federal-trade-commission/130211factareport.pdf.

Federal Trade Commission. 2012a. Google Will Pay $22.5 Million
to Settle FTC Charges It Misrepresented Privacy Assurances
to Users of Apple's Safari Internet Browser (Aug. 9). https://
www.ftc.gov/news-events/press-releases/2012/08/
google-will-pay-225-million-settle-ftc-charges-it-misrepresented.

Federal Trade Commission. 2012b. In the Matter of Facebook, Inc. (Aug. 10), File No. 092 3184. https://www.ftc.gov/enforcement/cases-proceedings/092-3184/facebook-inc.

Federal Trade Commission. 2010. Letter from Director David Vladeck to Peter Larson and Martin E. Shmagin (July 1). https://www.ftc.gov/system/files/documents/closing_letters/letter-xy-magazine-xy.com-regarding-use-sale-or-transfer-personal-information-obtained-during-bankruptcy-proceeding/100712xy.pdf.

Federal Trade Commission. 2010a. *Protecting Consumer Privacy in an Era of Rapid Change: A Proposed Framework for Businesses and Policymakers (Preliminary FTC Staff Report)* (December). https://www.ftc.gov/sites/default/files/documents/reports/federal-trade-commission-bureau-consumer-protection-preliminary-ftc-staff-report-protecting-consumer/101201privacyreport.pdf.

Feinberg, Joel. 1980. The Child's Right to an Open Future. In W. Aiken and H. LaFollette (eds.), *Whose Child?* Totowa, NJ: Rowman & Littlefield: 124–153.

Francis, John, and Leslie P. Francis. 2014. Privacy, Confidentiality, and Justice: Using Large-Scale Sets of Health Data to Improve Public Health. *Journal of Social Philosophy* 45, no. 3: 408–431.

Francis, Leslie P. 2008. Privacy and Confidentiality: The Importance of Context, *Monist* 91, no. 1: 52–67.

Francis, Leslie P., Margaret P. Battin, Jay Jacobson, and Charles B. Smith. 2009. Syndromic Surveillance and Patients as Victims and Vectors. *Journal of Bioethical Inquiry* 6, no. 2: 187–195.

Francis, Leslie P., and John G. Francis. 2010. Group Compromise: Perfect Cases Make Problematic Generalizations. *AJOB* 10, no. 9: 25–26.

Franks, Mary Anne. 2016. Democratic Surveillance. https://ssrn.com/abstract=2863343.

Freedominfo.org. 2012. 93 Countries Have FOI Regimes, Most Tallies Agree. http://www.freedominfo.org/2012/10/93-countries-have-foi-regimes-most-tallies-agree/.

Froomkin, Dan. 2015. After Two Years, White House Finally Responds to Snowden Pardon Petition—With a "No." *The Intercept* (July 28) [online], https://theintercept.com/2015/07/28/2-years-white-house-finally-responds-snowden-pardon-petition/.

Fuller, Tom. 2016. San Francisco Torn as Some See "Street Behavior" Worsen. *New York Times* (April 25) [online], http://www.nytimes.com/2016/04/25/us/san-francisco-torn-as-some-see-street-behavior-worsen.html?_r=0.

Fullerton, Stephanie, and Sandra S.-J. Lee. 2011. Secondary Uses and the Governance of De-identified Data: Lessons from the Human Genome Diversity Panel. *BMC Ethics* [online], http://bmcmedethics.biomedcentral.com/articles/10.1186/1472-6939-12-16.

Furletti, Mark. 2002. An Overview and History of Credit Reporting. Federal Reserve Bank of Philadelphia (June), file:///Users/u0035587/Downloads/CreditReportingHistory_062002.pdf.

Garfinkel, Simson. 2000. *Database Nation: The Death of Privacy in the 21st Century.* Sebastopol, CA: O'Reilly Media.

Garrard, Peter, and Timothy J. Peters. 2012. Multiple Sclerosis or Neuromyelitis Optica? Re-evaluation an 18th-Century Illness Using 21st-Century Software. *Journal of the Royal Society of Medicine Short Reports* 3, no. 1: 1.

Gay, Roxane. 2016. The Blog That Disappeared. *New York Times* (July 29) [online], http://www.nytimes.com/2016/07/30/opinion/sunday/the-blog-that-disappeared.html.

Gellman, Robert. 2015. Fair Information Practices: A Basic History (Version 2.15; Dec. 14) [online], http://bobgellman.com/rg-docs/rg-FIPShistory.pdf.

Gillon, Raanan. 1987. AIDS and Medical Confidentiality. *British Medical Journal* 294 (27 June): 1675–1677.

Gilman, Charlotte Perkins. 1979. *Herland.* New York: Pantheon Books (first published 1915).

Glancy, Dorothy J. 1979. The Invention of the Right to Privacy. *Arizona Law Review* 21, no. 1: 1–39.

Goldgeier, James, and Jeremi Sure. 2016. Revitalizing the U.S. National Security Strategy. *The Washington Quarterly* 38, no. 4: 35–55. https://twq.elliott.gwu.edu/sites/twq.elliott.gwu.edu/files/downloads/TWQ_Winter2016_Goldgeier-Suri.pdf.

Goldsmith, Jack, and Tim Wu. 2006. *Who Controls the Internet? Illusions of a Borderless World.* New York: Oxford University Press.

Gonzales, Roberto G. 2009. *Young Lives on Hold: The College Dreams of Undocumented Students.* The College Board, https://secure-media.collegeboard.org/digitalServices/pdf/professionals/young-lives-on-hold-undocumented-students.pdf.

Goodman, Nadia. 2015. This Is What Happened When We Posted Monica Lewinsky's TED Talk. *Ideas.ted.com* (Mar. 27) [online], http://ideas.ted.com/want-to-help-prevent-online-bullying-comment-on-facebook/.

Green, Robert C., et al. 2013. ACMG Recommendations for Reporting of Incidental Findings in Clinical Exome and Genome Sequencing. *Genetic Medicine* 15, no. 7: 565–574.

eenberg, Andy. 2016. The Father of Online Anonymity Has a Plan to End the Crypto War. *WIRED* (Jan 6) [online], https://www.wired.com/2016/01/david-chaum-father-of-online-anonymity-plan-to-end-the-crypto-wars/.

Greenwald, Glenn. 2014. *No Place to Hide: Edward Snowden, the NSA, and the U.S. Surveillance State.* New York: Henry Holt.

Hackett, Robert. 2015. No, NSA Phone Spying Has Not Ended. *Fortune* (Dec. 1) [online], http://fortune.com/2015/12/01/nsa-phone-bulk-collection-end/

Haggerty, Kevin D., and Minas Samatas, eds. 2010. *Surveillance and Democracy.* Abington, UK: Routledge-Cavendish.

Halamka, John. 2015. Hacked? Big Deal, I Made My Most Personal Data Public. *Politico* (July 15) [online], http://www.politico.com/agenda/story/2015/07/hacked-big-deal-i-made-my-most-personal-data-public-000140.

Hansen, Mark. 2007. The Toughest Call. *ABA Journal* (Aug. 1) [online], http://www.abajournal.com/magazine/article/the_toughest_call/.

Hardart, George E., and Wendy K Chung. 2014. Genetic Testing of Chilren for Diseases That Have Onset in Adulthood: The Limits of Family Interests. *Pediatrics* 134, Suppl. 2: S104–S110.

Harris, Shane. 2016. How Hackers Could Destroy Election Day. *The Daily Beast* (Aug. 2) [online]. http://www.thedailybeast.com/articles/2016/08/03/how-hackers-could-destroy-election-day.html?via=newsletter&source=DDAfternoon.

Hart, Anna. 2015. Jackie Collins Kept Her Cancer Secret— and So Did We. *The Telegraph* (Sept. 21) [online], http://www. telegraph.co.uk/women/womens-life/11879532/Jackie-Collins-kept-her-cancer-secret-and-so-did-we.html.

Harvey, Tom. 2015. Citing High Level of Fraud in Utah, Lawmakers Pass White Collar Crime Registry. *Salt Lake Tribune* (March 11) [online], http://www.sltrib.com/home/2278712-155/citing-high-level-of-fraud-in.

Hawthorne, Nathanial. 1850. *The Scarlet Letter.* Boston, MA: Ticknor & Fields [also many contemporary editions].

Heath, Brad. 2015. New Police Radars Can "See" Inside Homes. *USA Today* (Jan. 20) [online], http://www.usatoday.com/story/news/2015/01/19/police-radar-see-through-walls/22007615/.

Hennessy-Fiske, Molly. 2011. UCLA Hospitals to Pay $865,500 for Breaches of Celebrities' Privacy. *Los Angeles Times* (July 8) [online], http://articles.latimes.com/2011/jul/08/local/la-me-celebrity-snooping-20110708.

Herold, Benjamin. 2014. inBloom to Shut Down Amid Growing Data-Privacy Concerns. *Education Week* (April 21) [online], http://blogs.edweek.org/edweek/DigitalEducation/2014/04/inbloom_to_shut_down_amid_growing_data_privacy_concerns.html.

Ho, Anita, Anita Silvers, and Tim Stainton. 2014. Continuous Surveillance of Persons with Disabilities: Conflicts and Compatibilities of Personal and Social Goods. *Journal of Social Philosophy* 45, no. 3: 348–368.

Hoffman, Bruce. 1986. Defining Terrorism. *Social Science Record* 24, no. 1: 6–7.

Hoffman, Jan. 2013. Watchful Eye in Nursing Homes. *New York Times* (Nov. 18) [online], http://well.blogs.nytimes.com/2013/11/18/watchful-eye-in-nursing-homes/.

Hoofnagle, Chris Jay. 2016. Assessing the Federal Trade Commission's Privacy Assessments. *IEEE Security & Privacy* 14, no. 2: 58–64.

Hoofnagle, Chris Jay. 2016a. Letter to the FTC. https://www.ftc.gov/system/files/documents/public_comments/2015/09/00003-97142.pdf.

Hoofnagle, Chris Jay. 2016b. *Federal Trade Commission Privacy Law and Policy.* New York: Cambridge University Press.

Hoofnagle, Chris Jay, Jennifer King, Su Li, and Joseph Turow. 2010. How Different Are Young Adults from Older Adults When It Comes to Information Privacy Attitudes and Policies? (April 14), http://ssrn.com/abstract=1589864.

Hoofnagle, Chris Jay, and Jennifer M. Urban. 2014. Alan Westin's Privacy *Homo Economicus. Wake Forest Law Review* 49: 261–317.

Howard, Philip N., Aiden Duffy, Deen Freelon, Muzammil Hussain, Will Mari, and Marwa Mazaid. 2011. Opening Closed Regimes: What Was the Role of Social Media during the Arab Spring? *Project on Information Technology & Political Islam Working Paper* 2011.1. https://ssrn.com/abstract=2595096.

HSLDA. 2014. Major Victory for Student Safety and Privacy: inBloom National Database Shuts Down (April 29), http://www.hslda.org/docs/news/2014/201404290.asp.

Huber, Machteld, et al. 2011. How Should We Define Health? *British Medical Journal* 343: d4163.

Institute of Medicine (IOM). 2009. *Beyond the HIPAA Privacy Rule: Enhancing Privacy, Improving Health Through Research.* Washington, DC: National Academies Press.

Institute of Medicine Committee on Federal Research Regulations and Reporting Requirements. 2016. *Optimizing the Nation's Investment in*

Academic Research: A New Regulatory Framework for the 21st Century.
Washington, DC: National Academies Press.

Internal Revenue Service (IRS). 2016. Public Disclosure and Availability
of Exempt Organizations Returns and Applications: Documents
Subject to Public Disclosure (March 17). https://www.irs.gov/
charities-non-profits/public-disclosure-and-availability-of-exempt-
organizations-returns-and-applications-documents-subject-to-
public-disclosure.

Islam, Mohammad Badiul, and Renato Iannella. 2012. Privacy by
Design: Does It matter for Social Networks? In J. Camensich,
B. Crispo, S. Fischer-Hübner, R. Leenes, and G. Russello (eds.),
Privacy and Identity Management for Life. New York: Springer: 207–220.

Jackman, Tom. 2015. Anesthesiologist Trashes Sedated Patient—and It
Ends Up Costing Her. *Washington Post* (June 23) [online], https://
www.washingtonpost.com/local/anesthesiologist-trashes-sedated-
patient-jury-orders-her-to-pay-500000/2015/06/23/cae05c00-18f3-
11e5-ab92-c75ae6ab94b5_story.html.

Jacobs, James B. 2014. Juvenile Criminal Record Confidentiality. In
David S. Tanenhaus and Franklin Zimring (eds.), *Choosing the
Future for American Juvenile Justice.* New York: New York University
Press: 149–168.

Johnson, Bruce S. 1989. "A More Cooperative Clerk": The
Confidentiality of Library Records. *Law Library Journal* 81: 769–802.

Jolie Pitt, Angelina. 2015. Diary of a Surgery. *New York Times* (March
24) [online], http://www.nytimes.com/2015/03/24/opinion/
angelina-jolie-pitt-diary-of-a-surgery.html?smid=fb-nytimes&smty
p=cur&bicmp=AD&bicmlukp=WT.mc_id&bicmst=1409232722000
&bicmet=1419773522000&_r=0.

Jouvenal, Justin. 2016. The New Way Police Are Surveilling You:
Calculating Your Threat "Score." *Washington Post* (Jan. 10) [online],
https://www.washingtonpost.com/local/public-safety/the-new-
way-police-are-surveilling-you-calculating-your-threat-score/2016/
01/10/e42bccac-8e15-11e5-baf4-bdf37355da0c_story.html.

Kesan, Jay P., Carol M. Hayes, and Masooda N. Bashir. 2016.
A Comprehensive Empirical Study of Data Privacy, Trust, and
Consumer Autonomy. *Indiana Law Journal* 91: 267–352.

Kittay, Eva Feder. 1999. *Love's Labor: Essays on Women, Equality, and
Dependency.* New York: Routledge.

Klugman, Craig. 2016. Stinging Doctors: Recording Your Own Surgery.
bioethics.net (April 20) [online], http://www.bioethics.net/2016/
04/stinging-doctors-recording-your-own-surgery/.

Klugman, Craig. 2015. Why Doctors Should Audio Record Patient Encounters. *bioethics.net* (April 29) [online], http://www.bioethics.net/2015/04/why-doctors-should-audio-record-patient-encounters/.

Klugman, Craig. 2014. Nana Cams: Personal Surveillance Video and Privacy in the Age of Self-Embellishment. *bioethics.net* (July 7) [online], http://www.bioethics.net/2014/09/nana-cams-personal-surveillance-video-and-privacy-in-the-age-of-self-embellishment/.

Kukathas, Chandran. 2008. Cultural Privacy. *Monist* 91, no. 1: 68–80.

Kukathas, Chandran. 2003. *The Liberal Archipelago*. Oxford: Oxford University Press.

Kymlicka, Will. 1989. *Liberalism, Community and Culture*. Oxford: Clarendon Press.

Lahey, Tim. 2014. A Watchful Eye in Hospitals. *New York Times* (Feb. 16) [online], http://www.nytimes.com/2014/02/17/opinion/a-watchful-eye-in-hospitals.html?_r=0.

Lambert, Paul, ed. 2014. *Social Networking: Law, Rights and Policy*. Dublin: Clarus Press.

Lamont, Tom. 2016. Life after the Ashley Madison Affair. *The Observer* (Feb. 27) [online], https://www.theguardian.com/technology/2016/feb/28/what-happened-after-ashley-madison-was-hacked.

LaMotte, Sandra. 2015. Do Voters Have the Right to Know Presidential Candidates' Health Histories? *CNN* (Dec. 15) [online], http://www.cnn.com/2015/12/14/health/presidential-candidate-health-disclosure/.

Leiner, Barry M., Vinton G. Cert, David D. Clark, Robert E. Kahn, Leonard Kleinrock, Daniel C. Lynch, Jon Postel, Larry G. Robert, and Stephen Wolff. 2016. Brief History of the Internet. Internet Society, http://www.internetsociety.org/internet/what-internet/history-internet/brief-history-internet#VGC74.

Leonard, John. 2015. Privacy by Design: An Idea Whose Time Has Come. *Computing* [online], http://www.computing.co.uk/ctg/feature/2428799/privacy-by-design-an-idea-whose-time-has-come.

Lever, Annabelle. 2015. Privacy and Democracy: What the Secret Ballot Reveals. *Law, Culture and the Humanities*, http://papers.ssrn.com/sol3/papers.cfm?abstract_id=2500227.

Lever, Annabelle. 2007. Mill and the Secret Ballot: Beyond Coercion and Corruption. *Utilitas* 19, no. 3: 354–378.

Lever, Annabelle. 2006. Privacy Rights and Democracy: A Contradiction in Terms? *Contemporary Political Theory* 5: 142–162.

Liberty. 2016. Privacy. https://www.liberty-human-rights.org.uk/human-rights/privacy.

Lobanov-Rostovsky, Christopher. 2016. Sex Offender Management Strategies. Chapter 8 in *Sex Offender Management Assessment and Planning Initiative*, Office of Justice Programs, http://www.smart.gov/SOMAPI/sec1/ch8_strategies.html.

Locke, John. 1980. *Second Treatise of Government*. Edited with an Introduction by C. B. McPherson. Indianapolis and Cambridge: Hackett Publishing (Originally published in 1690). https://www.gutenberg.org/files/7370/7370-h/7370-h.htm.

Lohr, Steve. 2016. At Berkeley, a New Digital Privacy Protest. *New York Times* (Feb. 1) [online], http://www.nytimes.com/2016/02/02/technology/at-uc-berkeley-a-new-digital-privacy-protest.html?_r=0.

Luxton, David D., Jennifer D. June, and Jonathan M. Fairall. 2012. Media and Suicide: A Public Health Perspective. *American Journal of Public Health* 102, Suppl. 2: S195–S200.

Mack, Renata Lawson. 2014. The Federal Witness Protection Program Revisited and Compared: Reshaping an Old Weapon to Meet New Challenges in the Global Crime Fighting Effort. *University of Miami International & Comparative Law Review* 21: 191–239.

Mack, Renata Lawson. 1992. Lying, Cheating and Stealing at Government Expense: Striking a Balance between the Public Interest and the Interests of the Public in the Witness Protection Program. *Arizona State Law Journal* 24: 1429–1459.

Maier, Thomas. 2014. *When Lions Roar: The Churchills and the Kennedys*. New York: Broadway Books.

Majumder, Mary Anderlik, and Christi J. Guerrini. 2016. Federal Privacy Protections: Ethical Foundations, Sources of Confusion in Clinical Medicine, and Controversies in Biomedical Research. *American Medical Association Journal of Ethics* 18, no. 3: 288–298.

Mandel, Lee R. 2009. Endocrine and Autoimmune Aspects of the Health History of John F. Kennedy. *Annals of Internal Medicine* 151, no. 5: 350–354.

Marceau, Justin, and Alan K. Chen. 2016. Free Speech and Democracy in the Video Age. *Columbia Law Review* 116: 991–1062.

Marx, Gary T. 2016. *Windows into the Soul: Surveillance and Society in an Age of High Technology*. Chicago: University of Chicago Press.

Matthew, Dayna Bowen. 2015. *Just Medicine: A Cure for Racial Inequality in American Health Care*. New York: New York University Press.

Mayer-Schönberger, Viktor. 2009. *Delete: The Virtue of Forgetting in the Digital Age*. Princeton, NJ: Princeton University Press.

McChrystal, Michael K. 2015. No Hiding the Ball: Medical Privacy and Pro Sports. *Marquette Sports Law Review* 25: 163–180.

McKnight, Veronica E. 2015. Technology and the Fourth Amendment: Aerial Surveillance Precedent and *Kyllo* Do Not Account for Current Technology and Privacy Concerns. *California Western Law Review* 51: 263–291.

McLaughlin, Jenna. 2015. U.S. Mass Surveillance Has No Record of Thwarting Large Terror Attacks, Regardless of Snowden Leaks. *The Intercept* (Nov. 17) [online], https://theintercept.com/2015/11/17/u-s-mass-surveillance-has-no-record-of-thwarting-large-terror-attacks-regardless-of-snowden-leaks/.

Meyer, Robinson. 2014. Everything We Know about Facebook's Secret Mood Manipulation Experiment. *The Atlantic* (June 28) [online], http://www.theatlantic.com/technology/archive/2014/06/everything-we-know-about-facebooks-secret-mood-manipulation-experiment/373648/.

Mill, John Stuart, and Harriet Taylor Mill. 1869. *The Subjection of Women*. London: Longmans, Green, Reader, & Dyer.

Mondak, Jeffery J., and Jon Hurwitz. 2012. Examining the Terror Exception, Terrorism and the Commitment to Civil Liberties. *Public Opinion Quarterly* 76, no. 2: 193–213.

Moore, Barrington, Jr. 1984. *Privacy: Studies in Social and Cultural History*. Armonk, NY: M. E. Sharpe.

Muggah, Robert. 2012. Why Personal Security Should Be Part of the Post-2015 Development Agenda. IPI Global Observatory (Nov. 13) [online], https://theglobalobservatory.org/2012/11/why-personal-security-should-be-part-of-the-post-2015-development-agenda/.

National Conference of State Legislatures. 2016. Employer Access to Social Media Usernames and Passwords. http://www.ncsl.org/research/telecommunications-and-information-technology/employer-access-to-social-media-passwords.aspx.

National Consumer Law Center. 2016. Credit Reports. http://www.nclc.org/issues/credit-reports.html.

National Consumer Law Center. 2016a. Past Imperfect: How Credit Scores and Other Analytics "Bake In" and Perpetuate Past Discrimination (May). http://www.nclc.org/images/pdf/credit_discrimination/Past_Imperfect050616.pdf.

National Institutes of Health (NIH). 2016. Newly Launched Genomic
    Data Commons to Facilitate Data and Clinical Information Sharing
    (June 6). https://www.nih.gov/news-events/news-releases/
    newly-launched-genomic-data-commons-facilitate-data-clinical-
    information-sharing.
Newport, Frank. 2015. Gallup Review: U.S. Public Opinion on
    Terrorism (Nov. 17). http://www.gallup.com/opinion/polling-
    matters/186665/gallup-review-public-opinion-terrorism.aspx.
Nissenbaum, Helen. 2010. *Privacy in Context: Technology, Policy, and the
    Integrity of Social Life.* Stanford, CA: Stanford University Press.
Norman, W. J., and Will Kymlicka. 2000. *Citizenship in Diverse Societies.*
    Oxford: Oxford University Press.
Office of the National Coordinator for Health Information Technology
    (ONC). 2016. ONC Data Brief 33 (Feb. 2016), http://dashboard
    .healthit.gov/evaluations/data-briefs/trends-individual-
    perceptions-privacy-security-ehrs-hie.php.
Office of Sex Offender Sentencing, Monitoring, Apprehending,
    Registering, and Tracking, Office of Justice Programs, US
    Department of Justice (SMART). 2016. The National Guidelines for
    Sex Offender Registration and Notification. http://www.smart
    .gov/pdfs/final_sornaguidelines.pdf.
Ohm, Paul. 2014. Changing the Rules: General Principles for Data Use and
    Analysis. In Julia Lane, Victoria Stodden, Stefan Bender, and Helen
    Nissenbaum (eds.), *Privacy, Big Data, and the Public Good: Frameworks
    for Engagement.* New York: Cambridge University Press: 96–112.
Olegario, Rowena. n.d. Credit-Reporting Agencies: Their Historical
    Roots, Current Status, and Role in Market Development. World
    Bank Resources [online], http://siteresources.worldbank.org/
    INTWDRS/Resources/477365-1257315064764/2429_olegario.pdf.
O'Reilly, Tim. 2005. What Is Web 2.0. http://www.oreilly.com/pub/a/
    web2/archive/what-is-web-20.html.
Ornstein, Charles. 2008. Ex-worker Indicted in Celebrity Patient Leaks.
    Los Angeles Times (April 30) [online], http://articles.latimes.com/
    2008/apr/30/local/me-ucla30.
Orwell, George. 1949. *1984.* London: Harvill Secker.
Parker, Clint. 2015. Disclosing Information about the Risk of Inherited
    Disease. *AMA Journal of Ethics* 17, no. 9: 819–825.
Pasquale, Frank. 2015. *The Black Box Society: The Secret Algorithms
    That Control Money and Information.* Cambridge, MA: Harvard
    University Press.

Passikoff, Robert. 2015. Progressive Adds "Bad Driver" Surveillance to Snapshot Telematics. *Forbes* (Mar. 31) [online], http://www.forbes.com/sites/robertpassikoff/2015/03/31/progressive-adds-bad-driver-surveillance-to-snapshot-telematics/#6319c752f8e2.

Paule-Emile, Kimani. 2014. Beyond Title VII: Rethinking Race, Employment Discrimination, and Ex-Offender Status in the Information Age. *Virginia Law Review* 100: 893–952.

Perry-Hazan, Lotem, and Michael Birnhack. 2016. Privacy, CCTV, and School Surveillance in the Shadow of Imagined Law. *Law and Society Review* 50, no. 2: 415–449.

Peterson, Andrea. 2015. Google is tracking students as it sells more products to schools, privacy advocates warn. *Washington Post* (Dec. 28) [online], https://www.washingtonpost.com/news/the-switch/wp/2015/12/28/google-is-tracking-students-as-it-sells-more-products-to-schools-privacy-advocates-warn/.

Phillips, John P., Caitln Cole, John P Gluck, Jody M. Shoemaker, Linda Petree, Deborah Helitzer, Ronald Schrader, and Mark Holdsworth. 2015. Stakeholder Opinions and Ethical Perspectives Support Complete Disclosure of Incidental Findings in MRI Research. *Ethics and Behavior* 25, no. 4: 332–350.

Ponesse, Julie. 2014. The Ties That Bind: Conceptualizing Anonymity. *Journal of Social Philosophy* 45, no. 3: 304–322.

Potere, Michael. 2012. Who Will Watch the Watchmen?: Citizens Recording Police Conduct. *Northwestern University Law Review* 106: 273–316.

Powles, Julia. 2015. Right to Be Forgotten: Swiss Cheese Internet, or Database of Ruin? *The Guardian* (August 15) [online], https://www.theguardian.com/technology/2015/aug/01/right-to-be-forgotten-google-swiss-cheese-internet-database-of-ruin.

Pozen, David. 2010. Deep Secrecy. *Stanford Law Review* 62 (Jan.): 257–340.

Presidential Commission for the Study of Bioethical Issues (Presidential Commission). 2013. *Anticipate and Communicate: Ethical Management of Incidental and Secondary Findings in the Clinical, Research, and Direct-to-Consumer Contexts* (December). Washington, DC, http://bioethics.gov/sites/default/files/FINALAnticipateCommunicate_PCSBI_0.pdf.

Privacy and Civil Liberties Oversight Board (Oversight Board). 2014. *Report on the Surveillance Program Operated Pursuant to Section 702 of the Foreign Intelligence Surveillance Act.* https://www.pclob.gov/library/702-Report.pdf.

Rainie, Lee. 2016. The State of Privacy in America: What We Learned. Pew Research Center, http://www.pewresearch.org/fact-tank/2016/01/20/the-state-of-privacy-in-america/.

Rainie, Lee, and Maeve Duggan. 2016. Privacy and Information Sharing. Pew Research Center, http://www.pewinternet.org/2016/01/14/privacy-and-information-sharing/.

Rawls, John. 1971. *A Theory of Justice.* Cambridge, MA: Harvard University Press.

Reardon, Sara. 2015. US Tailored-Medicine Project Aims for Ethnic Balance. *Nature* (July 21, clarified July 24) [online], http://www.nature.com/news/us-tailored-medicine-project-aims-for-ethnic-balance-1.18023.

Review Panel. 2007. *Report: Mass Shootings at Virginia Tech* (August), http://www.washingtonpost.com/wp-srv/metro/documents/vatechreport.pdf.

Rhodes, Rosamond. 1998. Genetic Links, Family Ties, and Social Bonds: Rights and Responsibilities in the Face of Genetic Knowledge. *Journal of Medicine and Philosophy* 23, no. 1: 10–30.

Richardson, Henry S. 2012. *Moral Entanglements: The Ancillary-Care Obligations of Medical Researchers.* New York: Oxford University Press.

Richardson, Victor, Sallie Milam, and Denise Chrysler. 2015. Is Sharing De-identified Data Legal? The State of Public Health Confidentiality Laws and Their Interplay with Statistical Disclosure Limitation Techniques. *Journal of Law, Medicine & Ethics* 43, no. s1: 83–36.

Rodriguez, Michelle, Jason Morrow, and Ali Seifi. 2015. Ethical Implications of Patients and Families Secretly Recording Conversations with Physicians. *Journal of the American Medical Association* 313, no. 16: 1615–1616.

Roosevelt, Franklin D. 1938. Inaugural Address, March 4, 1933, as published in Samuel Rosenman, ed., *The Public Papers of Franklin D. Roosevelt, Volume Two: The Year of Crisis, 1933.* New York: Random House: 11–16.

Rose, David. 2014. *Enchanted Object: Design, Human Desire, and the Internet of Things.* New York: Scribners.

Rosenthal, Elizabeth. 2014. When Health Costs Harm Your Credit. *New York Times* (March 8) [online], http://www.nytimes.com/2014/03/09/sunday-review/when-health-costs-harm-your-credit.html.

Rothstein, Mark, and Abigail B. Shoben. 2013. Does Consent Bias Research? *American Journal of Bioethics* 13, no. 4: 27–37.

Rubel, Alan. 2014. Privacy and Positive Intellectual Freedom. *Journal of Social Philosophy* 45, no. 3: 390–407.

Rubin, Richard. 2015. What a Presidential Candidate's Financial Disclosures Do, and Do Not, Reveal. *Bloomberg Politics* (May 15) [online], http://www.bloomberg.com/politics/articles/2015-05-15/what-a-presidential-candidate-s-financial-disclosures-do-and-do-not-reveal.

Sales, Nathan. 2013. Regulating Cyber-Security. *Northwestern University Law Review* 107: 1503–1568.

Sanger, David E. 2016. U.S. Cyberattacks Target ISIS in a New Line of Combat. *New York Times* (April 24) [online], http://www.nytimes.com/2016/04/25/us/politics/us-directs-cyberweapons-at-isis-for-first-time.html?_r=0.

Satz, Debra. 2013. Feminist Perspectives on Reproduction and the Family. *The Stanford Encyclopedia of Philosophy* (Winter 2013 Edition), Edward N. Zalta (ed.), http://plato.stanford.edu/archives/win2013/entries/feminism-family/.

Saunders, Father William. 2000. The Seal of the Confessional. *Catholic Education Resource Center* [online], http://www.catholiceducation.org/en/religion-and-philosophy/catholic-faith/the-seal-of-the-confessional.html.

Scheer, Robert. 2015. *They Know Everything About You: How Data-Collecting Corporations and Snooping Government Agencies are Destroying Democracy.* New York, NY: Nation Books.

Seetharaman, Deepa, Jack Nicas, and Nathan Olivarez-Giles. 2016. Social-Media Companies Forced to Confront Misinformation and Harassment. *The Wall Street Journal* (Nov. 15) [online], http://www.wsj.com/articles/social-media-companies-forced-to-confront-misinformation-and-harassment-1479218402.

Sharp, Alastair, and Diane Bartz. 2016. Ashley Madison Owner to Pay $1.66 Million to Settle FTC Case. *Reuters* (Dec. 14) [online], http://www.reuters.com/article/us-ashleymadison-cyber-settlement-idUSKBN14325X.

Shelter. 2005. Full House? How Overcrowded Housing Affects Families. *Shelter* [online], https://england.shelter.org.uk/__data/assets/pdf_file/0004/39532/Full_house_overcrowding_effects.pdf.

Shlosberg, Amy, et al. 2014. Expungement and Post-Exoneration Offending. *Journal of Criminal Law & Criminology* 104: 353–388.

Shlosberg, Amy, Evan Mandery, and Valerie West. 2012. The Expungement Myth. *Albany Law Review* 75: 1229–1241.

Silverman, Jacob. 2015. *Terms of Service: Social Media and the Price of Constant Connection*. New York: HarperCollins.

Silverman, Rachel Emma. 2016. Bosses Tap Outside Firms to Predict Which Workers Might Get Sick. *Wall Street Journal* (Feb. 17), http://www.wsj.com/articles/bosses-harness-big-data-to-predict-which-workers-might-get-sick-1455664940.

Simmons, A. John. 1992. *The Lockean Theory of Rights*. Princeton, NJ: Princeton University Press.

Singleton, Solveig. 1997. How Big Brother Began. Washington, DC: Cato Institute. http://www.cato.org/publications/commentary/how-big-brother-began.

Skloot, Rebecca. 2010. *The Immortal Life of Henrietta Lacks*. New York: Crown Publishing.

Smedley, Brian D., Adrienne Y. Stith, and Alan R. Nelson, eds. 2002. *Unequal Treatment: Confronting Racial and Ethnic Disparities in Health Care*. Washington, DC: National Academies Press.

Sprenger, Polly. 1999. "Sun on Privacy: 'Get Over It.'" *Wired* [online]. http://archive.wired.com/politics/law/news/1999/01/17538.

Sweeney, Latanya. 2016. Matching Known Patients to Health Records in Washington State Data. http://dataprivacylab.org/projects/wa/1089-1.pdf.

Tabery, James. 2014. *Beyond Versus: The Struggle to Understand the Interaction of Nature and Nurture*. Cambridge, MA: MIT Press.

Talal, Andrew B. 2014. Drones and *Jones*: The Fourth Amendment and Police Discretion in the Digital Age. *California Law Review* 102: 729–780.

Thompson, Clive. 2016. The Early Years. *New York Magazine* [online], http://nymag.com/news/media/15971/.

Timberg, Craig, and Sarah Halzak. 2014. Right to Be Forgotten vs. Free Speech. *Washington Post* (May 14) [online], https://www.washingtonpost.com/business/technology/right-to-be-forgotten-vs-free-speech/2014/05/14/53c9154c-db9d-11e3-bda1-9b46b2066796_story.html.

Tumulty, Karen. 2009. Is Congress Being Too Tough on Nominees' Taxes? *Time* (Apr. 3) [online]. http://content.time.com/time/politics/article/0,8599,1889399,00.html.

US Courts. 2014. Report of the Director of the Administrative Office of the United States Courts on Applications for Delayed-Notice Search Warrants and Extensions. file:///Users/u0035587/Downloads/delayed_notice_search_warrant_2014_0%20(1).pdf.

US Courts. 2007. Report of the Director of the Administrative Office of the United States Courts on Applications for Delayed-Notice Search

Warrants and Extensions. file:///Users/u0035587/Downloads/
2007_delayed_notice_search_warrant_report_0%20(1).pdf.

US Department of Education Family Policy Compliance Office (FPCO).
2011. Addressing Emergencies on Campus (June 11), http://www2
.ed.gov/policy/gen/guid/fpco/pdf/emergency-guidance.pdf.

US Department of Justice (DOJ). 2015. Identity Theft. https://
www.justice.gov/criminal-fraud/identity-theft/
identity-theft-and-identity-fraud.

US Department of Justice (DOJ). 2014a. Law School Admission Council
Agrees to Systemic Reforms and $7.73 Million Payment to Settle
Justice Department's Nationwide Disability Discrimination Lawsuit
(May 20). https://www.justice.gov/opa/pr/law-school-admission-
council-agrees-systemic-reforms-and-773-million-payment-settle-
justice.

US Department of Justice (DOJ). 2004. Delayed Notice Search
Warrants: A Vital and Time-Honored Tool for Fighting Crime
(September). https://www.justice.gov/sites/default/files/dag/
legacy/2008/10/17/patriotact213report.pdf.

US Department of Justice, Civil Rights Division (DOJ). 2014. Testing
Accommodations, https://www.ada.gov/regs2014/testing_
accommodations.html.

US Department of Justice, Office of the Inspector General. 2016.
A Review of the Federal Bureau of Investigation's Use of National
Security Letters (March 2007). https://oig.justice.gov/reports/
2016/o1601b.pdf.

US Department of Labor (DOL). 2016. elaws: Drug Free Workplace
Advisor. https://webapps.dol.gov/elaws/asp/drugfree/drugs/
dt.asp.

Varone, Curt. 2012. New Jersey Enacts Cathy's Law Criminalizing
Photo Taking at Emergency Scenes. *Fire Law blog* (Aug. 9) [online],
http://www.firelawblog.com/2012/08/09/new-jersey-enacts-
cathys-law-criminalizing-photo-taking-at-emergency-scenes/.

Voss, Jeffrey. 2016 Networks of 'Things.' NIST Special Publication 800-
183 (July), http://dx.doi.org/10.6028/NIST.SP.800-183.

Wakefield, Jane. 2016. Social Media 'Outstrips TV' as News Source for
Young People. *BBC News* (June 15) [online], http://www.bbc.com/
news/uk-36528256.

Wang, Amy B. 2016. Can Alexa Help Solve a Murder?
Police Think So—but Amazon Won't Give Up Her Data.
The Washington Post (Dec. 28) [online], https://www
.washingtonpost.com/news/the-switch/wp/2016/12/28/

can-alexa-help-solve-a-murder-police-think-so-but-amazon-wont-give-up-her-data/?utm_term=.34aaead27fe9.

Warren, Samuel D., and Louis D. Brandeis. 1890. The Right to Privacy. *Harvard Law Review* 4, no. 5: 193–220.

Weill, Kelly. 2016. This Fertility App Is a Jackpot for Stalkers. *The Daily Beast* (Aug. 3) [online], http://www.thedailybeast.com/articles/2016/08/04/this-fertility-app-is-a-jackpot-for-stalkers.html?via=newsletter&source=DDAfternoon.

West, Robin L. 2009. The Harms of Homeschooling. *Philosophy & Public Policy Quarterly* 29, no. 3–4: 7–12.

Westin, Alan F. 2003. Social and Political Dimensions of Privacy. *Journal of Social Issues* 59, no. 2: 431–453.

Westin, Alan F. 1967. *Privacy and Freedom*. New York: Atheneum.

White House. 2015. *National Security Strategy* (February). (https://www.whitehouse.gov/sites/default/files/docs/2015_national_security_strategy.pdf).

Whitman, Christina B. 1985. Privacy in Confucian and Taoist Thought. In D. Munro (ed.), *Individualism and Holism: Studies in Confucian and Taoist Values*. Ann Arbor: University of Michigan Center for Chinese Studies. Available at http://repository.law.umich.edu/cgi/viewcontent.cgi?article=1020&context=book_chapters.

WikiLeaks. 2015. What is WikiLeaks (Nov. 3). https://wikileaks.org/What-is-Wikileaks.html.

Yik Yak. 2016. Yik Yak Privacy Policy (July 27). https://www.yikyak.com/privacy.

Yu, Persis S., and Sharon M. Dietrich. 2012. Broken Records: How Errors by Criminal Background Checking Companies Harm Workers and Businesses. https://www.nclc.org/images/pdf/pr-reports/broken-records-report.pdf.

Yung, Corey Rayburn. 2012. The Incredible Ordinariness of Federal Penalties for Inactivity. *Wisconsin Law Review* 2012: 841–870.

Zaleski, Katherine L. 2015. Withholding Information from an Anxiety-Prone Patient? *AMA Journal of Ethics* 17, no. 3: 209–214.

Zarya, Valentina. 2016. Employers Are Quietly Using Big Data to Track Employee Pregnancies. *Fortune* (Feb. 17) [online], http://fortune.com/2016/02/17/castlight-pregnancy-data/.

Zweig, Janine M., Meredity Dank, Pamela Lachman, and Jennifer Yahner. 2013. *Technology, Teen Dating Violence and Abuse, and Bullying*. Urban Institute Justice Policy Center (July), https://www.ncjrs.gov/pdffiles1/nij/grants/243296.pdf.

INDEX